Conversational Borderlands:
Language and Identity in an Alternative
Urban High School
BETSY RYMES

Inquiry-Based English Instruction:
Engaging Students in Life and Literature
RICHARD BEACH and JAMIE MYERS

The Best for Our Children: Critical Per-
spectives on Literacy for Latino Students
MARÍA DE LA LUZ REYES and
JOHN J. HALCÓN, Editors

Language Crossings: Negotiating the Self
in a Multicultural World
KAREN L. OGULNICK, Editor

What Counts as Literacy? Challenging the
School Standard
MARGARET GALLEGO and
SANDRA HOLLINGSWORTH, Editors

Critical Encounters in High School
English: Teaching Literary theory to
Adolescents
DEBORAH APPLEMAN

Beginning Reading and Writing
DOROTHY S. STRICKLAND and
LESLEY M. MORROW, Editors

Reading for Meaning: Fostering
Comprehension in the Middle Grades
BARBARA M. TAYLOR, MICHAEL F.
GRAVES, PAUL van den BROEK, Editors

Writing in the Real World: Making the
Transition from School to Work
ANNE BEAUFORT

Young Adult Literature and the New
Literary Theories: Developing Critical
Readers in Middle School
ANNA O. SOTER

Literacy Matters: Writing and Reading the
Social Self
ROBERT P. YAGELSKI

Building Family Literacy in an Urban
Community
RUTH D. HANDEL

Children's Inquiry: Using Language to
Make Sense of the World
JUDITH WELLS LINDFORS

Engaged Reading: Processes, Practices,
and Policy Implications
JOHN T. GUTHRIE and
DONNA E. ALVERMANN, Editors

Learning to Read: Beyond Phonics and
Whole Language
G. BRIAN THOMPSON and
TOM NICHOLSON, Editors

So Much to Say: Adolescents,
Bilingualism, and ESL in the Secondary
School
CHRISTIAN J. FALTIS and PAULA WOLFE,
Editors

Close to Home: Oral and Literate Practices
in a Transnational Mexicano Community
JUAN C. GUERRA

Authorizing Readers: Resistance and
Respect in the Teaching of Literature
PETER J. RABINOWITZ and
MICHAEL W. SMITH

On the Brink: Negotiating Literature and
Life with Adolescents
SUSAN HYNDS

Life at the Margins: Literacy, Language,
and Technology in Everyday Life
JULIET MERRIFIELD, MARY BETH
BINGMAN, DAVID HEMPHILL, and
KATHLEEN P. BENNETT DeMARRAIS

One Child, Many Worlds: Early Learning
in Multicultural Communities
EVE GREGORY, Editor

Literacy for Life: Adult Learners, New
Practices
HANNA ARLENE FINGERET and
CASSANDRA DRENNON

Children's Literature and the Politics of
Equality
PAT PINSENT

The Book Club Connection: Literacy
Learning and Classroom Talk
SUSAN I. McMAHON and TAFFY E.
RAPHAEL, Editors, with VIRGINIA J.
GOATLEY and LAURA S. PARDO

Until We Are Strong Together: Women
Writers in the Tenderloin
CAROLINE E. HELLER

Restructuring Schools for Linguistic
Diversity: Linking Decision Making to
Effective Programs
OFELIA B. MIRAMONTES, ADEL NADEAU,
and NANCY L. COMMINS

Writing Superheroes: Contemporary
Childhood, Popular Culture, and
Classroom Literacy
ANNE HAAS DYSON   (Continued)

LANGUAGE AND LITERACY SERIES (continued)

Opening Dialogue: Understanding the
Dynamics of Language and Learning in
the English Classroom
MARTIN NYSTRAND with ADAM
GAMORAN, ROBERT KACHUR, and
CATHERINE PRENDERGAST

Reading Across Cultures: Teaching
Literature in a Diverse Society
THERESA ROGERS and
ANNA O. SOTER, Editors

"You Gotta Be the Book": Teaching
Engaged and Reflective Reading with
Adolescents
JEFFREY D. WILHELM

Just Girls: Hidden Literacies and Life in
Junior High
MARGARET J. FINDERS

The First R: Every Child's Right to Read
MICHAEL F. GRAVES,
PAUL van den BROEK, and
BARBARA M. TAYLOR, Editors

Exploring Blue Highways: Literacy
Reform, School Change, and the Creation
of Learning Communities
JOBETH ALLEN, MARILYNN CARY, and
LISA DELGADO, Coordinators

Envisioning Literature: Literary
Understanding and Literature Instruction
JUDITH A. LANGER

Teaching Writing as Reflective Practice
GEORGE HILLOCKS, JR.

Talking Their Way into Science:
Hearing Children's Questions and
Theories, Responding with Curricula
KAREN GALLAS

Whole Language Across the Curriculum:
Grades 1, 2, 3
SHIRLEY C. RAINES, Editor

The Administration and Supervision
of Reading Programs, SECOND EDITION
SHELLEY B. WEPNER, JOAN T. FEELEY, and
DOROTHY S. STRICKLAND, Editors

No Quick Fix: Rethinking
Literacy Programs in America's
Elementary Schools
RICHARD L. ALLINGTON and
SEAN A. WALMSLEY, Editors

Unequal Opportunity:
Learning to Read in the U.S.A.
JILL SUNDAY BARTOLI

Nonfiction for the Classroom:
Milton Meltzer on Writing, History,
and Social Responsibility
Edited and with an Introduction by
E. WENDY SAUL

When Children Write: Critical Re-Visions
of the Writing Workshop
TIMOTHY LENSMIRE

Dramatizing Literature in Whole
Language Classrooms, SECOND EDITION
JOHN WARREN STEWIG and CAROL BUEGE

The Languages of Learning: How
Children Talk, Write, Dance, Draw, and
Sing Their Understanding of the World
KAREN GALLAS

Partners in Learning: Teachers and
Children in Reading Recovery
CAROL A. LYONS, GAY SU PINNELL,
and DIANE E. DEFORD

Social Worlds of Children Learning to
Write in an Urban Primary School
ANNE HAAS DYSON

The Politics of Workplace Literacy:
A Case Study
SHERYL GREENWOOD GOWEN

Inside/Outside: Teacher Research and
Knowledge
MARILYN COCHRAN-SMITH
and SUSAN L. LYTLE

Literacy Events in a Community of Young
Writers
YETTA M. GOODMAN
and SANDRA WILDE, Editors

Whole Language Plus: Essays on Literacy
in the United States and New Zealand
COURTNEY B. CAZDEN

Process Reading and Writing:
A Literature-Based Approach
JOAN T. FEELEY,
DOROTHY S. STRICKLAND,
and SHELLEY B. WEPNER, Editors

The Child as Critic: Teaching Literature in
Elementary and Middle Schools,
THIRD EDITION
GLENNA DAVIS SLOAN

The Triumph of Literature/The Fate of
Literacy: English in the Secondary School
Curriculum
JOHN WILLINSKY

Literacy for a Diverse Society:
Perspectives, Practices, and Policies
ELFRIEDA H. HIEBERT, Editor

The Complete Theory-to-Practice
Handbook of Adult Literacy: Curriculum
Design and Teaching Approaches
RENA SOIFER, MARTHA IRWIN,
BARBARA CRUMRINE, EMO HONZAKI,
BLAIR SIMMONS, and DEBORAH YOUNG

CONVERSATIONAL BORDERLANDS

*Language and Identity
in an
Alternative Urban High School*

BETSY RYMES

Teachers College, Columbia University
New York and London

Published by Teachers College Press, 1234 Amsterdam Avenue, New York, NY 10027

Chapter 6 is a revised version of: Rymes, B., (1996), Naming as social practice: The case of Little Creeper from Diamond Street, *Language in Society, 25*(2), 237–260. Copyright Cambridge University Press. Used with permission.

Chapter 8 is a revised version of: Rymes, B., (1996), Rights to advise, *Linguistics and Education, 8*, 409–437. Copyright Elsevier Science. Used with permission.

Library of Congress Cataloging-in-Publication Data

Rymes, Betsy.
    Conversational borderlands : language and identity in an alternative urban high school / Betsy Rymes.
        p. cm. — (Language and literacy series)
    Includes bibliographical references (p.   ) and index.
    ISBN 0-8077-4130-2 (cloth : alk. paper) — ISBN 0-8077-4129-9 (pbk. : alk. paper)
        1. Urban schools—United States—Case studies.   2. Urban youth—United
States—Education.   3. Urban youth—United States—Attitudes.   I. Title.   II. Series.
    LC5131 .R96 2001
    373.12′913—dc21   2001027751

ISBN 0-8077-4129-9 (paper)
ISBN 0-8077-4130-2 (cloth)

Printed on acid-free paper

Manufactured in the United States of America

08   07   06   05   04   03   02   01   8   7   6   5   4   3   2   1

Contents

Introduction   vii

1. School in the City   1
City School   2
Charter Schools and School Reform   6
Doing Fieldwork in Educational Borderlands   12

2. Dropping Out   20
A Developing Context for Talk   20
Discourse Genres at City School   22
Narrative and Identity   23
Narratives at City School   25
The Role of Ethnicity in Charter Schools and Narrative   26
Emerging Genre: The "Dropping Out" Narrative   27
The External Form of the Dropping Out Genre   28
Themes Brought Up Through Stories   36
Summary   38

3. The Language of Dropping Out   40
The Grammatical Repertoire of the Dropping Out Genre   40
Indexical Resources of the Dropping Out Genre   53
Summary: The Genrefication of Moral Discourse   56

4. Reframing Dropping Out Narratives   57
Reinforcing Dropping Out Themes   59
Debunking Dropping Out Themes   63
The Ramifications of Reframing   71

5. Dropping In: Narratives of School Success   73
The Institutional Emergence of Dropping In Stories   75
The Conversational Emergence of Dropping In Stories   76
The External Form of Dropping In Stories   77
Grammatical Resources of the Dropping In Genre   81
A Debunker in the Midst   87
Narrative and Reform   89

 6. **Names**   **92**

      Gang Names and Nicknames at City School   *93*
      Alternative Readings of Names   *105*
      City School's Approach to Names and Graffiti   *109*
      Naming, Narrative, Identity, and Reform   *111*

 7. **When Friends Aren't Friends**   **113**

      Mario's Dropping In Perspective   *114*
      Conflicting Commitments in Dialogue   *116*
      Negotiating Conflicting Commitments
          with Reference Terms for Friend   *117*
      Deconstructing a Gang Member's Moral Frame   *127*
      Language, the Contact Zone, and School Reform   *127*

 8. **Rights to Advise**   **131**

      Conversational Borderlands:
          Students and Teachers at City School   *132*
      Indexical Language   *132*
      Indexical Forms and Conversations About Jail   *133*
      Genrefication of Moral Discourse and Emergent
          Mutual Understandings   *145*

 9. **School Closure**   **148**

      What Happened?   *148*
      Two Versions of Pablo's Story   *152*
      A Third Version of Pablo's Story   *154*
      City School's Demise   *158*

10. **On Teaching and Reform**   **162**

      Interactional Coauthorship:
          Recommendations for Teachers Working with Adolescents   *163*
      Institutional Coauthorship:
          Recommendations for Charter School Reform   *169*
      Putting It All Together:
          Students, Teachers, Reformers, Researchers   *174*

References   177
Index   185
About the Author   193

Introduction

This book is about a unique school, City School, and the community that evolved there. City School was a charter school, one that catered to those students statistically most unlikely ever to finish high school, and one that failed after only a year and a half in operation. This book reveals how the young men and women at City School communicated with each other and with their teachers about their lives. Through close analysis of the language of this school, I examine the forces that drew these young men and women back to high school to adopt new and mainstream goals and led some of them to leave school once again. The choices made by City School students—by any students, I will argue—has much to do with how the teachers in this school and their students interact. Therefore, part of this book will address the ways that students and teachers talk with and about each other as well as how students at City School tell stories and construct their identities through language.

The ways in which stories are told and the identities they create are also influenced by the unique school environment in which they take place. Therefore, this book is also about how talk and stories shape these students' identities, as well as how school reform and educational context shape which stories emerge. In this way, this book links societal-level issues of school reform (and the charter school movement in particular) with interactional level—even word-level—issues of language, presentation of self, and adolescent identity.

Goals of the Book

This book has three main goals. The primary goal is to illuminate adolescent identity and its relationship to school. I do so by analyzing the narratives of teenagers who are former high school dropouts, but who have dropped back into this innovative charter school. A second goal is to illustrate how a context created by a reform movement—a charter school—uniquely shapes the kinds of interactions that can occur there. The agenda of reformers obviously and intentionally shapes policy and curricula. But my analysis also shows how reform, perhaps less intentionally, shapes the language within schools, the kinds of stories students tell there, and even certain ways of being and becoming human within school. A third goal of this book is to illustrate a research methodology through which we can begin to understand these human effects of school reform. This microethnography of City School exemplifies one way to study how an innovative school shaped (and was shaped by) students' language and lives.

Synopsis of Chapters

Nine months after my first visit to campus, many of the first students I had spoken with were no longer at City School or were feeling strong pressures to leave. They had become sad examples of the difficulty of City School's mission: Federico Valdez (also known as "Little Creeper") was missing. Friends I spoke to in his neighborhood said he might be in jail. Ned Maldonado ("Cubby") had moved to a distant suburb with his girlfriend who was pregnant. Juan Felix ("Largo") and Danny Fernandez ("Sider") were still in school, but Largo's girlfriend had become pregnant, and he wasn't sure he could continue attending. Rosa Morales ("Sunshine") was still in school, but missed many days to stay home with her 2-year-old baby, whose grandmother didn't trust the child care of strangers. After his first few weeks, and two weeks after I had met him, Jesse Navarro no longer came to school. He had been murdered in his neighborhood.

These are the stories of some of City School's first students, and they display the challenge City School and its teachers confronted. Chapter 1 introduces these challenges and how this unique charter school was formed to meet them. By exploring student talk as it emerged in the context of City School, the following chapters illuminate the kinds of student realities that any urban school must both recognize and reckon with. Chapters 2 and 3 introduce one genre of story—I have called it the "dropping out" story—told by students at City School. My analysis will illustrate how these stories collectively invoke moral frameworks through which protagonists' societally condemned acts are rendered humane choices. Chapter 4 analyzes how fellow students debunk or reemphasize the ideologies implicit in the dropout narratives by reframing stories upon their completion. These examples reveal how the audience for these narratives (peers and researcher) coauthor the stories to create new identities for the primary narrators. Chapter 5 illustrates how "successful" students (as identified by teachers and administrators) speak the language of "dropping in," another distinct and localized genre. These "success stories" show a conspicuous absence of the "dropping out" perspective. Yet the coexistence of these radically different story genres at City School reveals how the institution itself acts as a coauthor in the stories told at City School.

Paradoxically, while City School was formed to honor the perspectives and voices of the students, its mission was also to change those perspectives. Thus, as the succeeding chapters illustrate, student and teacher discourse inevitably exhibits a tension between the desire to provide educational opportunity, to alter the current life trajectory of many of the students (the "dropping in" perspective) and the necessity to honor the values of those to be educated (the "dropping out" perspective). Student and teacher discourse dances around these perspectives as they try to skirt or identify with one or the other. Chapter 6 explores how students either identify with or deny a "dropping out" identity by examining their use of gang nicknames in and out of school. Chapter 7 looks at student conversations to illustrate the creative ways in which reference terms (e.g., "homes," "ése," "vato," "roll dog") can be used to display a paradoxical allegiance to both the dropping out and the dropping in points of view. Chapter 8 analyzes conversations between teachers and students to illustrate that certain ways of speaking have the power to create credibility and trustworthiness by displaying alignment with speakers, awareness of a particular reality, and an orientation to certain local, peer group assumptions. Chapter 9 describes City School's closure (due primarily to financial problems), and also examines how teachers and administrators invoke different genres to narrate the school's demise.

Recommendations to Readers

Just as this book has multiple goals, so its readers may have different reasons for reading it. A complete narrative in itself, I most highly recommend reading this story from cover to cover. However, some readers might be engrossed in the linguistic details of my discourse analysis, while others might shrink from them. For the former, I recommend a close reading of the interior chapters, 3 though 8, where I detail the linguistic resources used to narrate and debunk identity, and to forge coalitions within a conversation. For the latter, your understanding of the City School story will not be compromised if you skim through explanations of the linguistic detail and focus on the overarching narrative. More specifically, for readers interested in qualitative methods and school ethnography, or who are designing or conducting a similar study, I recommend focusing on Chapters 1 and 2, which describe how I entered the field. For those most interested in school reform and the lessons this school has to offer, I recommend a focus on the overarching description of this school (as presented in Chapters 1 and 2), its demise (as presented in Chapter 9), and my own recommendations for teachers and reformers (as presented in Chapter 10). Also, most chapters conclude with a summary of the implications for school reform.

Acknowledgments

In this book, I explore how school can be both a place that, to paraphrase Richard Wright (1937), "revitalizes one's being and whips one's senses to a high, keen pitch of receptivity" (p. 138) as well as a place that contains the ever-present potential to disappoint one's spirit. This is a tension I have also noticed in my own schooling, and I am deeply indebted to the teachers and mentors who have raised my receptivity to its highest pitch. In this regard, I am most especially grateful to Elinor Ochs, who first illustrated for me the capacity of language both to support community and to afford change, and who continues to be one who whips my senses into shape. Also instrumental to the thoughts and writing of this book, has been the support and critique of Alessandro Duranti, John Schumann, Kris Gutierrez, Asif Agha, Marcyliena Morgan, Mike Rose, Stephen Yenser, and JoBeth Allen. Most practically, the research on which this book is founded was funded by a fellowship from the National Science Foundation, and the final product is the result of the gentle guidance and great editorial suggestions of Carol Collins and Cathy McClure.

I am also endlessly indebted to the students, teachers, and staff of City School, who graciously facilitated my research and allowed me to roam the halls freely and take part in their lives for the 18 months of City School's existence. I hope this book, in some measure, perpetuates the initial goals of this community, to create real educational opportunities, inspiration for new lives, and, most practically and simply, keep kids in school.

CONVERSATIONAL BORDERLANDS

Language and Identity
in an
Alternative Urban High School

CHAPTER 1

School in the City

A new school. . . . It will destroy this community.
—William J. Mavropoulos,
a spokesman for Grupo Latino Echo Park

One does not expect to find a high school in downtown Los Angeles. Daily, thousands of cars are deposited among the tall buildings and swiftly funneled into underground parking, their drivers whisked up interior elevators to work. At the end of the day, well-engineered entrance ramps carry the cars back to homeward-bound freeways. These cars crisscross each other, making elaborate and split-second negotiations, but interaction between people, it seems, is an indoor activity here. The vision of high school students carrying backpacks, walking and talking in groups, seems incongruous with this urban efficiency.

Should one turn off of Hill Street, and head west under the 110 freeway, there is a scene equally incongruous with traditional schooling. Much of this neighborhood was evacuated and leveled years ago for the ambitious and ill-fated "Central City West" project that was to include public housing, a new high school, and a shopping area. Today, a large barren hill, visible from the freeway, forms a buffer zone between the urban poor and the swift pace of downtown traffic. A deteriorating cement wall holds part of the hill together and has been tagged with graffiti from the local gang, "Diamond Street." A corner of the field houses have become an ad hoc outdoor living room—a lounge chair, bent into permanent recline, drained twelve packs, old car mats. Nearby, a dirt alley hides a recently stripped car. Atop a hill, centering the neighborhood, a small and feeble oil rig slowly pumps and clinks. One might notice now the acrid sulfuric odor in the air.

Around the corner stands evidence of a life shared by some of the young men and women of this neighborhood, a life that lures them away from school. An aqua blue house, only officially evacuated, towers above the street, marked with the Diamond Street gang roll call and a silver Diamond Street logo painted a full story tall (Figure 1.1). The foundation wall of the burnt-out garage, painted deep red, lists another set of names under the letters "R.I.P": those gang members who have died "for the neighborhood." On the other side of the neighborhood, beneath another wide, barren hill, graffiti taggers congregate at Belmont

1

FIGURE 1.1: Diamond Street House with Gang Roll Call.

Tunnel, a relic of L.A.'s extinct public rail system, a former link to downtown (Figure 1.2). This space has now become a landmark, well-known and oft-cited in literature on the L.A. underground art scene (cf., Davis, 1992; Martinez, 1993). It provides thousands of square feet of cement wall for graffiti "pieces" (short for masterpieces) created by local spray-can artists. They've covered every inch.

CITY SCHOOL

From this neighborhood, downtown's skyscrapers are clearly visible on the other side of the freeway, but for the people who live here, the opulence and opportunity suggested by those skyscrapers is distant, even irrelevant, to their lives. The complicated relationship between young men and women of this and similar L.A. neighborhoods, and the paths to financial security and academic success was meant to be addressed by City School. ("City School" and all other proper names in this text, apart from references and citations, are fictitious.) In the center of downtown, on one of its busiest streets, this alternative charter school promised to offer young men and women from such neighborhoods, estranged from the goals of mainstream society, access to education and middle-class careers. Neither part of the official business of downtown, nor part of the

FIGURE 1.2: Belmont Tunnel.

traditional public school system, City School came to embody a liminal realm, the potential contact zone between economic opportunity and economic disenfranchisement—between downtown's high-rises, and the bulldozed lots just across the freeway. Designed especially for students who had dropped out of or been expelled from their former schools, and for young mothers or pregnant teens, City School explicitly encouraged these young people to return to high school and earn their diplomas. By recognizing and working in concert with the strong forces that pull these young men and women away from traditional high school, City School planned to offer a substantial, and substantially different kind of education for them.

City School began on the fourth floor of what looked like an abandoned business that had been converted into storage space—gray and dingy, no sign announcing the school, no marquis listing students of the week or the next date for parents' night. The acquisition of this site and the school's genesis is a story of the strategic melding of business and educational interests. Negotiations surrounding the new school began when Carlton Hobbes, an administrator at a local university, was having lunch with a friend that owned a bank downtown, near the original location of the school. The banker mentioned that he had several trade schools he couldn't operate privately anymore, vacant facilities now, in need of use. Hobbes, who had a history of being involved in outreach projects to bring inner-city high school students to the university, suggested that those facilities could be used to help disadvantaged youth, and the banker was interested.

A few days later, Calvin Romaine, a former student at the university and a protégé of Hobbes, brought some young men from the nonprofit youth organization where he was working, to the university and they went to visit Hobbes in his office. Here Hobbes told Romaine about the vacant schools available and they began to think about forming a nonprofit organization for at-risk youth. Meanwhile the banker spoke with his neighbor, Paul Dennis, a psychologist at another local university, who also was interested in forming a new school for the at-risk students out of the now obsolete trade school. Eventually all four got together and made a deal. Hobbes, Dennis, and Romaine each pitched in $100 dollars and formed a nonprofit organization; later Hobbes talked to his friends at the school district headquarters and their organization became a school.

While City School emerged through the cracks of the city's infrastructure, efforts of city officials to develop a new school across the freeway (also part of Central City West) had been stymied for years—in large part by neighbors, who did not welcome the addition of another high school, but feared it. Their neighborhood already housed a large high school, with a dropout rate of 25–30%, which neighbors referred to as a "warehouse" full of potentially violent and dangerous teenagers. Schools, redefined as warehouses of undesirables, were unwelcome in this part of town, and the addition of another meant more potential problems: in the words of one neighbor, "crime, gang rivalries, and a parking squeeze." While the overcrowded neighborhood had been arguing for more public housing for nearly 20 years, they did not want a new high school. The opinion of local activists, their understanding that with school comes neighborhood violence, echoes not only the sensationalistic media portrayals of inner-city schools, but the findings of a long-term sociological study as well. As John Devine (1996) has written in his ethnography of urban schools in New York, lower-tier schools can come to function as warehouses, and the boundary between the school and the street, and the violence of each, is porous.

As the city was locked in controversy over their massive new school and housing project, Hobbes and Romaine were quietly transforming the vacant downtown building into a different sort of educational community. What had once been a banker's albatross became an administrator's social program, and then, his protégé's school. The banker's empty business academy now awaited a new population—the very students dropping out of the local high school, students that neighbors did not want around. In the heart of urban Los Angeles, with a list of former dropouts waiting to be admitted, what sort of community would be defined by this new school? How would the inhabitants be affected? Who would they be? Whether this school, born out of contingent opportunity, a meeting between a business executive and a higher education administrator, would provide safety and education for the disadvantaged and in many ways unwanted would be determined over the coming 19 months.

As I walked into the former business academy on my first visit to City School, a student/office intern stood behind the reception window where I signed in, while other students, all apparently in their late teens, milled about before going to classes. As Hobbes and Romaine had envisioned, these young people were all ethnic minorities, and as evidenced by the bustling child care center directly across from the reception area, many of them had children. For young women with children there were few other educational options. Many teenagers drop out even before they have their babies—while pregnant teens could feasibly continue to attend regular schools, the stigma of pregnancy often forces them to leave. Special "pregnancy schools" exist, but usually women over 17 are not allowed to attend.

Many of the students at City School didn't have babies, however. Other factors had led them to leave their former schools. As I would soon find out, for many students, loyalties to gangs (like Diamond Street) or tagging crews (groups of young people, similar to gangs, whose defining concern is propagation of their collective, written graffiti mark, or tag) and fellow grafitti artists (like those who congregate at Belmont Tunnel) had initially pulled them away from other schools, or led to their expulsion. Still other students had left their previous schools to work. A young man I had met tending the parking lot on the first floor couldn't afford the luxury of full-time school. He was working to support his family, and planning to attend City School too. Working kids, teens with babies, gang members, taggers—these were the students for whom Hobbes and Romaine planned to provide an education.

By working on the margins of the educational system, Hobbes and Romaine had managed to found a school for traditionally underserved minority students. Now five recently hired teachers were attempting to stem a tide of dropouts, young men and women who had already been failed by their traditional public schools. Statistically speaking, theirs was an impossible goal. The neighboring high school's dropout rate (the 25–30% cited above) was not encouraging, and the more general statistics gathered about this very demographic—ethnic minorities, teenage mothers, the urban poor—can be demoralizing. Even on cursory examination, dropout rates reflect gross and seemingly insurmountable inequalities, inevitably along socioeconomic and racial lines (cf., Fine, 1991; Kohl, 1967; Kozol, 1991; Monti, 1994). These dropout statistics, published annually, debated by policy makers, and printed in newspapers, also tend to create a homogeneous picture of inner-city schools largely as places of failure, devoid of meaningful interaction. But these statistics, by design, are also generalizations. As far as minority education goes, these generalizations are often overly broad and negative, sweeping over pockets of potential (Rose, 1995).

The goal of a many small, nontraditional schools is precisely to defeat such generalizations (cf., Meier, 1995, 1999) and to tap the potential in those students who traditionally drop out. Hobbes had deliberately founded a small school for this purpose, and the teachers at City School often mentioned that these students were, to them, the most fascinating to teach, though often the most difficult to reach. Many of these students, failed disproportionately by schools, have, by necessity, forged alternative, powerful, and highly self-sustaining identities that are not so easily documented through statistical reports (Heath & McLaughlin, 1993; Trueba, Spindler, G., & Spindler, L., 1989). City School's goal, and one of the goals of my own research, was to find a way through to these young people by recognizing the complexity of their lives and the power of their non-school commitments. This complexity is not easily captured by statistics or generalizations, which are often exaggerated by the media (Jankowski, 1991).

But the forms students' alternative support systems take are often highly incompatible with continuing their education. For many young men and women, for example, ties to youth gangs provide much more substantial sources of self-esteem than school experiences they have had (Alvarez, 1993; Harris, 1988). Gangs also provide more promise of financial reward (Monti, 1994) or ethnic identity (Davidson, 1996; Mendoza-Denton, 1996; Talty, 1995) than a life committed to success in schools typically does. When young peoples' own families provide little financial or emotional stability, gangs (not schools) fill this void as well (Cooper, 1994; Jankowski, 1991), leading to a lifestyle that ultimately may be incompatible with school. Young women may seek a sense of belonging in such gangs or through starting families of their own (Harris, 1988). Whether young people who drop out of school join a gang or not, school provides little that is relevant or emotionally meaningful for them.

In general, these are the young men and women for whom City School wanted to provide an education, working not only to educate them, but also to attend to their different social, emotional, and practical needs. Through an awareness of the unique and tangible concerns of their students, City School promised to provide them with skills for mainstream success without taking away or denigrating their nonmainstream identities. City School would be saturated with meaningful interaction.

CHARTER SCHOOLS AND SCHOOL REFORM

The kind of interaction *within* City School and the very possibility for the genesis of such an educational community emerged out of a reform-oriented climate that fostered the idea of charter schools as an economically and politically feasible means to educational innovation (Alexander, 1993; Amsler & Mulholland, 1992; Bierlein & Mulholland, 1994; Diamond, 1994; Hill, 1994; Little Hoover Commission, 1996; Sautter, 1993; Shankar, 1988). After Hobbes and Romaine had started their school, they needed funding to keep it running. They were interested in securing state funds, but they did not want to be subject to the curricular mandates and top-down management style of public schooling. Charter legislation, which had recently gone into effect, allowing the formation of ten new charter schools in the Los Angeles Unified School District, was designed to provide state resources for just such innovative programs. For Hobbes and Romaine, this was a policy plum that provided them a unique opportunity to create—and fund—a school designed for the disadvantaged and underserved students in the public school system, those students the local neighborhoods were currently "warehousing." One month after opening, City School applied for and attained charter status.

Charter Schools as Real Innovation

What is a charter school? Put most simply, a charter school is "an independent public school of choice, freed from rules but accountable for results" (Manno, Finn, & Vanourek, 2000, p. 736). Charter schools are state funded like all the public schools, but in contrast to traditional schools, they have freedom from state guidelines. While they are required to present a thorough and detailed charter stating their goals and criteria for success, the means by which schools attain this success is open. This definition is simple enough, but it does not fully convey the real signature of the Charter School movement—genuine, truly innovative change. When City School received its charter in 1993, the momentum of the Charter School movement was building, and as policy papers, research reports, and strong opinion emerged, so did the inevitable refrain of "innovation." The late Albert Shankar, former president of the American Federation for Teachers, was a key proponent of charter schools primarily because he saw charter schools as the only form of school restructuring that involved the innovation demanded in our radically changed times. "The point is," Shankar wrote in 1988, "that it's time to question or justify every assumption we have had about schooling for the last 150 years" (p. 94). Charter schools, Shankar wrote, were a vehicle for such innovative rethinking.

With Shankar's enthusiastic and public endorsement, the Charter School movement—and a renewed call for educational innovation—began. By 1993 (the year City School received its charter), there were three charter schools up and operating (all in Minnesota), and California had just passed the law allowing a total of 100 charters to be granted in the state. In 1992 and 1993, policy and research reports hailed charter schools as a "truly different alternative," "innovative" (Amsler & Mulholland, 1992, pp. 1–2), satisfying the need for "break the mold schools," "exciting, promising, and revolutionary" (Alexander, 1993, p. 764), and a "new breed of public schools" (Sautter, 1993). By 1994, California had 45 charter schools, and in that year President Clinton officially endorsed charter schools in his State of the Union address. With endorsement ranging from President Clinton to Albert Shankar to Lamar Alexander to Gary

Hart, charter schools were catching on, and their reputation as real "innovation" appealed to both sides of the political spectrum.

While the idea of real innovation was crucial to charter schools' initial popularity, "innovation" has been a key concept on which charter schools have been attacked as well. Just as "innovation" can be seen as valuable for reformers of any stripe who are looking for something different, it can also be seen as problematic by critics on either side of the political spectrum. On the one hand, critics don't like innovation. Teacher unions, school boards, and school superintendents have argued that this innovation occurs at the expense of good jobs for teachers and real accountability, or that it threatens the future of the entire public education system (Manno, Finn, & Vanourek, 2000). On the other hand, critics who like innovation have argued that despite the heavy rhetoric of innovation, most charter schools are really not innovative at all (Good & Braden, 2000a; Wells et al., 1998a). Instead, many charter schools are simply a veiled form of elitist school choice legislation. This critique of innovation has caused much discussion. While a primary rationale for charter schools was to create a bureaucratic structure that would encourage innovation resulting in more educational opportunities for underserved minority populations, as the demographics of current charter schools suggest, they have also become a new way to preserve the status quo (Kolderie, 1994).

This critique, that charter schools are just a new way of funding schools for students who are already doing well, has become increasingly well documented. And hints of this problem were already apparent during the time of my study. When City School came into existence, four of Los Angeles's ten governmentally designated slots for charter schools were located in Pacific Palisades, an affluent neighborhood in which parents had begun to send their children to private schools when the overpopulated inner-city schools began bussing students to the suburbs. Palisades High began to lure back affluent neighborhood children by creating charter schools within the school (Pyle, 1995), essentially a form of internal tracking (cf., Oakes, 1985). Aside from City School, the city's nine other charter schools attracted successful students, generally highly motivated, with parents actively involved in their education (*Los Angeles Times,* 1994). In this way, charter schools, yet another educational option, had the potential to act as already common magnet schools, offering educational options for those already educationally successful, and taking successful students out of inner-city schools (cf., Devine, 1996).

City School as Real Innovation

In contrast, City School was one of a small number of "second- or third-chance" schools that "offer some students an enclave for education by tailoring opportunities that are not as readily available in the public school system" (Good &

Braden, 2000a, p. 246). City School specifically advertised itself to students that no other school would accept, mentioning school dropouts, expelled students, young mothers, and pregnant students in their enrollment brochure. Throughout its tumultuous 18-month existence, City School's student population was composed exclusively of low-income ethnic minorities, many of whom had spent time in jail or juvenile hall, had babies, or were active gang members. A year after its founding, 15% of City School's students were on parole and 85% had arrest records (*Los Angeles Times*, 1994). However, "tailoring opportunities" to fit the needs of this population, prone to absenteeism, inevitably behind grade level in all subjects, and most importantly, habitually identifying as non–school oriented, proved extremely challenging to City School.

The founders of City School clearly rose to the occasion of charter school fervor, founding a school downtown for at-risk students when seemingly no school could ever have been created for these kids through the usual means. After all, the city, the state, and the school system had been fighting for 20 years over placing a school in this area. Still, some readers may be skeptical. It sounds too easy. How could a few men get together and found a school over lunch? This is another hallmark and another point of criticism of charter schools. For many critics, school charters are simply too easy to get. Some states have become so enthralled with the idea of social capital created by a community of eager teachers and administrators, set loose to "innovate," that in their enthusiasm they have failed to even require coherent or complete proposals from charter school founders (Good & Braden, 2000b). In the case of City School, requiring a more coherent fiscal plan, and more closely monitoring City School's progress possibly could have saved the school, which, after only 16 months as a charter school, dissolved upon district audit, collapsed under mountains of debt.

The Paradoxes of Innovation

City School makes vivid some of the paradoxes of charter school legislation. Charter school legislation is designed precisely to allow creative thinking people like Hobbes and Romaine to seize opportunity and act to create new and innovative schools, in cases where a huge bureaucratic machine would not be able to. However, this same pathway to swift, innovative action is potentially an invitation to irresponsibility and negligence. In the case of City School, this lack of oversight led to fiscal disaster. Similarly paradoxical, charter school laws allowed Hobbes and Romaine to found a school for students that no other school system seemed capable of educating. However, the same school could be seen as enabling further inequity. That is, charter school laws granted City School permission to conduct, essentially, an educational experiment (one that ultimately failed), with little oversight, on those students already so disadvantaged by the system. While one strategy is to use charter schools as pilot school settings for research and development, "sometimes a charter school that was not intended for R&D ends up serving that purpose" (Manno et al., 2000, p. 742). In the case of City School, the students who were involved in this charter school experiment ended up, after 16 months, without a school to attend, further discouraged by the system that was trying to educate them. Yet another paradox, and one fundamental to the kind of community that evolved at City School, was the complex curricular problem of educating students by building on students' disaffection from schooling. Inside this school, curriculum was designed to build on students' identities, to bring their concerns into a school context. However, most of what students oriented to, after years of negative educational experience, was the desire to be away from school.

One reason charter school legislation is so controversial is because it attempts to tackle these complex dilemmas of public education that, for so long, more limited school reforms have tried to gloss over. As Shankar made clear in 1988, simple, one-size-fits-all solutions like the calls for higher standards, more testing, or back-to-basics are not going to work in the complexity of today's school system. One look at the population of City School makes these solutions instantly ridiculous. Creating higher standards, for example, will not help a student who has been expelled from three different schools for fighting. Getting back to basics will not help a student who has excellent math skills, but has only used them to calculate fractions of ounces for drug sales. More testing on reading in English will not access the bilingual abilities of many of today's schoolchildren. Charter schooling is one way of institutionalizing more unique forms of accommodation to the infinite variety of schoolchildren using the public schools today. And City School exemplifies a school that sought out precisely this sort of variety.

These policy-level paradoxes were not only reflected in the institutional trajectory of City School. They were also evident in the kinds of interactions that took place inside the school, between teachers and students, every day. As teachers there struggled to fulfill their charter school mission to serve a population at-risk (and already failed by many other public schools) they came face-to-face with the contradictions of their own mission. Teachers and students alike found themselves in a unique environment, where students considered societal risks were grouped together for the sole purpose of succeeding in that same society. If a school attracts a population with unique needs, the school must be innovative in meeting those needs. Everyday, teachers at City School faced students who demanded new ways of teaching. How did teachers meet this demand? How did students respond to an entirely unique educational environment? This is a question about what goes on, not on a macro policy level, but on an interactional level, inside the classrooms of charter schools. However, despite the burgeoning literature critiquing charter schools, "little research exploring how students perform in charter schools has been produced" (Good & Braden, 2000b, p. 745). Furthermore, the research that has been done claiming to be more comprehensive skims the surface (e.g., Wells, 1998a, 1998b). Unfortunately, while there is much debate at the policy level about what should be changed in charter school legislation (cf., Good & Braden, 2000a) with the exception of the students and teachers who work and interact there, it seems nobody really knows what is going on inside charter schools.

Innovative Reform Calls for Innovative Research

The research at City School documented in the chapters that follow is one small contribution to this lack. I am not documenting "performance" of students in City School of the kind Good and Braden (2000a) are probably calling for. I do not focus on test scores, measures of language proficiency, or even graduation rates. Instead, I investigate the interactional terrain of City School. I look at the kinds of narrating that goes on between students, and how teachers access the identities students develop through narrative. I also examine how institutional context, the pressures of charter school legislation, and ultimately a district initiated audit influence the talk that goes on inside one charter school. By doing so, I illustrate how charter school legislation at times facilitated the creation of a truly unique educational context, and at times led to the censorship of certain voices and ways of thinking. The narratives and conversations I analyze here are a product of the charter school environment, and illustrate the dilemmas inherent in today's public schools by giving voice to those students usually thought to be "pushed out" (cf., Fine, 1991) or silenced.

As my study began, City School was just beginning its journey into schooling. At City School, in contrast to traditional public schooling, there were fewer scripted behaviors (cf., Gutierrez, Larson, & Rymes, 1995; Gutierrez, Rymes, & Larson, 1995) or codes to follow, and teachers often actively encouraged students to talk about (and me to record) their lives outside of school. As a result, some typically unheard voices came to the fore. By closely examining the interactions of these students and teachers, and by linking the policy level of school reform (charter school legislation) with interaction level issues of language, presentation of self, and adolescent identity, this research displays the real impact of charter school reform, in one school, for the students who experience it.

The Impact of City School on Charter School Reform

While City School failed, charter schools are probably here to stay. City School, in 1993, was one of the first charter schools in the nation. Eight years later, over 2,000 charters have been granted in the United States. Clearly this is a movement with some momentum. But even after 8 years of charter legislation, there is no prescribed procedure for starting and maintaining an ideal charter school, and the direction of charter school legislation and action remains malleable. The movement is getting some history, however, and with history comes lessons. A school like City School, viewed closely, but with the 20/20 vision of hindsight, can provide some insight into the charter schools of the future.

One of the initial goals of charter school laws was to allow unheard voices and uneducated children to be heard and to receive an education. I argue, throughout this book, that the types of interactions at City School that brought new voices forward were made possible by charter school innovation. Despite this small success, City School's closure looms much larger in charter schools' collective history. City School, unfortunately, has become one of the examples of charter school failure held up in report after report as an example of, if not why charter schools in general are terrible, why charter schools need to change (Little Hoover Commission, 1996). City School, as a failure, can easily provide data for both of these arguments. But I wish to argue that its impact is more significant. City School's greatest impact, I hope to show, is in the attention it drew to the concerns of youth in Los Angeles, and the possibility for voicing those concerns and hearing them in classrooms.

DOING FIELDWORK IN EDUCATIONAL BORDERLANDS

Uncovering Language, Institution, and Identity

As Renato Rosaldo (1989) has observed, "[C]lassic norms of analysis make it hard to study zones of difference within and between cultures. From the classic perspective, cultural borderlands appear to be annoying exceptions rather than central areas for inquiry" (p. 28). While Rosaldo was speaking primarily about the dilemma faced by traditional anthropologists trying both to understand a community's individuals, while making useful generalizations about its practices, his statement is equally applicable to City School. The students at City School reveal themselves in such a variety of ways, and identify with such a complexity of worlds that they rapidly frustrate the desire, in the manner of "classic" social science, to generalize about categories like "ethnic minority," "high school dropouts," "gang members," "parolees," "graffiti artists," "teen mothers," "at-risk youth," or "high and low achievers." As the story of City School's founding suggests, even the category of "school" was being redefined here. In turn, the City School community proved to be a constantly changing mix of ways of speaking, dressing, acting, and telling stories. To understand City School, what drew students here, and whether these students would stay, was to understand precisely those "zones of difference" so annoying to the classic perspective. My own approach to understanding nuanced local categories of identity would be to record interaction between members of the City School community and to study, in turn, the way in which such interactions, and my recording of them, was guided by the institution and unfolded over time.

While conversation and collaborative construction of identity came to be the focus of my research, the actual conversations I recorded and subsequently analyzed were also determined by my circuitous routing through City School. Rather than attempt artificially to pin down a definition of "typical" interaction at this school, or the identity norms for students and teachers, I recorded the way that identity and notions of typicality were structured through language as well as the institutionally circumscribed nature of these interactions. The institution, as it grew and changed, afforded varying opportunities for students and teachers to interact. Therefore, recording many different situations of language use at City School revealed the value not only of the minute interactional variables observable through a videotaped clip, but also those institutional variables that facilitate interaction and regulate the types of language used and in turn, the way that a conversation evolves. Over the course of my research, I began to see how the constantly changing culture within the City School community created changing expectations in any interaction, and how, in turn, language practices reshaped those expectations. Through this approach, almost any interaction at City School was meaningful—the "borderlands" and "annoying exceptions" described by Rosaldo, became integral to my research.

Discourse Analysis: Language as Lens

Analysis of language-in-use was my ticket of entry into these borderlands. In the chapters that follow, I will elaborate in more detail on the linguistic tools that facilitated my investigation. I will look specifically at *genre*, *narrative*, *grammar*, *naming*, and *indexicality* as linguistic resources students and teachers at City School use to establish individual identity and negotiate their social roles within this unique community.

These linguistic resources provide a lens through which to view multiple layers of context that make up the complex social arena of City School. Throughout my analysis, I use these tools to emphasize the concept of *coauthorship*. Discourse analysts have begun to reveal how localized views of "reality" are constructed and deconstructed (sometimes in a matter of seconds) through coauthored narrative. Conversation analysts have shown how speakers shape their utterances in minute detail according to the reactions of their listeners— their gestures, eye gaze, and conversational responses (Goodwin, 1979). This shaping has been called "recipient design" (Schegloff, 1972) and implicates not only the current speakers, but also any knowledge (or assumptions) the speakers have of their interlocutors' backgrounds and individual or cultural experiences. Because speakers are always designing their utterances according to their interlocutors' reactions, the audience becomes "coauthor" of the speech of any individual; the way in which speakers present themselves is as much a function of who they are speaking to as who they "really" are as individuals (Duranti, 1986).

Duranti (1986) has also observed that, while individual speakers accomplish certain local goals through interaction, these individual speakers simultaneously work within the goals of some larger institutional discourse structure. A young man's narrative, for example, may take a very different form when relayed to his parole officer than when told among his friends, and the difference between these two situations points to the institutionally situated nature of meaning. Therefore, narrative and micro-level linguistic analysis, as well as attention to "coauthorship" when combined with longitudinal study within a community, can provide insight into both the individual construction of goals and the institutional goals those individual voices may serve. City School, where traditional modes of schooling were being challenged in institutionalized ways, was an ideal location to study how language and conversation structure individuals' presentation of self, and how those same language practices are shaped by the institution within which they occur. Therefore, my research examines the effects of both interpersonal and *institutional* coauthorship.

Despite my attention to coauthorship, this research is *not* based on any sort of assumption that language itself creates reality or that language is more important than the events that happen to real people (the violence, for example, involved with gang activity, or the "Savage Inequalities" documented by Kozol [1991]). The focus on language here is neither meant to relativize all violence nor to belittle the larger forces that lead to the lack of positive life choices available to a large and particular section of the population, and most of the students at City School. Instead, my research is grounded in a methodology, both anthropological and linguistic, and profoundly empirical, which uses language as a means to explore culture and change (cf., Duranti, 1994; Ochs, 1988; Schieffelin, 1990). Microanalysis of language practices provides the researcher an empirical *entré* into the complex reality of communities. In this study, language, as viewed through videotaped and audiotaped interactions, provides a means to see the manner in which identities are formed and changed (and, certainly, masked) within everyday activities at City School.

Entering the Field

On my first visit, after signing in and standing bewildered in the front lobby, a student brought me to the office of a teacher/administrator, Laura, with whom I had an appointment to discuss how I could enter this community and begin my research. At the end of that visit, Laura invited me to start attending an "economics" class held every Thursday night. The following Thursday, and for the next 4 weeks, I attended this as a participant/observer, taking part in all the activities as we created a mock community and ran our own businesses.

Through participation in this class, I gained a familiarity with students and school that would enable me to start recording, but, in this context, I also felt ineffectual as a researcher. Over the next 4 weeks, I worked side-by-side with students, as we exchanged "money," started new "businesses," or went "bankrupt." My interaction with the students focused exclusively on the economics tasks, and soon my role became that of unofficial teacher's aide, someone students could turn to for help or guidance in the classwork. But I felt I couldn't engage in talk about other topics since that would detract from the teacher's agenda. Gradually I became aware of what I was not learning about the school and the individual students by confining myself in the classroom. For students, school is often about peer groups and socializing at least as much as about "education" (cf., Eckert, 1989; Shuman, 1986; Sizer, 1984). Without knowing more about students' lives outside of the classroom, I would be missing a lot of what was happening inside the classroom.

Through this initial classroom experience, I felt, firsthand, the shortcomings of interactional research that looks exclusively at the classroom. While, in the manner of typical classroom research, I could have analyzed the interaction in this classroom with an eye toward curricular reform, without more knowledge about the students in this classroom, any recommendations I could glean would very likely be irrelevant. Indeed, the best classroom research looks to what students bring to the classroom with them and how their local knowledge relates to classroom activity. Discourse studies in schools have begun to reveal the immense complexities involved, the unique interactional complexion of each classroom (Mehan, 1985; Shuman, 1986), and the kinds of local discourse practices which school instruction needs to orient to in order to be more effectual (Gutierrez, 1995; Heath, 1982; Phelan, Davidson, & Yu, 1998). These studies have focused on the way in which interactions structure not only what is taught, but also who has access to that information. Those who, for example, aren't familiar with certain classroom question-and-answer routines (Philips, 1983) or certain presupposed cultural practices (Gutierrez, Rymes, & Larson, 1995) may fall behind. These classroom studies illustrate some of the interactional foundations for the statistics that show disproportionate amounts of school failure among ethnic minorities. They also indicate that the researcher must look outside of the classroom to understand what is going on inside it.

Therefore, rather than focusing my own research on the classroom, I wanted to understand who would be speaking in such classrooms, what young people within a school community felt about their participation there. I needed to ask the questions and understand these students in ways that classroom teachers ordinarily do not have the luxury of time to do. With this in mind and with the help and encouragement of Laura, I organized a discussion group on Friday mornings when there were no classes scheduled. In this informal group, students could come and talk and I would be able to begin audio- and videotaping our interactions. Laura selected several students she thought should go, and I telephoned them to ask that they come.

I did want to ask students questions, but I did not ever approach them with a questionnaire or interview schedule. Instead, our interactions unfolded slowly, I spoke as little as possible, and encouraged the students to respond to one another, and not simply address me. This is known as a "spontaneous interview" process, notoriously uncomfortable for everyone involved (Wolfson, 1976); my first few discussions were tense, and the students were reticent, as they didn't know me very well and were not sure why they were there. Even in this strange atmosphere, however, they gradually began to open up, and I became more acquainted with their views of juvenile hall, the "hole," car-jacking, neighborhood loyalties, and the pervasive word, "respect." While I initially planned to learn about students' views of City School, these students spoke very little about their current school experiences, but had much more to say about their lives outside of school, and the events that led up to their departure from other schools. The narratives told by these students form the basis for Chapter 2, "Dropping Out," and the corpus analyzed there.

Both the institution (most obviously, by selecting these particular young people and allowing me to record them) and my presence as a researcher played important roles in shaping these stories. These roles, and the role of students' ethnicity, will be more fully analyzed in Chapters 2 ("Dropping Out") and 3 ("The Language of Dropping Out"), where those stories are discussed in detail. However, much of the way these discussions unfolded, while certainly guided by my presence and the encouragement of teachers at City School, was also determined by the students. The students eventually turned our sessions into an opportunity to meet up with their friends, hang out, plan their weekend activities, and, occasionally, to finish schoolwork. During the first 3 weeks, I encouraged attendance by calling several students the night before I came to remind them about our date, but soon other students, unbidden by telephone calls, began to drop in. We changed the location of our talks so we could be in a room the students preferred. We started listening to "oldies" during the sessions, and some students began drawing while we talked, which involved, for many, drawing their graffiti tag on paper. Over time, the sessions were defined more by the students than by my research agenda. I was, to borrow the title from Charles Briggs's (1986) book on language and ethnography, "learning how to ask"— precisely by not asking. As a result, I began to learn more about the students. Frequently, when I videotaped in the school, students would flash these tagged papers or throw gang hand signs, "representing" for the camera. The ubiquity of these names led me to focus on this aspect of their lives and, later, to see what meanings these signs held outside of this room, among teachers, school administrators, and in students' neighborhoods. Chapter 6 ("Names") discusses the power that these visual signs hold for students *and* teachers. This is just one example of how the emergent nature of these discussion sessions turned them into lessons for me about how the students portrayed themselves and wanted to be perceived by others.

As I stepped out of the classroom and into the noninstructional discourse at City School, my discussion sessions allowed me to see the importance of peer relationships to students. Much of what I learned in those first months was afforded through the videotapes I made, which allowed me to go back to the students' conversations and view them repeatedly, trying to make sense of students' stories and the way they were told. My preliminary videotapes with these young people began to reveal how the audience, their reactions, and their presumed experiences shaped the way that these students spoke about their lives and individual histories. By looking at the language used to form and contest peer groups and the norms associated with them, I saw student and institutional identities as they emerged and changed through interaction outside the formal boundaries of classroom lessons. As my study continued I hoped to see how these conversations related to students' interactions in other settings at City School. If audience shaped the way students presented themselves, exactly who became an audience for these students' stories, and how they participated in their telling, would be crucial.

Following the Community Trajectory

When I began to record classroom interaction 6 months later, I was far more aware of conversations at the margins of the classroom, and the kinds of priorities students brought with them to class. I began to record discourse in and out of the classroom and not only between student peers, but also between students and their teachers, and between students who do not ordinarily interact with one another. In this way I hoped to learn how conversation, and in particular, the types of conversation afforded by this school context, influenced the students. The conversations analyzed in Chapters 7 ("When Friends Aren't Friends") and 8 ("Rights to Advise") are drawn from these tapes.

During my last 5 months at City School, another opportunity for taping arose. Laura, the same teacher who had organized my initial Friday talk sessions was now interested in having me tape another set of interviews with students who had completed an intern program at the school. Again she selected the students I would interview initially. Unlike the first students I interviewed, however, she referred to these young men and women as her "success stories" and thought that it was important that I document their views of the intern program. I agreed, but tried for the most part to follow the format of my initial interviews, letting the students talk among themselves. I had them discuss their intern experiences, but I also encouraged discussion of other aspects of their lives and their perspectives on school. These stories form a dramatic contrast to the initial stories I gathered and form the corpus for Chapter 5 ("Dropping In: Narratives of School Success").

As these final interview sessions most sharply delineate, my presence at City School was by permission of the school, and was therefore guided by what the school allowed and sometimes even encouraged me to see. My continued presence was also guided by my own interest as a researcher into the social and linguistic forces that pushed students in and out of school. After my initial interview sessions, the school gradually became larger and that December, five months after receiving charter status, the school moved to a new location. In January they completely restructured their program. By this time, however, I had come to record not discussion with me, but spontaneous interactions in and around the school. I began by recording classes and the impromptu conversations within them, and continued by recording discussions at the boundaries of classes, before classes started, and between classes. As the school began to self-destruct, schedules and classrooms, any outward structure constantly in flux, I recorded almost anything that looked interesting: Exchanges at the metal detector, sudden arguments, final good-byes between teachers and their students. Then, 12 months after relocating, the school was closed for good. The students were left with a sign on the door to notify them school was shut down, and another sign listing possible Graduate Equivalency Degree (GED) programs. After the school closed and the community had dispersed, I found it much more difficult to find students and to talk. In the following few months, however, I spoke to teachers and administrators, recording their perspectives on why the school had closed and how it had failed.

My research began one month after City School officially received their charter school status, and continued as City School occupied two different campuses, redesigned their curriculum, expanded from a school with 50 students to one of nearly 500, and after 18 months, closed their doors. After the school had its first set of graduates, it also set up the Associates Program to ease students through the transition from high school graduation to a secure job or a place in college. This program provided a year of support for these graduates as they interned at various institutions, learned computer skills, and were coached in life skills. This program would also be a highly controversial expenditure when the school closed down after being audited by the school district. The perspectives of some of the "associates" and the questions raised about this program will be discussed in Chapters 5 and 9, respectively. I visited the school regularly between July 1993 and January 1995, when the school closed, and continued to talk about the school with teachers and staff while the school closed down and over the following summer. Though the school's life was short, few of the students were there through the duration. Some dropped out and returned, and many had only sporadic attendance. This constant change is reflected in the nature of many of the interactions I recorded. Classes often took on a very spontaneous format, necessarily adjusting to unexpected numbers. Teachers had to be ready to accommodate between 2 and 40 students. Similarly, students had to be ready for the size, format, and even the scheduling of their own classes to change without warning. The most debilitating example of this phenomenon occurred in January 1995, when a sign appeared on the door of the school:

<blockquote>

ATTENTION
TO ALL CITY SCHOOL
STUDENTS

The School is Closed. Please
come back on Monday 9
o'clock. L.A.U.S.D. will be
here to help you find a
convenient school to go to.
L.A.U.S.D. will be here from
9:00 A.M. to 10:00 A.M.

</blockquote>

As this note suggests, students who had dropped in ultimately faced the fact that their school itself had dropped out of existence. This final failure reflects an unsteadiness I experienced as a researcher at the school throughout my field-work and through the stories and experiences of the students I talked with and recorded. By tracing the trajectory of this school and the voices within it, this research aims to provide one picture of urban schooling and its inherent dilemmas. I examine primarily the voices of the students whom City School was meant to serve, and secondarily, the voices of the teachers who struggled to fulfill City School's complicated mission.

The failure of the City School provides one sort of closure to this research, but there is no closure to the problems the school tried to address. The neighborhood across the 110 freeway is still locked in protest over the construction of another "warehouse" for high school students. The violence that took the lives of three of City School's students continues to threaten. Schools that try, above all, to create and maintain order within a complex urban environment continue to push out those students who threaten order. In the end, the contradictions, which found an uneasy coexistence within City School, are still unresolvable, but the multiplicity of perspectives and their composite wisdom remains.

CHAPTER 2

Dropping Out

At Central they sent me to King,
King, got the same thing. Fights.
Went to Emerson High and the same thing happened there
                                                                    —Ned, 1993

Friday morning at 9:30 the classroom was quiet, unoccupied. Piles of books and papers were heaped on the teacher's desk, and two long tables and assorted empty chairs, randomly arranged, took up most of the space in the room. With the exception of Jaime, the student intern who had escorted me to the room, the entire school seemed empty and Laura, the teacher who had encouraged me to organize a Friday morning student-discussion group, was not in her office. The teachers, Jaime explained, were in meetings all Friday, and the students didn't generally have classes. Despite the ominous early quiet, I began to unpack my video and audio-recording equipment, arrange the tables, set up the coffee and muffins I had brought, and read through the questions I had written up. Half an hour later, there were still no students in sight, and I began to roam about the school.

A DEVELOPING CONTEXT FOR TALK

Though a school with no students present on Friday may surprise traditional sensibilities, this kind of innovative scheduling was a practice similar to the system's continuation schools, established at the turn of the century to provide an education for those students who had been expelled from the traditional public school. These schools provide a certificate of graduation based on the accumulation of credits and, as Dierdre Kelly (1993) writes, "continuation education usually involves a flexible and reduced school schedule, individualized instruction, extra counseling, small class size, open-entry/open-exit . . . and a curricular emphasis on personal growth and vocational and academic goals" (p. 12). In many ways, this description could adequately describe City School as well.

But the calm halls of city school, and the way I freely wandered through them, contrasts with other descriptions of continuation schools as places where "surveillance is at a premium" (Kelly, 1993, p. 10) and where, often surrounded by tall barbed-wire-crested fences, students can feel imprisoned. But City School was not a typical school—not even a typical "alternative school." The halls—or more accurately—the hall (there was only one), lined with framed photographs of notable African Americans, was peaceful and vacant. The school layout rendered "surveillance" of students, even had it been a goal, nearly impossible. Furthermore, the front office was run not by a suspicious adult, but by a student. Nevertheless, the bathrooms were free of graffiti, and unlike the segregated locked faculty bathrooms and defaced student bathrooms of many L.A. public schools these were shared by students and faculty. The halls of City School reflected neither the surveillance-happy continuation school described by Kelly, nor the rigidly scheduled traditional school to which continuation schools provide an alternative. So far City School appeared to be, as its founders had hoped, and as the charter movement trumpets, truly innovative.

Still, I hoped, at least, to see some students. At 10:15 I wandered back to the classroom I had set up and nobody had shown. But 15 minutes later, a young woman walked in, slowly, and took a seat. I introduced myself, offered her a muffin, which she refused, and we began to talk. She had been the first on my list, and we had spoken on the phone twice, but this was our first face-to-face meeting. I soon found that the questions I had written down more often led to awkward silence than to much conversation. I was relieved when 5 minutes later another student arrived, a young man I hadn't phoned during the week, but whom Laura, the teacher helping me to organize this group, had encouraged to come. The three of us continued talking, and I began recording. I was happy to have at least two students here, but the young woman, Elizabeth, was very reticent, and the new arrival, Jesse, seemed almost too exhausted to stay awake. As I soon found out, he had been released from Juvenile Hall at 4 o'clock that morning and had been up—and at City School—since. Still, he too refused coffee and muffins. After an hour of awkward talk, the students were ready to leave, so I said thanks and began to pack up my equipment. The students seemed eager to go, leaving the box of muffins untouched, researcher dismayed.

The next week, however, I arrived early again, and by around 10:30, four students had shown up. Despite the increase in numbers, however, our conversation seemed forced. I was relieved that the next week I would be out of town. I told the students I would call them when I got back and we could arrange the next Friday session in 2 weeks.

When I returned from vacation, there was a message on my answering machine from Laura. Jesse Navarro, one of the students with whom I had been meeting, had been murdered in his neighborhood. Suddenly, Laura deemed my Friday discussion groups, which I had felt were failing, very important. If nothing else, they would keep these young men and women out of their neighborhoods on Fridays. Sitting and talking with a researcher in a safe place like City

School was preferable to roaming dangerous streets. This decision on Laura's part began to change the demographic of my discussion group. Suddenly large men loomed in the foreground and tiny Elizabeth, who had never spoken much anyway, shrunk into the background of my tapes. These were the men that City School was hoping to save from a life in the streets, to save from the by now clichéd but still applicable prediction that otherwise they would end up "in jail or dead."

By the third meeting, I had also found a conversational tack that led to more fruitful discussion. Instead of asking about the students' experiences at City School, or more general conceptual questions about past and future, goals and fears, I began to ask about the experiences that had led them to leave their previous schools. This simple but concrete question generally elicited stories about previous schools—stories that the other students would add to, or follow with similar anecdotes of their own. These stories also provided me as a researcher and interviewer with enough raw material to begin to ask more relevant questions about their lives. In this way, the initial narratives, no matter how brief, afforded further conversation, and conversation of a certain type.

DISCOURSE GENRES AT CITY SCHOOL

These stories were elicited partly by the questions I devised, but their emergence was also facilitated by City School's institutional origins and the goals of the people working there. The school itself generously granted me a room and a morning to talk with students. This would never have been possible in the hectic daily schedule of an ordinary public school, where any interruption in the structure of the day can create at best bureaucratic complications and at worst, total chaos.

Furthermore, because the school's initial goal was to provide an education for those students who were not being served by such traditional schools, teachers knew about neighborhood violence and saw themselves as responsible for keeping their students away from it. Thus, my own discussion group also became a form of intervention. The students I was encouraged to include in the Friday discussion group were not only a particular set of students in Los Angeles; they were also a particular selection of City School students. These were the students Laura felt were most in need of something—anything—to do on Friday, when classes were not officially in session. This was a select group, and as I learned gradually, they told a characteristic genre of story.

This chapter illustrates that genre, which I have called the "dropping out" story, its emergence in the context of my research at City School, and some of its salient characteristics. The dropping out story genre is marked by a set of themes which are communicated through distinct story structure, characteristic grammar and lexicon, and a set of phrases that develop shared meanings. But a genre of talk can be characterized by formal criteria only to a degree. Genres are also dynamic ways of speaking, emergent through talk, and shaped to be appropriate for a particular context (Bakhtin, 1986; Hanks, 1996). For example, a "sob story" may be a narrative genre that emerges among intimates, but would not be likely to emerge in a job interview.

Similarly, the dropping out genre discussed in this chapter emerged through a certain institutional setting, a particular conversational context that facilitated the telling of such stories, and a participation framework that structured these stories during their telling and reframed them after. In short, students' self-presentations, communicated through stories that draw on recurring patterns of narrative structure and language use, emerge through intricate institutional and interpersonal "webs of interlocution" (Taylor, 1989), to be teased apart below.

NARRATIVE AND IDENTITY

Studies in narrative have long recognized that a story is shaped by history and institutional forces, as well as the listeners present at the time of its telling. In these days of radically politicized trial-by-jury (Gates, 1997) and a highly sophisticated advertising industry (commercials don't even bother trying to appear truthful anymore) (cf., Parmentier, 1994), few people believe that any story is a complete or wholly accurate portrayal of reality. As the novelist Margaret Atwood (1997) has succinctly pointed out, "we are in an age that questions narrative." Despite such questioning, however, people have never ceased to tell and to listen to stories. Telling stories, in fact, was the one activity that saved my small discussion groups at City School, and provided me with my first insights into the students and the school.

Even though all stories are necessarily incomplete, they convey a great deal about the individual doing the narrating. They may even tell more about the narrator through their particular inaccuracies (this is what lawyers hope for when impeaching the credibility of a witness). In general, how a person chooses to tell a story—what is selected or omitted, the inflection on verbs, the tone of one's voice, the repetition of certain words—creates an emerging self-portrait, an entertaining, gripping, depressing, or harrowing presentation of self and the world one inhabits (Capps & Ochs, 1995). Gesture, bodily orientation, and demeanor also contribute to an individual's presentation of self. Erving Goffman's (1959) early work takes particular interest in the theatricality of daily life—and finds most revealing not the information people give through talk, but the impression people *"give off"* through particular ways of interacting. Similarly, through the stories students began to tell at City School I began to learn about the students, not only through the information contained in their stories, but also from the way in which information was selected and conveyed, how students' stories were intricately crafted to create a particular impression.

While every tellable occurrence potentially leads to infinite storied versions, none of which can claim Platonic truth, stories do emerge from an experienced world, and often very real and frightening events. The necessarily selective nature of narrative form and content does not deny the existence of such realities. Almost all the young men and women I spoke to, for example, had been victims of gang violence and/or spent time in juvenile hall. Many of the women had babies with absent fathers. Most students had been in multiple fights. Their scars were real, as were their babies and the time spent away from school, in jail or juvenile hall. And these young men and women were not only victims. They were also perpetrators. Many had inflicted violence on others, stolen cars, robbed houses. These students' experiences with violence, the justice system, and parenting demand narration. While narrative cannot possibly relay "exactly what happened," it can help the narrators reconcile themselves to events that can't be made sense of otherwise. This ability to narrate events, to establish our own situated and partial understanding of an often unsettling and demoralizing, even dehumanizing life, maintains an individual's sanity, and creates an individual's stance toward the future, and a strategy for coping with necessary hardship and disappointment, or making sense out of extraordinary events (Bruner, 1990).

Through its temporal unfolding, narrative also creates a speaker's emergent identity. Narrative meaning is evolving, not static or traditionally logical, and allows the individual to portray life as a continuum of necessary choices, with moral milestones along the way. In Bruner's (1990) terms, narrative itself is an "act of meaning," and the events of a narrative lead into one another through "narrative logic." Through narrative, events that might not fit together in a traditionally logical sense can follow smoothly from one another in the temporal unfolding of a story (Bruner, 1991). One's life emerges not as a smattering of unrelated experiences, but more as a linear quest, which gives shape to an individual's sense of self (MacIntyre, 1984). Charles Taylor (1989) contrasts the essential and "punctual self," the self as static entity, with the narrating, forever reforming "moral self." Because of the inherent temporality of narrative, the march toward inevitable closure, the cause and effect suggested by a temporal sequence of events, the narrative impulse is equally a moral impulse. As Taylor argues, we cannot narrate our lives without coloring the events of our life choices with moral overtones. In this way, narrative serves as a "source of the self" and in particular, a moral self.

This self, however, also emerges through its relationship with others. Our histories and the experiences we have shared with other people shape the sorts of stories we tell and with which we identify (Taylor, 1989). Particular groups of people tell particular types of stories, and two stories about the same event can be told very differently, revealing different assumptions on the part of the tellers, and different moral understandings of characters and events within a narrative (Sacks, 1984). Similarly, adolescent peer groups also maintain unspoken rules about who can rightfully relay certain types of stories, who can be portrayed as a hero or a villain (Goodwin, 1990; Shuman, 1986).

How we tell a story about ourselves is often controlled by how our audience responds. As M. H. Goodwin (1982) has written about stories told by children in Philadelphia, the "primary organization of the descriptions in them, as well as responses to them, is to be found not in the properties of the past events being described but rather in the structure of the present interaction" (p. 811). In other words, and as any experienced storyteller knows, factual accuracy can become a minor issue in the telling of a good story, but attention to the responses of one's interlocutors, and an accurate projection of their moral assumptions, can be crucial.

NARRATIVES AT CITY SCHOOL

While my discussion sessions at City School began as interviews, the students were not there to answer only to me. They also had to present an image for their friends who were also in the room. In fact, the presence of their friends helped to transform the later sessions into lively events, rather than the stilted discussions I conducted for the first 2 weeks. Often, the way these students' stories unfolded were critically shaped by actual verbal contributions of their peers. At other times, this shaping was not so obvious—the videotapes have captured how students shape their stories both for me and their peers, as they flash a sheepish glance at me, attempt to involve their peers through eye gaze, or blatantly disattend by turning away from the group. Depending on the students' primary audience, stories were told differently. Often, while students seemed to be shaping their stories for their friends who were present, when prompted by my follow-up questions to provide further explanation they would provide a far more detailed contextualization of the event. Their peers would often add to the story at this point, explaining to me, the novice, the universal nature of the circumstances described in the story.

As this interactional shaping reveals, students' different versions of stories are also guided by their particular motivations (Smith, 1981). As Ochs, Smith, and Taylor (1989) have discussed in their analysis of stories told at the dinner table, one of the motives served by a particular version of a story is that of the primary author to "look good," or in Charles Taylor's (1989) terms, to present their version of "the good" (in a moral sense) and narrate their adherence to it. The motive to look good can take on more practical dimensions in more institutional circumstances—"looking good" during a police interrogation, for example, or on the witness stand, can be a matter of life or death; in a job interview "looking good" can secure employment.

As such examples suggest, the nature of "looking good" changes dramatically with the setting of the storytelling, and leads to different *genres* of story. Through gathering stories in different circumstances at City School, I found that the first stories I gathered were very particular versions of students' previous experiences, and oriented to certain standards of looking good. The fact that this particular genre of story was being told revealed a great deal not only about the speakers and their peers, but also about City School. This institution, by drawing peers together and allowing me to sit in and record, had also helped to coauthor these stories. Just as the stories told by an individual "give off" impressions of the individual and that teller's motivations, these stories also "give off" impressions of the institution. Laura knew that my videotapes were going to be viewed by local university professors, and that the university was an important founding father of City School. Like any good storyteller, Laura was concerned with presenting a favorable portrait of the institution and, through association, herself. Laura encouraged a certain type of student to attend these groups—the urban student, threatened daily by violence, expelled from all other schools, relying on City School for a last chance at a high school diploma. While I had no intention on focusing on violence or gangs when I began this project, these topics often came up when Laura would describe my research to other people at the school. At this point in City School's history, Laura felt my research could dramatize a particular view of the school, and the moral responsibilities it was shouldering. She even articulated to me, frequently, the value of this group and what it would show about the school: This was a place where those students threatened with violence in other schools, even in their own neighborhoods, could find a safe haven. The harrowing stories told on Fridays would illustrate City School's importance. As I later recorded other stories, which were even more obviously institutionally selected, but meant, in contrast (but also at Laura's urging), to illustrate the dramatic reform wrought by City School (the dropping-in stories of Chapter 5), this role of institutional shaping emerged again. While individual identities were being shaped and conveyed through storytelling, they were also being shaped by, and simultaneously creating an identity for, the school.

THE ROLE OF ETHNICITY IN CHARTER SCHOOLS AND NARRATIVE

So far I have discussed how the factors of the institution, the policy context from which it emerged, my research discussion group, and students themselves and peer pressures all worked together to create a certain generic kind of story. What was the role of students' ethnicity in the kinds of stories that emerged?

The role of ethnicity is deeply intertwined with the goals of this particular charter school and the other contextual factors of these narratives. As I mentioned previously, this school was specifically designed to serve minority students. From the point of view of the founders, new and innovative schools are the only realistic way to serve minority populations effectively since, so obviously, the status quo has not been working for this population. However, one major criticism of charter schools has been that they create either "bastions of affluence" or "ghettos comprised of racial and ethnic minorities" (NCREL Report, 1997). City School, with a student body that was two thirds Latino and one third African American, would probably qualify as the latter.

Furthermore, inadvertently, my initial discussion group had become another homogenous group within the school. All of the students in this Friday morning discussion group were Latino. They were all born in the United States, and all had parents who were born in Mexico. They came to school on Friday to meet with me and, primarily, to socialize with each other. What does it mean that these students came together, and that these students, together, told a certain generic type of story about their lives? These questions will be of continued presence throughout the discussion of these stories and the others included in the book, because it is through these storytellings that, I argue, identity emerges.

However, though it is important to know that these students are all of Hispanic origin, this work focuses less on how identities are essentially preexistent and more on how aspects of identity become relevant in unfolding interaction, how identities are produced by social actors who actively construct who they are through the stories they tell (cf., Kroskrity, 1999). Taking this perspective, the narrative analysis that follows highlights the aspects of identity that the participants themselves highlighted, through their own telling, as most relevant. In most of the stories analyzed here, ethnicity is not highlighted by the participants.

EMERGING GENRE: THE "DROPPING OUT" NARRATIVE

These students' construction of identity is most salient through the genre of the "dropout story." This genre emerged in a specific and documentable way through these discussion groups.

As I had come to understand over the first several weeks, one question led to the most talk in these conversations. When I asked about previous schools and why the students had left, students eventually told stories in which they described the circumstances that made it impossible for them to return to or remain in school. These stories, in turn, led other students to tell similar stories. While my first prompting didn't always lead to very detailed or involving stories, the topic itself encouraged more discussion. Often, after a minimal, three-sentence story, for example, I would ask another question, which encouraged further explanation, and frequently led to another story, a longer version of the one just told, or another story by another student. These stories, while encouraged by my initial questioning, fed into one another. Other students, even some of the most reticent, inevitably joined in to provide explanations for circumstances I didn't seem to understand. These stories unfolded in conversation, and my questions, as well as the contributions of peers, fed into and promoted the telling of a series of stories of a certain form, creating a conversational domino effect. My own prompt was always about previous schools, but was not uniformly phrased. Although none of these prompts explicitly requested a "story," students generally used a narrative form to formulate their responses. These initial narratives are generally very brief, but structured according to a shared pattern.

THE EXTERNAL FORM OF THE DROPPING OUT GENRE

While these stories were embedded in and guided by the conversational contexts, they also had narrative structure and boundaries of their own. The analysis in this chapter draws on 12 of these stories, narrated primarily by eight students—four men and four women, all Latino/as between the ages of 15 and 18—Jerry, Manny, Federico, Ned, Rosa, Sylvia, Fran, and Wendy. While I lump these tellers together artificially as "subjects" here, their individual characters will emerge as the reader becomes familiar with their narratives, gathered from 11 Friday morning discussion groups, audio and video recorded over the course of 4 months. As an introduction to the narrative form of these stories, four representative stories are presented below and discussed in rudimentary detail. Chapters 3 and 4 will draw, in finer analytic detail, on excerpts from all 12 narratives. While each student's narrative described unique experiences, taken together these narratives form a chronological and collective unfolding of these students' presentation of leaving traditional public schools.

Despite the emergent nature of these narratives, narrative itself is an ordered way of speaking, subject to formal criteria. Like literary narrative, stories told in conversation, while emergent from a particular history and subject to differing interpretations, also have an internal, independently analyzable structure (Klein, 1999). For Stein and Policastro (1984), a minimal story contains four parts: (1) the setting; (2) an initiating event; (3) an attempt or plan; and (4) a consequence. Labov (1972) describes a minimal narrative as containing more features, including a "coda" which, though not required of a complete story, is also present in most of the 12 stories in this corpus. Labov describes this coda as the bridge between the world of the story (typically, for Labov, told in past tense) and its characters, and the (present tense) interaction and the participants in the current conversation. While Labov saw the coda as inconsequential to stories themselves and remarked on its frequent omission, the coda plays an important role in this analysis. Rather than leading out of the story world, the coda, by signaling the end of the speaker's version of the narrative, invites interlocutors' responses to the story, and can lead to subsequent reframing of the story (discussed in detail in Chapter 4). This reframing puts a new spin on the events of the initial story, or leads to subsequent, related stories.

As the multiple and differing descriptions of external story structure suggest, these are formal descriptions of talk that is, in great part, an emergent phenomenon. Nevertheless, there are general norms of storytelling in conversation to which, as Sacks (1974) has shown, speakers and listeners orient. Interlocutors expect a climax, or jokingly interrupt after a story "abstract" or "setting" has been relayed—the joke itself being that they are interrupting an expected story structure. Thus, even when narrative order is not followed, participants orient to the normative formal criteria for spoken narrative. So, while narrative form is emergent in context, formal patterns of the sort described by Labov and Waletzky (1967), Labov (1972), Mandler (1984), and Stein and Policastro (1984) also play a part in shaping them.

Spoken narratives, however, can also play with presupposed narrative form, recombining given elements for certain effects (Capps & Ochs, 1995). The dropping out stories also illustrate how elements of the typical story structure generally blend into or displace one another. Stories in this corpus all feature an "initiating event" to which the teller responds, and many times the initiating event is not described as an action or event, but as a problematic setting which in itself necessitates a reaction. Because of the blended nature of the setting and problematic event, I have followed Capps and Ochs and labeled this component the "central problematic experience." The particular way in which the story form emerges here contributes to my characterization of this set of stories as a unique genre. The general outline of the dropping-out story is as follows:

1. Abstract (not always present)
2. Setting/central problematic experience
3. Response (behavioral and/or psychological)
4. Consequence
5. Coda (not always present)

This pattern can be illustrated in even the shortest of the stories in the corpus. The story below was the first relayed in these discussion groups and follows a question I asked about Federico's previous school, which, as Federico explains here, he attended for only one week (see Table 2.1 for transcription conventions).

TABLE 2.1: Transcription Conventions

Symbol	*Meaning*	*Example*
[	Overlap	Betsy: You [wouldn't- Ned:　　　[Just get my butt it kicked 　　　　　　every day.
=	Sentence continuation across an interruption	Mario: Well do your time while their 　　　　ass is out here= Luis:　(shit) Mario: =you know getting smoked on
(0.2)	Silence interval	Rosa: I just (0.2) hit him
—	Brief, self-interruption	Ned: It's— it's like—
↑	Rising intonation	Ned: . . . they'll ↑kick your ass
.	Falling intonation (Periods are *not* used conventionally within transcripts.)	Manny: . . . they socked me.
CAPS	Raised volume	Mario: I want to have a FAMily.
?	Final rising intonation	Ned: . . . so they socked me?
,	Continued intonation (Commas are *not* used conventionally within transcripts.)	Ned: naw, I don't want no trouble
(xxx)	Item of doubtful transcription	Rosa: All you can go do there is like 　　　*ditch*, *skip*, (xxx).
(( ))	Description of scene	Jerry: Well. I got kicked out. 　　　((sheepish glance to Betsy))
Italics	Item of analytic focus	Fran: If they want you bad *they'll* 　　　*be waiting for you.*

"Everybody Rushed Me"

abstract	FED: I lasted only for a week there.
	MANNY: A week.
setting/problematic	FED: Our neighborhood started having shit
experience	with that neighborhood down there, so I
	went over there to the bus so they came
	and hit me up. I said my neighborhood
	and they said fuck that so they socked
	me. Everybody rushed me. Hn.
response	Then the next day we, we and the homeboys
	went down
consequence	and they got me.
coda	So that's it.

As this narrative suggests, the use of a story form can contribute to meaning, not because the form itself contains predetermined meaning, but because individual narrators can work with a form to foreground or background certain elements, to suggest causal relationships. Form is most meaningful then because it is subject to variation. The way Federico's story fits into a generic story form reveals how the story uniquely presents a picture of the teller. The story begins by describing an ongoing state of affairs out of which this particular antagonism emerged. That is, the sentence "Our neighborhood started having shit with that neighborhood" does not explicitly describe the problematic occurrence, yet. Rather, it sets the scene in a particularly problematic way, and illustrates the way in which setting can foreshadow coming problematic experiences, or, in the words of Capps and Ochs (1995), "precast" events as problematic. Out of this ongoing state of "having shit" it seems inevitable that problems will arise, and indeed, the problematic experience, the initial fight, emerges out of this setting. Narrative form, by implying a connection between the scene-setting and the problematic experience, enables the storyteller, in this case, to convey the inevitability of gang antagonism.

The narrative form also enables the author to make a contrast between the violence of which the author was a victim and the violence the author perpetrated in response. In this story, Federico describes the problematic experience at relative length and detail. He explicitly narrates the violence inflicted by "that neighborhood," describing how they "socked" him and "everybody rushed" him. However, Federico describes his own response to this event only obliquely. Following the elaborately narrated problematic experience, the response ("The next day we, we and the homeboys went down") is not fully articulated, nor is it attributed to Federico alone, but to "we and the homeboys." While presumably Federico is describing the last fight he had at school, the fight that led him to be expelled, he does so by first prefacing his actions with the explicit violent actions of others, and describing his own response ("we and the homeboys went down") with reduced detail or clarity. This euphemistically narrated response, however, leads directly into the consequence: "they got me."

While Federico does tell the story of his last fight at school, complying with my request, he uses the story form to contextualize his actions in ways that mitigate his own role: first, rather than describing his own role in instigating gang fights, he describes a preexistent setting that leads inevitably to the initial problematic experience, and second, while he describes the problematic experience in explicit detail, he only minimally describes his own part in the retaliatory fight that followed.

In many of these stories, the setting and problematic event dominate the narrative, and the author's own response is minimized. Often, the setting and problematic event are intertwined to create an ominous sense of inevitable threat. This is the case in the story below, where Ned describes the problematic setting that eventually caused him to bring a knife to school. Ned's description of the school atmosphere turns the setting itself into the event worthy of reaction and contextualizes Ned's decision to arm himself:

"Knife Story"

setting/problematic experience	NED: Its— it's like— it's like you know you don't want trouble but you'll kick it and an' like naw, I don't want no trouble but they'll pick you and pick you until you get mad and get up and what's up? And then get in a fight and they'll ↑kick your ass. Guys right there when I was there I remember guys get stabbed in the bathroom and stuff and I'll be like da, I ain't going to the bathroom alone so I got it. They'll chase me. Once I'll get out of school I'll jump the fence and run home. They'll chase me though but the next day I'll get (black) cause they kicked my ass three times right there. Cause they got me from the back boom boom boom and my face was all messed up and my aunt told me don't go to school and I go alright so I went back and they got me in the halls.
response	That's when I took the knife.
consequence	And they arrested me.

In one rapid-fire list, Ned narrates a pervasive atmosphere at the school ("guys get stabbed in the bathroom and stuff"), the frustratingly repetitive nature of it ("they'll pick you and pick you"), and his own repetitive problematic experiences at the school ("they got me from the back" "they got me in the halls") to create a pervasive setting full of highly problematic events. He presents this accumulation as a problematic experience in itself, one that led to his ultimate response. To contextualize his decision to bring the knife, Ned creates a scenario in which this seems all he could do when circumstances themselves forced him to make this decision of self-defense. Like Federico in the story above, in this story Ned spends few words describing his own response, but many building up to it. Ned's response is also worded in a way that emphasizes its causal connection to the preceding events: "*that*'s when I took the knife," echoes Federico's "*then* the next day we— we and the homeboys went down," both in its minimized expression of the author's offense and in its casting of the author's minimal action as a response to preceding offenses perpetrated by others.

In other stories, the long narration of a problematic event is not followed directly by a behavioral response, but by what Capps and Ochs (1995) call a "psychological response," which leads to certain behavior. The narration of this psychological response, like the lengthy narration of the problematic experience, further contextualizes the author's subsequent actions, providing a warrant for them—for an unleashed fist or a knife in one's pocket. In another story told by Ned, for example, he describes what happened after he was caught with a knife at his first high school. After listing the many schools he attended subsequently, and his frustration at waiting to get a job, he narrates his own psychological response: "I just got bored and started getting crazy" (see Vigil [1988] for a more detailed discussion of what "getting crazy" means in Latino gangs). This response explicitly describes his reaction to the cumulative problematic experiences, and serves as an explanation for the behavioral response that followed: another fight. Like the two stories above, this response is preceded by a lengthy description of a series of problematic experiences.

"I Just Got Bored"

setting/problematic experience	NED: Gu— took me to Rampart. And then, they, told me my records were over there? So I waited, to Roosevelt, got in a fight over there, went to Hollywood High, 'cause I went to uh City Hall? And they told me if I go to school? I can get a job. So I go. You know, go to school go to the job, like that. But I go you know and

	then I went and no job was— no job was coming.
psychological response	So I just got bored and started getting crazy
behavioral response	and then I got in a fight up there
consequence	and then I heard about this an I go.

As in the previous story, in this story Ned's response follows an extensive list of problematic events, his journey from the Rampart Police Station to Roosevelt High to Hollywood High to City Hall and subsequent promises about a job that would be "coming." Nestled within this lengthy narration of unelaborated places to and from which Ned was shuttled in and out, is another fight, here couched as simply a problematic experience ("I got in a fight"), one more in the series of trials. This list of inevitable familiar troubles leads narratively into his psychological response: "I just got bored and started getting crazy." This response explicitly marks Ned's reaction to the list of events he has described, and simultaneously provides a warrant for the behavioral response that followed: another fight, the fight after which he came to City School. As in the previous stories, Ned's behavioral response is minimally narrated and arrives on the heals of a lengthy stretch of problems Ned has faced. The top-heavy problematic experience section and the narration of his own psychological response mitigate his own role in leaving school.

Similarly, in the story "I Got Mad," Rosa tells about the time she hit a teacher. After describing at length how he had chased her around the school, grabbed her arm, and refused to let go, Rosa describes her own psychological response ("I got mad") as a preface to her subsequent behavior ("and I just hit him").

"I Got Mad"

setting/problematic experience	ROSA: Me and her started getting in a fight, and when I— when when when we— when we stopped fighting, they said a teacher's coming a teacher's coming so I ran you know. I was trying to get away eh— and he was chasing me. An' then, and so he wouldn't let go of my hand and I was telling him let go let go and he goes no your going with me an I was go get her, sh— she started it and she wouldn't let me go— he wouldn't let me go so,
psychological response	heh heh, I don't know I got mad

behavioral response	and I just (0.2) hit him.
consequence	That was why I didn't go to school, cause I knew he was looking for me.

Like Ned in the previous story, Rosa contextualizes her final behavioral response in two ways: She elaborates at length on the teacher's pursuit, the problematic experience, and she describes her own psychological response to this experience. By including her psychological response, she provides a warrant for her final action, hitting the teacher.

Both "I Just Got Bored" and "I Got Mad" illustrate moments when the speaker explicitly narrates a psychological response that comes on the heels of a series of problematic experiences and contextualizes an upcoming behavioral response. In describing their psychological responses these authors use words that define mental states: "mad," "bored," and "crazy." In other cases, the internal response to the problematic event or setting is less explicitly narrated. This is the case in the story below, where Fran narrates her own anticipation of actions, her internal premonition of further trouble, a psychological response that is blended into her description of the problematic setting and which also provides a warrant for her behavioral response: leaving school.

"I Got Fed Up"

setting/problematic event/ *psychological response*	FRAN: Too much problems there I couldn't even hang. Time for me to get (on/out). (0.2) Before they kicked me out. I would have to— tired of (changing myself up) before they kicked me out. (0.5) Couldn't hang with them. I been there three years and them three years I never graduated.
	. . .
	That school's fucked *up*.
	All you can go do there is like ditch, skip, (xxx).
behavioral response	That's about it.
consequence	Now I'm here. Getting myself straight.

In this description of the events that led Fran to leave school, the setting, as it becomes the problematic experience, also becomes colored with "psychological response." Although Fran does not use psychological adjectives like "bored," "mad," or "crazy," the way she describes the school is colored with emotion and her own internal predictions of subsequent problems. Her description of the setting also features a projection of what would probably happen to her there—

that she would get kicked out. She describes the school as a place where she felt constantly unsettled, always ready to be expelled or get in some kind of trouble, a place she had been for 3 years and never graduated, where she was making little tangible educational progress. Thus, her subsequent "that school's fucked *up*" is not a neutral description of the school setting, but a description both of the school and of Fran's psychological response to it, her own experience of the school as highly problematic. In describing the setting, Fran indirectly and simultaneously conveys her psychological response to it. Her behavioral response, to "ditch and skip" then, makes sense in the unfolding terms of her narrative. Ultimately, the consequence of this response is to come to City School where she, presumably, will start "getting [her]self straight."

As the examples above illustrate, the "kernel stories" can be analyzed as self-contained story forms, and the story form itself is one resource these authors draw on to portray themselves in common ways. Though these stories describe different events, and use different words, they arise out of a particular discourse setting and share distinctive textual structures that contribute to my characterization of them as a particular discourse genre. All of these authors responded to my question of previous school experiences by framing those experiences in particular ways, using the narrative structure as one resource to do so. In all of the stories printed above, authors use the narrative form to render their own problematic actions understandable, the result of an accumulation of unfortunate events, the inevitable outcome of the weight of an unbearable setting or series of problematic experiences—the endless pursuit by unsavory others, be they rival gang members, teachers, school officials, or other students. Through this narrative form, particular themes emerge.

THEMES BROUGHT UP THROUGH STORIES

The stories shown above have begun to illustrate the formal rudiments as well as the conversational emergence of this genre. This genre can also be characterized by certain themes constructed through these conversational and formal means. All of these stories create a sense of the protagonist's unwilling but inevitable resort to violence. Related to this theme, all these stories also present an omnipresent and ever-threatening setting that the protagonist copes with.

An Unavoidable Resort to Violence

The temporal and structural demands of storytelling pull the story in a certain direction, and necessitate a particular moral framing of the events. For example, because Federico is telling his story in response to a particular question, he must narrate his participation in the fight described above, even though his role was a violent one, a role he may not want to articulate fully in my presence. But the way he narrates illustrates his own moral framing of the events. Though my question and the temporally ordered nature of narrative pull Federico's story in a particular direction, Federico controls the way this temporal unfolding is colored, and even uses the temporally suggested cause-and-effect relationship between the two fights in his story to make sense of his own necessary resort to violence. He describes himself not as a ruthless avenger of the gang who attacked him *first*, but as a rightful protector of his own well-being—his own violence is told as a *subsequent* act of self-defense. When he "went down" the next day to start another fight, he was acting reasonably, given the onslaught of violence he had faced the previous day and would likely face in the future should he choose not to retaliate.

Similarly, Ned, after facing repeated beatings at his school, finally decided to protect himself by bringing a knife. Rosa, faced with a teacher who would not "let go" ultimately had to hit him. And Fran, after 3 unproductive years in a "fucked-up" school, finally had to leave. In these stories, narrators portray their responses as reasonable actions for any person faced with unreasonable violence or unbearable, unavoidable situations. This is a theme that emerges repeatedly in these stories and the expression of which is facilitated by the temporal unfolding of narrative.

A Context of Omnipresent Threat

Another related theme apparent in the stories analyzed above, and common to many of the "dropping out" genre, is the way in which the problematic event is cast. The violence that elicits a response is given an aura of omnipresence. This is portrayed in the external story structure through the extended nature of the setting and problematic event. Internally, this omnipresence is further exaggerated through the use of indefinite pronouns like "everybody" and "everywhere" or an indexical "they" that comes to mean "everybody"—as in "they would have kicked her ass you know?" or "they got me." In other stories this omnipresence is accentuated, not through the extended narration of a problematic event, but through the extended narration of a setting *as* problematic event, often elaborated in an story addendum with statements like "that's the way it is" or "there's still always trouble." Because of these circumstances, fights seem, as one student described it, to "start for no reason." In certain cases, before describing a specific problem at one school, a student will narrate a catalogue of schools from which they have been expelled (as Ned's epigraph exemplifies), universalizing the generally problematic atmosphere that exists at all of them and which inevitably led to the student's departure.

Mitigating Responsibility

As discussion so far suggests, when violence does occur in these stories, it is usually contextualized in a way that mitigates the teller's responsibility for it. Narrators often distribute their responsibility for violence by narrating their own violent acts as necessary to preserve the well-being or reputation of others— either other gang members or younger siblings. Within these stories narrators rarely narrate themselves as unilaterally acting violently. For example, in "Everybody Rushed Me," when faced with a problematic event, Federico retaliates not as an individual, but as part of "we" when he says, "the next day, we went down." Needless to say, this violence is not narrated very explicitly either, and the grammatical resources for maintaining ambiguity in such cases will be explored in the following chapter.

"Everybody Rushed Me" also illustrates one way that violence is portrayed as necessity—prompted by the need to protect the reputation of one's gang. As Federico describes the initiating event, his neighborhood was involved in a conflict with another neighborhood. Then one day, Federico narrates, "they came an' hit me up." This event—getting hit up—encapsulates an entire ethic of gang behavior that necessitates that gang members act as individuals in order to preserve the reputation of the group. Getting "hit up" occurs when someone approaches an individual from a rival gang and asks him where he is from (that is, to which gang he claims membership). The individual has two options: he can either say "nowhere," thereby disappointing his gang and leading to later violence at the hands of former friends, or admit a rival gang affiliation and take a beating on the spot. Getting "hit up" always necessitates a violent response, not simply to protect one's own dignity as an individual, but to protect the viability one's gang, the group on whose behalf one is fighting. In the above story, Federico does not hesitate to claim his gang loyalties ("I said my neighborhood"). Within the ethic of getting hit up, he has behaved honorably. This theme of violence as performed on behalf of the group extends to family as well, as gang members often narrate their role in a gang as one of protection— either of their neighborhood or of their family, and in particular, of younger siblings.

SUMMARY

The narratives that emerged during my first months of fieldwork were revealing of the lives of the students, the institutional context in which they evolved, and the shaping role of my own presence. The themes that these stories conveyed— tellers' violence as a necessary response to inevitable, omnipresent, preexistent violence, and the tellers' minimization of responsibility for their own individual acts, would probably strike even the most casual listener of these stories. As I listened, I liked these young men and women. I didn't see them as unruly or violent, but as young people trapped in a cycle of escalating and unpleasant circumstances. My own responses hinged on storytellers' portrayal of their own actions as understandable, even honorable, given certain circumstances. Some of these themes are communicated only obliquely in the stories themselves, but reworded and explicitly articulated in the extended addenda that follow, usually at my prompting.

Given the potential of narrative to reveal not necessarily the "truth" but details about narrating individuals and groups, and the goals of these individuals and the institutions within which they operate, the themes shown in these narratives are powerful. Even as City School tried to keep these young men from the violence in their neighborhoods, even change them, by placing them in the Friday morning discussion group and encouraging their attendance at City School in general, their narratives describe the inevitability of violence or victimization that has threatened many of them. By describing the conversational unfolding of these stories, however, before describing these general themes, I hope to have conveyed that these are not immutable themes that necessarily or interminably dominate the lives of these young men and women. Rather, these themes, by virtue of the context of their telling, were essential to *these* stories, and the students' self-portrayals in these meetings. These portrayals, these lives, are always subject to change.

CHAPTER 3

The Language of Dropping Out

*They kicked my ass three times right there 'cause they got me
from the back, boom boom boom, and my face was all messed
up and my aunt told me don't go to school and I go alright.*
                                                    —Ned, 1993

Although the dropping out narratives emerge according to context, after hearing several, they begin to form a more stable impression: The themes seem immutable, and the roles narrated come to embody characteristic types. This impression of a typical reality conveyed through these stories can be traced through closer examination of the linguistic resources systematically drawn on to create the "dropping out" genre. While the students' individual stories are unique, the similarities across these stories suggest the stability of a genre. The typicality of these stories is what Bakhtin (1986) has defined as a speech genre:

> Each separate utterance is individual, of course, but each sphere in which language is used develops its own *relatively stable types* of these utterances. These we may call *speech genres*. (p. 60, emphasis in original)

This chapter goes about tracing exactly what makes a "relatively stable type" by identifying the characteristic linguistic features of the "dropping out" narrative genre. This genre draws on characteristic grammatical forms, as well as patterns of textual structure. These linguistic and indexical resources construct the common themes—they form the founding "stability"—of the dropping out genre.

THE GRAMMATICAL REPERTOIRE OF THE DROPPING OUT GENRE

The thematic trends outlined in the previous chapter emerged not only through the events relayed in stories, but also through the way that speakers selected, highlighted, mitigated, or tempered events through their telling. By narrating their own role in leaving school in ways that render their actions reasonable, these authors present themselves as individuals who have, despite expulsion from other schools, time spent in jail, ties to gangs, or their numerous fights, behaved honorably. Grammar plays a key role in this crafting of narrative selves.

In research described in *Language in the Inner City*, Labov (1972) looked at the grammatical complexity of narratives in order to distinguish between genres of stories told by different sociological categories of people: children and adults, African Americans and European Americans, middle and working classes. To make such distinctions, he began to look not only at the external form, but also at the "internal structure," the syntactic makeup of narrative, to see how speakers create compelling stories. Today, Labov's work on narrative is frequently called into question, precisely because of the elicited nature of his narratives. The elicitation (he asked subjects to describe a moment when they were in danger of death) as well as the presence of the researcher no doubt contributes somewhat to the way that these narratives were structured both internally and externally. While Labov acknowledged that the narratives are influenced by the research format (they would be different if the interviewer wasn't structuring the situation), he also claimed that narrators typically got so lost in telling the story that the manner of its elicitation was moot. In this research, Labov still saw the narrative as a rather monologic construction, rather than one constructed, as the dropping out stories clearly are, by the participation framework, specifically, the presence of peers and/or a researcher as coauthors. Labov's neglect of the phenomenon of coauthorship, however, does not negate the patterns he identified. The forms he recorded were certainly there, though the reasons these patterns exist may be more complex than his categorical sociolinguistic distinctions suggest.

Like Labov's narratives, the narratives told in the Friday discussion groups employ a particular patterned use of grammatical forms. That is, they share a grammatical repertoire, and this grammatical repertoire co-occurs systematically with certain narrative events or even particular words. And like Labov's narratives, these are a certain "genre" of narrative. This narrative genre is particular not only to the kinds of students being interviewed, but also (and this is what may thwart a larger sociolinguistic project like Labov's, of linking this genre to race, ethnicity, or social class) by the setting itself, my own presence, and the institutional preconditions of our meeting. A consciousness of the influence of elicitation and the interactional setting may hinder attempts to generalize these grammatical traits sociolinguistically. However, the existence of any particular genre of narrative reveals much about the reproduction and flexibility of social identities and the role institutions take in this reproduction or change.

In the Friday discussion groups, my presence is muted, as is the role of charter school reform, or, for that matter, the latest media report on City School. No banner hangs over our conversation telling students to make City School look good. No school staff member holds up signs saying "laugh" or "clap" or "groan," as if the storytellers' peers were a studio audience. But these presences are apparent in the way that stories are told and received. Storytellers carefully craft language to render the events of their lives *simultaneously* reportable to their peers *and* to me, the researcher, and to whatever institutional agenda they see me representing. This typically means they must discuss events of gang retaliation or the fights in which their peers know they were involved, but they must also temper these descriptions to make them palatable for me. They must "look good" for both their peers and for the researcher. Generally authors manage both of these audiences by describing the events in question, and using grammatical tools to limit their own agency in these events, rendering their role in narrated actions more ambiguous.

Throughout this process, together, students coauthor not only each others' narratives, but a narrative genre. Just as a single story is coauthored in conversation, across multiple conversations, a narrative *genre* is coauthored into existence. The presence of this genre tells something not only about its multiple authors, but also about the institutions and individuals that engendered that particular sort of story. Instead of pinpointing a genre on a demographic group, my goal is to understand how multiple influences shape that genre, and to use genre as a tool for understanding context (in this case, the context of the charter school). In other words, instead of saying something like "This is the kind of story Latinos tell," I want to say, "This is the kind of story that students in this institutional context, under these social influences, tell." Uncovering the role of context (including the role of the genre's coauthors) involves first examining the grammatical repertoire that makes up the genre. What is "this kind of story"? Describing precisely that is the goal of the remainder of this chapter.

Creating Ominous External Inciting Events

Tellers of dropping out stories often minimize their own role in school troubles by maximizing the role of the external inciting events. As the analysis of the stories' formal layout has already begun to illustrate, speakers often portray violence or the decision to leave school as the result of inescapable circumstances that predate the story itself and frame the author's response as necessary, even inevitable. While the form the narratives take—the extended narration of the central problematic event—is one resource speakers use to portray the inevitability of their response, systematic deployment of certain grammatical forms is another formal resource that speakers draw upon to convey a sense of inevitability. As detailed in the sections that follow, certain patterns of grammar, common across speakers and stories, portray ongoing strife, project the inevitability of trouble, create a sense of immediacy, emphasize timeless truth, identify ubiquitous antagonists, and narrate problems as "everywhere."

Portraying Ongoing Strife. Progressive aspect functions grammatically to describe "ongoing, durative" actions (Chalker & Weiner, 1994). The dropping out genre is marked by the frequent use of progressive aspect, particularly during the setting and problematic event section of the narrative, but during the recasting of events in the addendum as well. The use of this grammatical structure *in conjunction* with particular story components and characters becomes a genred locution, shared by tellers of the dropping out stories. For example, when Fran describes the school atmosphere that eventually caused her to drop out, she portrays the relentless and projectable pursuit of an ambiguous "they" by using progressive aspect:

FRAN: If they want you bad *they'll be waiting for you.*

This excerpt illustrates the generic "dropping out" use of future progressive *in conjunction* with troubling events. "They" in this example refers to the students at school who are always try*ing* to catch you off guard and beat you up. Using this pronoun in conjunction with the progressive emphasizes the omnipresent danger of these pursuing peers.

In other stories, progressive aspect is used not to describe ongoing gang rivalry or the teller's pursuit by other students, but, as in Rosa's story about her fight with the teacher, the durative nature of teachers' negative behavior, and the ongoing need to avoid it. Rosa begins her story of her final fight at school in the midst of the action already hiding from a teacher:

ROSA: Because I *was hiding* from this teacher.

As she goes on to explain, the teacher was relentlessly pursuing her. She conveys the enduring nature of his pursuit through further use of progressive aspect:

ROSA: An—and *the teacher was chasing me?* And I an—I tried to get away
    from him an I didn't want to get in trouble so *he was pulling me.*

As she continues to struggle, Rosa uses progressive aspect to describe her own repeated but futile attempts to get away from the teacher:

ROSA: and *I kept telling him* to to to let go and he wouldn't let go.

In this last excerpt, Rosa even emphasizes the habitual nature of the progressive aspect by using the lexical aspect marker "kept" in place of the "be" component of progressive aspect. Ultimately, the teacher's enduring pursuit, even in the face of Rosa's repeated pleas, leads her to sock the teacher, but her final violent act (and the one that led to her departure from school) is narrated as the result of repeated attempts to tell the teacher to let go, and the enduring, stubborn nature of the teacher's pursuit. As Rosa continues, she narrates her own decision to leave the school permanently as a result of this teacher's enduring presence:

ROSA: and *he was looking for me* that's why I couldn't go there anymore
      'cause I knew if I would go there I would get in trouble.

In the subsequent framing of this story, Rosa continues to emphasize the enduring quality of this teacher's pursuit through the use of progressive aspect. When I questioned her motivation not to go back, she reemphasizes the teacher's pursuit and a tactic generally used by teachers to track down students in trouble, looking them up in the yearbook:

BETSY: S— So you just left, and never went back, they didn't kick you out or
      anything?
ROSA: They didn't know about what—they didn't know me.
BETSY: Oh.
ROSA: I just knew who he was but he didn't, know me. *He was just looking
      for me* though and *he was looking for me in the yearbook* but I'm not in
      the yearbook 'cause I didn't take no pictures.
MANNY: That's a good thing. Not to take pictures in the yearbook.

As Rosa explains to me why she had to leave school, she again describes the durative nature of the teacher's pursuit ("He was looking for me . . . looking for me in the yearbook"). Manny's recognition of the yearbook avoidance tactic suggests that this teacher's pursuit strategy is considered common enough that many students don't have their yearbook pictures taken.

Fran also emphasizes the relentless pursuit of teachers, using progressive aspect, and the same verb, "looking," to describe how the teachers operate:

FRAN: I know they were about to kick me out. They were just *waiting— look-
      ing after me all the time*.

Fran even accentuates the durative aspect of the school officials' actions here by appending the adverbial "all the time."

Ned uses progressive aspect to describe the enduring state of his boredom while he went to school and waited for a job, the lack of which led to another durative state, getting crazy:

NED: *No job was coming* so I just got bored and started *getting crazy*.

When another student, Jerry, begins to describe the school he used to attend, he doesn't even formulate "complete" sentences, but relies on progressive aspect to communicate the atmosphere of his life there, and the preexistent, enduring quality of antagonism from other students:

JERRY: *Getting* chased, *getting* beat up.

Jerry's use of the -ing ending and the repetitive parallel structure of his statements echoes the uses of the progressive aspect seen in the other excerpts. In another creative use of the progressive, Federico manages to create a habitual, ongoing event out of even the *beginning* of an antagonism by replacing the auxiliary "be" of the progressive with the verb "started." In this way Federico narrates the preexistent nature of his conflict with the rival gang:

FED: Our neighborhood started *having* shit with that neighborhood down
    there?

As Federico goes on to narrate, in some time in the past, an ongoing state "started" ("having shit") and as the use of progressive aspect indicates, it has continued ever since. The durative nature of this rivalry (as grammatically marked through progressive aspect) led to his own violent actions, and ultimately, to his expulsion from school.

   Projecting the Inevitability of Trouble. As some of these examples above have already suggested, the inevitability of trouble is also communicated in these stories through the use of hypothetical constructions that project the future, or through more direct grammatical marking of future actions. For example, Rosa narrates her decision to leave school as a natural response to what she supposes would be the future actions of her teacher. She expresses her projection through a conditional clause:

ROSA: and he was looking for me that's why I couldn't go there anymore
    'cause I knew *if I would go there I would get in trouble.*

After Federico's story "Everybody Rushed Me," I explicitly ask him to project a specific outcome had he *not* retaliated the next day. His response echoes the projections of other dropping out stories: He may not have been suspended from school, but he would have faced more painful consequences:

BETSY: Oh. So what would have happened if you had just never went down
    the next day?
FED: *I wouldn't get suspended.*
BETSY: You [wouldn't—
FED: [*Just get my butt it kicked every day.*

As Federico's projections suggest, his fight, though it did lead to his departure from school, was necessary to prevent further victimization. In describing her need to leave school, Fran characterizes the ominous school atmosphere in terms of projected actions, using both a conditional clause, and the future progressive:

FRAN: *If* they want you bad *they'll be waiting for you.*

And Rosa, when describing the circumstances that led to her fight with another girl, projects the intentions of the other gang:

ROSA: I got in a fight right? 'Cause they *were going to beat up* on my little
     sister.

Generally speaking, however, this projection of the actions of others may act as a self-fulfilling prophecy which, in fact, solidifies the intentions of others, by acting on them before they occur (Goodwin, 1990; Greenfield, 1980). This projection of actions becomes a powerful resource for constructing identity in relation to other people.

   Creating Immediacy.   Generally speaking, people consider narratives to be told about previous events, and therefore to be told in the simple past tense. In actuality, however, few narratives consistently maintain past tense, and frequently, departures from the past are precisely what keep interlocutors interested in a story. Labov (1972) described any departure from simple past tense as a more sophisticated contribution to the narrative, a case of evaluative coloring that leads to the narrative's reportability. Through analysis of stories told at the dinner table, Ochs (1993) has shown how present tense makes storied events more relevant by extending past experiences forward into the present, and Capps and Ochs (1995) illustrate how departures from the past tense can serve more particular communicative functions in the narratives of an agoraphobic woman, noting, for example, how the phrase "here I am," followed by a list of unbearable circumstances, depicts narrative events as more spatially and temporally immediate to interlocutors. While generally their subject narrates her panic events as taking place in distant locations (not the place where the story is being told), "here" brings these events into the spatial realm of their telling and the present tense "am" achieves temporal immediacy.
   The use of present tense in the dropping out genre of narratives also is used in a particular way—to create a more universal aura to the problematic settings described. The impression of the omnipresence of trouble is created through precise deployment of the *present tense of a certain repertoire of verbs* in combination with the appearance of a *certain repertoire of subject position occupants* (indefinite, plural, or generic noun phrases). Thus, through a combi-

nation of tense, lexicon, and story components, these tellers use the present tense to narrate "general timeless truths" (e.g., "Water freezes at 0° C," as described by Celce-Murcia & Larsen-Freeman, 1983, p. 62). When used in this way during the "setting/problematic experience" portion of a narrative, the present tense marks events as timeless truths about existence in a particular high school or neighborhood. In Ned's knife story, for example, he uses the present tense *in combination with* a generic, plural noun phrase ("guys") to set the scene of school as one that inevitably includes violence:

NED: guys *get stabbed* in the bathroom and stuff

Fran also uses the present tense in combination with a generic "you" to describe the kinds of habits the school would lead anyone to develop:

FRAN: *All you can go— just go do there* is like ditch, skip. That's about it.

The use of present tense also emerges after the story coda, when all the conversationalists reflect on the story and the relevant timeless truths the story has evoked. While Labov (1972) noted that the coda generally functions to take interlocutors out of the story time, the present tense ruminations in the aftermath of dropping out narratives almost always reflect back on the stories, highlighting the general and timeless ramifications of the narrated events. These often universalizing reflections also function to reinforce the theme of unavoidable threat. For example, after Rosa describes the need to protect her sister, she finishes with a present tense, universalizing description of "the way it is."

ROSA: You jump me today I'll jump you tomorrow. And *that's the way it is.*

In this excerpt, Rosa uses the present tense in "that's" in combination with the noun phrase "the way" which refers, of course, to more unpleasant interactions between a generic "you" and antagonistic others ("you jump me today I'll jump you tomorrow"). Again, present tense in combination with a particular generic noun phrase creates a genre in which trouble seems omnipresent. The cyclic nature of troubles is usually agreed upon in the Friday discussion groups, and after Rosa's statement, another student ratifies her depiction of the events, repeating slowly to herself "that's . . . the way . . . it is."

Similarly, after Ned's "Knife Story," and at my prompting, both Ned and Federico switch into global present tense explanations for why people are driven to such extremes at their schools:

NED: There's a *lotta* gangs [going there
FED: [There's a lotta gangs. You know you might get
   along with one but *there's a few you don't get along.* So that's when
   the— the problem starts see.

Rather than describing their fights as particular to certain inciting events, Federico and Ned describe the conditions that lead to fights as enduring and ever
present. In a similar way, after Fran describes leaving school, she goes on to
elaborate the conditions at that school. Her use of the present tense suggests
these problems were not hers alone nor particular to the time of her departure
from school, and another student present, Willow, picks up on her description
of the school and augments it with her own present tense description:

WILLOW: Belmont is a real touchy school. Real touchy. You can't do one little thing 'cause it's already coming into a fight.

At times my own questions reverted to past tense to discuss Fran's experiences
of high school. The past, however, suggests that "a single, completed action"
has occurred (Celce-Murcia & Larsen-Freeman, 1983, p. 63). Fran and her
peers, however, will not follow my lead in constructing events this way. Even
after my questions about specific past events, students' responses pulled the
events back into the general, timeless simple present:

BETSY: So who did you fight with there?
FRAN: Hm?
BETSY: Who did you fight with?
FRAN: Oh heh heh heh
WILLOW: *Who don't you fight with!*
   At Belmont *who don't you fight with.*
FRAN: *Who don't you fight with. You got all kinds of people with their
   attitudes—*

Both Fran and Willow reassert the timeless threat present at their former high
school, and avoid my construction of their troubles there as specific to one
particular fight or problematic encounter. All of these uses of present reinforce
the theme of unavoidable trouble that led these young men and women to leave
school.

   Emphasizing Timeless Truth.   In the examples just listed, we can see the
emergence of a genred locution: nonspecific noun phrases systematically occur-
ring in combination with present tense. The timeless truths expressed through
simple present in these stories are also emphasized when, in place of the "you"

or "guys" seen in the above examples, "it" and "there" appear as subjects of the present tense. These speakers use nonreferential "it" and "there" (also known as "existential" it and there) to convey ever presence of particular unpleasant environmental conditions. Indeed, nonreferential "it" is also referred to as "ambient" or "environmental" it (Celce-Murcia & Larsen-Freeman, 1983, pp. 281–282), and used to describe atmospheric conditions like time, temperature, or weather (e.g., "it's hot outside," "it's late"). In these narratives, the use of ambient "it" in combination with the present tense evokes a particularly trying or antagonistic atmosphere, as when Fran discusses her ongoing problems in and out of school:

FRAN: I mean *it's rough*. You know how it is. *It's rough*.

or when Rosa describes the circular nature of gang retaliation:

ROSA: You jump me today I'll jump you tomorrow. And *that's the way it is*.

Ned uses environmental "it" to create an ambient sense of the conditions at his school:

NED: *It's like* you know you don't want trouble but you'll kick it and and like naw, I don't want no trouble but they'll pick you and pick you until you get mad and get up and what's up? and then get in a fight and they'll kick your ass.

Even though Ned narrates a series of very particular experiences here, he frames those experiences with an ambient "it's like" suggesting the more generalizable, atmospheric nature of those events.

Nonreferential "there" also accentuates the atmospheric overtones of present tense "be." For example, Fran uses nonreferential "there" to describe the inescapable nature of trouble:

FRAN: *there's* still always trouble

And Ned and Federico use existential "there" with the present tense to evoke the omnipresence of gangs at their school:

NED: *There's a lotta gangs* [going there
FED: [*There's a lotta gangs*. You know you might get along with one but *there's a few you don't get along*. So that's when the the problem starts see.

These nonreferential forms convey a general presence, an atmospheric surround within which "the problem starts."

Identifying Ubiquitous Antagonists.   Indefinite pronouns also frequently appear in subject position in these narratives to describe the narrators rivals, creating a sense that countless others are acting on the protagonist. Federico, for example, describes the problematic experience as one caused not by a particular person or group of people, but by "everybody":

FED: I said my neighborhood and they said fuck that so they socked me?
      Everybody rushed me. Hn.

Similarly, Fran describes the way "everybody" is always in bad moods, and Drew, another student present, ratifies her description of the kind of people that "everybody" tends to be:

FRAN: *Everyone* they're always on the rag.
DREW: *Everybody* thinks they're champions.

Later in this conversation, the general nature of Fran and Willow's pursuers has developed to such a level that I, and one of the students listening, have lost track of who "they" are, and we try to get a more specific identification from Willow:

WILLOW: If they really want you bad they'll be waiting for you.
BETSY & STUDENT: Who?
WILLOW: Pschhh. *Whoever* heh.

The indefinite nature of the pursuers here seems to be their most salient descriptive characteristic. When asked for specifics, "whoever" appears to be the most relevant way of portraying them. Willow's scoffing "pschh" even suggests that the question of who "they" really are misses the point. "They" are not a specific person, but potentially anyone. In this way, storytellers use "indefinite" pronouns definitively—to portray pursuers who narrators experience as "everybody."

Narrating Problems "Everywhere."   Just as narrators' use of "everyone" conveys a ubiquitous and embodied threat, these students' use of "everywhere" conveys how this threat permeates the spaces they inhabit. In the two examples below, Fran continues to describe the environment she eventually had to leave:

FRAN: It is that jealousy around that school *everywhere*. No matter what you gotta—

Here, "jealousy," generally an adjective used to modify animate, usually human nouns, is not attributed to a particular person, or even to "everyone," but to the general atmosphere of the school. Jealousy is "around" that school "everywhere." The atmosphere is so permeated with unpleasant traits that problems are inevitable:

FRAN: Even *everywhere* you go you always have problems. And here I wasn't even gonna come here no more? I was fed up with it? But alright.

Problems are "everywhere" and "always" present. This indefinite place referent creates a context where problems and necessary reactions are inevitable.

In these depictions of events in schools as ever present and unavoidable, "everybody" becomes suspect, and the situation becomes one that pushes students to certain reactions, and ultimately to their consequent status as "dropouts."

Mitigating Agency

The previous catalogue of examples has begun to illustrate the genrefication of discourse patterns in the narratives of dropping out. These young men and women use particular grammatical forms in systematic ways to convey the ominous and inescapable nature of the circumstances to which they respond. As the stories have already illustrated, students portray their reaction far less elaborately or explicitly than they portray the inciting problematic experience. This section illustrates more specifically, how narrators limit their own role in responding to the problematic experience by grammatically limiting their own agency. For example, these narrators do not tell stories in which they explicitly identify themselves as agents in the fights that led them to leave school. Instead, these narrators systematically draw on a particular repertoire of grammatical forms and deploy them in patterned combination with certain lexical and discourse structures to mitigate their own agency and as a result, their responsibility for the violence or unpleasant circumstances they narrate. This section will focus on one grammatical element that contributes to this self-portrayal: "Logical connectors" or "Resultative discourse markers," which occur as bridging elements between the problem and response components of the story and indicate that the speaker's actions follow other instigating circumstances ("*So* I hit 'im," "*then* the next day we went down," "*that's when* I brought the knife"), and suggest a cause-effect relationship between events which are temporally ordered.

While the patterned use of progressive aspect, the present tense of "eternal truths," atmospheric "it," the ominous indefinite pronouns "everyone" and "any-one," and the indefinite place referent "everywhere" set up situations as inevitably troublesome, the use of causally connecting discourse markers shows how these speakers narrate their actions as a result of such circumstances. In these narratives, clause external discourse markers afford speakers' narration of their own potentially reprehensible actions as the result of external circumstances. The discourse marker "so," for example, "often precedes information understood as resultative," that is, as the outcome of reported events (Schiffrin, 1987). The discourse meaning of "so" can be paraphrased (in certain contexts) to mean "as a consequence" (Celce-Murcia & Larsen-Freeman, 1983, p. 327). In these narratives, then, the discourse marker "so" further aids in portraying the speaker's own agency as an act of self-defense. Rosa, for example, uses "so" to indicate that her own violent response is a result of previous unreasonable antagonism.

ROSA: and then she goes "I'm gonna fuck her up" *so* I socked her, right?

The same resultative function of "so" is employed in one of Federico's narratives:

FED: and I seen all these *vatos* coming towards me
I say I'm not gonna let this guy go.
So I was just banging his head

In this excerpt, Federico portrays his own violence as a direct result of "all these *vatos* [guys]" coming at him. Again, the resultative "so" indicates that these agentive acts are the result of some other, external force. In Rosa's narrative, this external cause takes the form of another girl's threatening statement about Rosa's sister: "I'm gonna fuck her up"; in Federico's narrative this cause is the attack of "all these *vatos*." The use of "so" thereby links problematic events with the speakers' responses to them and mitigates speakers' responsibility for their own violent actions. While the speakers' actions, in isolation, may seem illogical, even reprehensible, these speakers narrate these acts as narratively logical based on the cause-and-effect relationship suggested by the discourse marker "so."

"Then" is another logical connector that can be used "to introduce the consequence" (Celce-Murcia & Larsen-Freeman, 1983, p. 327) and in this way functions, like "so," as a bridge between the problematic event and the teller's response to it. In "Everybody Rushed Me" for example, Federico uses "then" to indicate his actions "the next day" were a consequence of previous antagonism:

FED: Everybody rushed me. Hn. *Then* the *next* day we, we and the homeboys went down.

Federico's use of "then," in combination with "the *next* day" frames his actions as retaliation for what had occurred the *previous* day.

Sometimes the logical connection is not so specifically marked lexically, but implied through the positioning of events. In the following example (and the epigraph for this chapter), the word "and" functions to logically connect the repeated violence against Ned, with his aunt's suggestion and his ultimate decision to leave school.

NED: They kicked my ass three times right there 'cause they got me from the back, boom boom boom, and my face was all messed up *and [so]* my aunt told me don't go to school *and [so]* I go alright.

In these narratives, "so," "then," and in certain contexts, the word "and" (with an implied "so") serve to link formal narrative components to illuminate and even morally justify the speaker's actions.

INDEXICAL RESOURCES OF THE DROPPING OUT GENRE

The previous sections have illustrated how certain grammatical forms are used systematically within this narrative genre. Shared grammatical repertoires in and of themselves do not communicate the narrative themes discussed. Rather, the way that the speakers systematically organize these resources communicates the thematic concerns of this genre. The use of indefinite pronouns like "everybody" or present tense verbs does not, alone, indicate mitigating circumstances or reduced speaker agency, but lexical forms, in combination with grammatical categories, do acquire localized meaning in these discussion groups through their patterned deployment. The following sections build on the formal characterizations outlined thus far in order to illustrate the tension between grammatical and lexical form and interactional practice, and how narrative meanings and social identities emerge from this tension. As these narratives illustrate, "the interplay between the formal system and the social world of which it is a part serves to organize and prefigure certain kinds of experience" (Hanks, 1996, p. 181). Thus, "fashions of speaking" emerge—in this case the "dropping out" discourse genre.

Indexically Constructing Generic Identities and Events

One way form and the social world interact to construct meaning in this genre is through the use of indexical pronouns. An "indexical" is a word that relies on context for its meaning. While "apple" always means "apple" regardless of context, the meaning of a word like "everybody" or "it" depends more on the situation of speaking. These words act as an "index" to a meaning that is available only by looking at the context in which the words occur. The meaning of an indexical word isn't something you can look up in a dictionary. Rather, indexical meaning emerges in conversation, and often speakers construct the meaning of an indexical word collaboratively. Here, I provide a brief synopsis of the way that indexical value accumulates over the "dropping out" genre of narrative. In this narrative genre, certain pronouns take on generic value when systematically deployed in particular grammatical roles. The use of general expressions like "the same thing" and "everybody" or pronouns like "you," "they," and "it" imply generalized categories of problems and identities that extend, by analogy, across different narratives of this genre. Thus, generic identities and events are created through conventional indexicality (or, in Peirce's [1931] terminology, "hypoindexicality"), and ways of construing these indexicals are conventionalized through this discourse genre. In other words, the patterning of subjects and objects across these narratives provides evidence that all these young men and women tend to speak in similar ways when they talk about dropping out of school.

"They Got Me": Generic Villains. Across all these narratives, "they" is noticably and exclusively used as agent of active verbs. The repetition of this configuration in which "they" has power over the speaker (e.g."they got me") endows the referent of "they" with an indexically categorical, negative value. More specifically, whenever the verb "get" is used in its most agentive form (with the meaning of "catch"), the speaker is featured as the object of someone else's action. Through such patterned usage, the individuals referred to as "they" emerge as ominous and omnipresent figures who impose themselves on the speaker in these narratives, as in the examples below:

NED: cause *they got me* from the back boom boom boom
NED: *they got me* in the halls, that's when I took the knife.
FED: *they got me* [so] after that they found out who it was so they kicked me
out of Belmont.
FED: Then the next day we, we and the homeboys went down and *they got me*.

In all these uses of "get," "they" is co-referential with either police, school officials, or rival gang members, and the verb "get" is used in parallel with being either kicked out from school or otherwise victimized by rivals.

In two cases, the subject of "get" is explicitly "the cops" and "the police."

As might be expected, the cops are not cast as benevolent protectors, but as additional rivals, just like the generic "they."

JERRY: The *police* just went and *(get/got) me.*
     Handcuffed me. Took me in.

Jerry describes here how the police arrested him during school. In the context of the story, the police have already violated Jerry by opening his locker and searching for "Mary Jane" (marijuana), which they found, after which they came and "got" Jerry.

   These examples of the accumulated indexical value of "they" and "get" illustrate that the verb "get" or the pronoun "they" do not, in isolation, convey the presence of an indomitable and oppressive other, but that their repeated co-occurrence in this genre creates the impression of omnipresence and the capacity "they" have to "get" whoever they want.

   "Everybody" was Socking Me.   Similarly, the presence of the indefinite pronouns like "everybody" and "everyone" does not in and of itself convey omnipresent threat in the narratives, but when we examine what kinds of things "everybody" does, we see how these narratives begin to give that impression:

FED: *Everybody* rushed me. Hn
FED: *Everybody* was socking me hitting me
FRAN: *Everyone* they're always on the rag
MANNY: *Everybody* thinks their champions.
WILLOW: If they really want you bad they'll be waiting for you.
BETSY AND STUDENT: Who?
WILLOW: Pschhh. *Whoever* heh.

Like the generic "they" who always "gets" the speaker, "Everybody" repeatedly appears in subject position of a particular category of verb: verbs that suggest negative action or demeanor. Furthermore, these verbs take the form of omni-presence by being expressed in the simple present tense of "timeless truths" or the durative progressive aspect. Thus, while formal grammatical resources are called upon, their meaning arises through their repeated collocation with indexi-cals like "everybody" and verbs like "to sock" or "to be on the rag."

   "They Got Me": Generic Victims.   As shown above, when tellers use the verb "get" (in the sense of "catch"), not only is "they" exclusively in subject position, but "me is the object of "they's" negative actions. Even though these are stories about the students' final fights in school and descriptions of the actions that lead to their dismissal, "they" are always doing the "get[ting]" and

"me" is always the one "[being] got." Similarly, "me" is the victim of "everybody": As Federico narrates, "*everybody* rushed *me*" and "*everybody* was
socking *me*."

SUMMARY: THE GENREFICATION OF MORAL DISCOURSE

This chapter and the previous one have illustrated that the expression of certain
themes in these narratives has a genred organization. These narrators systematically use grammatical forms and indexical repertoires (e.g., categorical use of
"they" and "everybody") and textual structures (e.g., the extended narration of
a problematic experience, the parallel structure of certain verbs, subjects, and
objects). More importantly, through this systematic usage, they construct a negative and threatening environment and cast themselves as behaving in necessary
and unavoidable ways. Although these young men and women often tell stories
about their own reprehensible acts, they win the sympathy of their interlocutors
through narrative construction of their own orientation within a moral framework identifiable through this narrative genre.

CHAPTER 4

Reframing Dropping Out Narratives

In a way, see, that's what I'm saying. . . . that's what makes him think 'I look cool,' you know?

—Manny, 1993

The "dropping out" narratives have been characterized so far as playing to certain themes: students depict settings as pervasive, omnipresent, and unbearable; they minimize their own responses to such conditions; and they describe their own actions as performed by others. In these stories students emerge as underdogs, trapped in a cycle of violence or antagonism, forced to act to protect not only themselves, but also others to whom they are loyal. In many encounters with students outside of the Friday sessions, I would ask about these themes and I often had them reaffirmed. But a closer look at these students' stories and their conversational framing reveals points of difference and contention between members of the City School community. While these were all students for whom traditional education had proved unsatisfactory, the reasons for their dissatisfaction, and their perspectives on their pasts, though in many ways similar, were also significantly different. Laura encouraged a certain kind of student to come to the Friday discussion sessions (those she saw as likely to get in trouble if elsewhere), but these young men and women were not all the same, and their allegiances to the themes described in Chapter 2 were of varying degrees. This chapter looks at how some students reveal their differences and fine-tune their self-portrayals through their different reactions and re-tellings of each others' stories.

One category that all of these students' self-portrayals resists is that of "dropout." So far the term "dropping out" has been used rather uncritically to describe the kind of stories told by these young men and women. The term "dropout," however, strikes a false chord for many reasons. The term has been problematized widely in the literature on school reform. In her book *Framing Dropouts*, for example, Michele Fine (1991) finds the term "dropout" to be inaccurate because it places too much responsibility for dropping out on the student. A more accurate description of dropouts, she finds, is the term "push-outs"—due to the expunging nature of the conditions these students leave. As she has written, the questions we should ask of these young men and women is not "Why did you drop out?" but, rhetorically, "Why in the world would you ever stay?" The narratives seen so far seem to echo this point of view. The students have portrayed a set of conditions that are unbearable, and the events that lead to their departure from school as unavoidable. They do seem to have been pushed out, often from one school after another.

But as previous chapters have discussed, much of a story's content is determined both by the way it unfolds in context and the way it is subsequently elaborated on by interlocutors. Similarly, identities such as "dropout" or "pushout" are partially constructed in particular situations. Thus, whether these stories communicate the identity of "pushout" or "dropout," for example, is determined not only by the authors themselves, or what that author is "really" like (some identity detachable from context), but also by their present interlocutors, and the way that subsequent talk reinterprets their stories. By examining how these "dropping out" stories are reframed in narrative, this chapter looks at how young men and women orient to the themes described in Chapter 2, but how, through subsequent speech activity they reinforce, revise, or contest those themes.

As Chapter 2 illustrated, the structure of narrative is one resource narrators draw on to create a particular genre of story and a picture of themselves as acting as best they could, given the nature of their experiences or the inevitable threat embodied by a school setting. The common linguistic features of these narratives and their patterned deployment distinguish these stories as a discourse genre. Another feature that distinguishes between discourse genres is the way those genres are received, and the degree to which they are open to reconstrual. Because different discourse genres are embedded in different institutional and societal contexts, the extent to which these genres can be reconstrued differs. Official discourse—for example, a verdict delivered in a courtroom—is relatively closed to reconstrual. The verdict is embedded in a larger activity, the trial, which is, in turn, part of a larger cultural institution that defines it. Because of the official nature of the trial discourse, its conclusions are more "finalized" than those made in less formal discourse (Bakhtin, 1986; Hanks, 1996).

Like a "verdict" embedded in a "trial," the dropping out narratives are also embedded within a larger activity, the discussion group in which they are told, and the reception of these stories is another component that defines them as a distinct discourse genre. Compared to a verdict delivered by a judge during a trial, these narratives are a nonofficial genre, far more open to reconstrual by interlocutors. While the narratives may achieve formal closure through a coda, they inevitably contain blank spots or missing parts that frustrate closure, and lead to follow-up questions once the story reaches its formal completion point. Furthermore, the story itself, due in part to its unofficial nature, is open to revision by its interpreters. Within this story genre, narrative closure, even when marked formally with a coda like "so that's it" or a conclusive "there" is always available for reopening, and reconstrual. Unlike a verdict, the reconstrual of these stories can begin immediately, and need not go through official channels like an appeals process. Even Labov (1972), who treated stories as much more monological productions than the concept of coauthorship suggests, recognized the dialogic function of the coda, at least as a means of indicating a turn is over, that the storytelling is complete, and that others may take a turn.

While codas in these stories often claim story completion (and achieve it, formally), they rarely achieve closure within the ongoing activity. All of the stories told in the discussion group are addressed, interpreted, and revised in subsequent talk. Rather than leading away from the kernel story, the codas in these stories lead to subsequent speech activities that answer interlocutors' questions or address their interpretations. This subsequent talk often recasts events in the story long after the initial story coda suggests closure.

In summary, the "dropping out" narratives are never "finalized," but upon their coda (or other transition to conversation), reworked, following my own and the tellers' peers' attempts to clarify details or to revise or contest the content of the story or the way it was told. In particular, interlocutors pinpoint those narrative resources particular to the dropping out genre and use those same resources either to debunk the narrative perspective they construct, or to flesh out that view. In this way the themes of this genre can be either debunked or reified in subsequent framing of the story. This is accomplished by redoing the grammatical/indexical strategies that construct those themes and identities.

REINFORCING DROPPING OUT THEMES

The examples in the following sections indicate that subsequent story frames can reinforce the themes of the "dropping out" genre, drawing on the same grammatical and indexical repertoire to add credence to the same thematic claims.

Subsequent Framing Provides an Opportunity to Look Good

In Ned's "Knife Story," the subsequent speech activity reinforces the moral framing of the "dropping out" genre as I try to understand why, if Ned was the victim rather than the perpetrator of violence, he was the one kicked out of school. As the story ends, my reformulation of the story's upshot prompts further explanation as to why Ned was arrested for a knife if he had only taken it out to "show someone" and had been forced to bring it for self-defense:

Subsequent Framing of the "Knife Story"

Reformulation   BETSY: So you just took the knife to (0.2) defend yourself.

NED: Yeah an' they told me why did you
        bring your knife

SUBSEQUENT FRAME   and I told them heres to you guys to (psxx)
                       where you guys were— Where were you guys
                       when I was getting beat up? Eating donuts?
                       And I'm like "go (xxx)"

simple present of eternal   'Cause it's true.
truths

My reformulation provides Ned with an opportunity to further frame his story, and he goes on to describe the exchange he had with the security guards. They, like me, were interested in why he brought the knife, and he (hypothetically) explains to them, like he just has to me, that he had to bring the knife to defend himself. Ned asks the security guards hypothetically, "Where were you guys when I was getting beat up? Eating donuts?" The security guards, it seems, are not attending to the needs of the students and are not aware of the pervasive atmosphere of violence they should be protecting students from—if they were, students presumably wouldn't have to protect (and arm) themselves.

Ned's vague but finalizing, "'Cause it's true" suggests the global nature of his complaint. Still, he doesn't explain why exactly they arrested him, so my questioning continues, demanding explicit finalization to the story. Next, I ask Ned for an original responsible party for the final offense. If he brought the knife to defend himself, there must have been some reason "they" were after him, and why the officials weren't concerned about his reasons for having a knife. Ned locates responsibility for the final problem (getting caught with a knife) in long-standing rivalries, which have no distinct origin. Federico adds his voice to the subsequent framing here, articulating the general nature of the problem:

Further Framing of the "Knife Story"

SUBSEQUENT   BETSY: So, like why were those guys after—
FRAMING

progressive, on-going   chasing you?
pursuit

Simple present of eternal   NED: Cause they knew I was from another
truths   gang.
durative progressive   BETSY: Uh huh. *Is that the thing with Bel-*
                                 mont they have
durative progressive   like two different gangs *going* there or . . . ?

Simple present of eternal truths + nonreferential there	NED: *There's* a lotta gangs [*going* there FED: [*There's* a lotta gangs. You know you might get along with one but *there's a few you don't get along*. So that's when the problem starts see.

My questions here also draw from the dropping out repertoire: In trying to understand how Ned ended up bringing the knife, I am seeking a problem in the setting, and formulating possible answers using the present tense and the present progressive, suggesting the ongoing nature of the problematic atmosphere at Ned's previous school. Ned picks up on my use of the progressive and escalates the description of pervasive gang activity at Belmont: To my suggestion that they have "two different gangs going there" Ned immediately emphasizes that it is not just two but "a lot" and Federico continues: With so many gangs, there will be a few who fight one another. As Federico explains, "the problem" starts in the distant past, in a pervasive setting, where inevitably, a few gangs "don't get along."

By now, I had begun to understand the present depiction of this particular high school as one with a lot of unavoidable gang confrontation. My own contribution to the subsequent story framing, "Is that the thing with Belmont?" also displaces responsibility onto an entire institution and the sorts of activities it affords: The problem is a "thing with Belmont," not a specific action performed by Ned or Federico. As portrayed by Ned and Federico, and by other students in the other stories, generalized settings, and ongoing, preexistent problems led to fights or other unavoidable responses, which ultimately led to subsequent expulsion from school or the decision to drop out. In the excerpt above, my own participation in the subsequent framing conforms to this genre, suggesting that the genre itself is partially shaped in the moment and between speakers.

Subsequent Framing Followed by Counter-Reframing

Sometimes, however, my participation or that of other students contests the students' mitigated portrayal of their actions and questions the moral positioning within these stories. Although remarks in the subsequent speech activity at times begin to reframe the stories, in some cases the storyteller or peers join in to reemphasize the "dropping out" themes. In the following example, I attempt to reframe Federico's depiction of his fight by raising the possibility that he not retaliate to the previous day's attack by rivals. In his responses to my question, Federico uses the inevitability of retaliatory butt-kicking to reveal how, though he did start a fight (he "went down") the next day and was suspended as a result, even this was not something over which he had control:

*Subsequent Framing and
Counter-framing of
"Everybody Rushed Me"*

SUBSEQUENT FRAME	BETSY: Oh. So what would have happened if you had just went down the next day?
	FED: I wouldn't get suspended.
providing a warrant for	BETSY: You [wouldn't—
action	FED: [Just get my butt it kicked every day.

Even if Federico had managed to stay in school by never starting the fight the next day, when he "went down" with his homies, he would have faced another sort of trouble. Though he would not have been suspended, he would have ended up getting beaten up everyday from that day on. Even though pressed to describe his involvement more fully, Federico emphasizes the necessity of his violent action, and stresses the circumstances that precipitated it.

While Federico's story may have come out any number of ways, in this counter-reframing, the violence of the "other" is emphasized. Follow-up questions other than my own may have enabled Federico to reframe this story in other ways, but mine, which focused on the nature of his involvement, led him to further minimize it. As the following "debunking" section will illustrate, Federico's peers are not so hesitant to accentuate the nature of his violent involvement and his own responsibility for starting the fight. But in my presence, this sort of storytelling does not occur in the initial "dropping out" narrative. Instead, the subsequent frames function to flesh out two goals the formally bounded story may not have fully met: (1) the need (in response to my questions) to narrate the violence that occurred and which led to the student's expulsion; and (2) the need to justify morally or mitigate that violence by contextualizing it or narrating it in a particular way—in short, the need to "look good" (cf., Ochs, Smith, & Taylor, 1989) for both their peers and the researcher. Often, "looking good" and describing why one was expelled from school are difficult goals to maintain simultaneously. Therefore, the subsequent story frames act as a means to mediate further between these two narrative goals. While the examples above illustrate how subsequent talk can flesh out the moral framing of the initial "dropping out" narrative, alternatively, subsequent speech activity can reframe the story more fully, and put a new spin on the narrated events.

DEBUNKING DROPPING OUT THEMES

Coauthors Debunk Stories

As the examples so far have illustrated, at times subsequent speech activity reinforces narrative themes. But subsequent speech activity can also be used to contest those themes. This "debunking" activity also draws on the genred locutions of the dropping out narratives, but uses these ways of speaking for a different effect—to deconstruct the storyteller's self-portrayal and reveal the moral positioning taking place in the "dropping out" genre. The talk that occurs after the formal closure of "Everybody Rushed Me," for example, illustrates how follow-up questions on my part led to reframing of the story by peers. Although Federico's coda, "So that's it" suggests closure and a return to the nonstory world, his interlocutors immediately force him to reenter the story. After finishing his story, responses to my questions fill in the blanks left through the indirect and necessarily incomplete way in which Federico narrated certain events. The process of moving from narrative to its subsequent frame is illustrated below, and this transcript will be excerpted in pieces in the following discussion:

"Everybody Rushed Me"

abstract	FED: I lasted only for a week there
	MANNY: a week.
setting/problematic	FED: Our neighborhood started having shit
experience	with that neighborhood down there. So I
	went over there to the bus so they came
	and hit me up I said my neighborhood
	and they said fuck that so they socked
	me. Everybody rushed me. Hn.
response	Then the next day we, we and the homeboys
	went down
consequence	and they got me.
coda	*So that's it.*
SUBSEQUENT	BETSY: Did you start the fight, er—
FRAMING	FED: No, they— they did.
	BETSY: So how did you get kicked out?
	MANNY: Cause [the next day he started it.
	FED: [Cause the next day I went
	down. The next day I started a fight.

As Federico tells this story, he calls on the linguistic resources typical of the dropping out genre. As indicated in the annotated excerpt below, he uses pro-

gressive aspect to describe preexisting, durative troubles, and the indexical
"they" and "everybody" to explicitly narrate the problematic experience and
the consequence to his response. He also mitigates his own role in the story
by embedding the exchange in the "getting hit up" event, and using the pronoun "we" as the agent of the responsive action, rather than an agentive and
singular "I."

Genred Particulars of "Everybody Rushed Me"

progressive aspect	F: Our neighborhood started *having shit* with that neighborhood down there.
indexical "they" as villain	So I went over there to the bus so *they* came and hit me up I said my neighborhood
indexical "they" and "everybody" as villain	and *they* said fuck that so *they* socked me? *Everybody* rushed me. Hn.
resultative logical connector "then"	*Then* the next day
acting in concert with others ("we"), as subject of a nontransitive verb ("went").	we, we and the homeboys went down
indexical "they" as villain	and *they* got me.
coda	So that's it.

With hindsight and analysis, this narrative clearly describes Federico's fight
with a rival gang and subsequent suspension from school, but as my questions
at the time indicate, immediately after Federico finished telling about the fight,
I still wasn't clear as to who had been responsible for starting it, or, for that
matter, what "we—we and the homeboys went down" was meant to describe.
Federico tactfully leaves this phrase open to reconstrual—perhaps even allowing
for differing interpretation by his peers and by me. He does not explicitly narrate
himself as agent of a transitive verb, but instead uses the innocuous "we went
down." Furthermore, through the use of the pronoun "we," Federico never explicitly states his individual responsibility.

During the subsequent talk, however, I begin to reframe Federico's portrayal of events. I immediately ask who initiated the fight, looking for an explicit
statement of responsibility. Nevertheless, as with the nature of "getting hit up,"
the origin of the fight depends on the extent of history one is willing to consider,
and any answer to my question could be correct, depending on the day you start
counting. Exonerating himself, Federico answers with "They did," immediately
pinning responsibility on the villainous other. But my next query again poten-

tially pins responsibility for the ensuing violence explicitly on Federico: If "they" started the fight, why did Federico get kicked out of school? At this point, Manny, a listening peer, explicitly remarks on the responsibility Federico didn't immediately attribute to himself, naming the day when the fight was started (the "next" day), and explicitly pinning the responsibility for that fight on Federico: "The next day *he* started it."

As the story reframing continues, Manny explicitly rejects Federico's attribution of responsibility to the villainous "they," and insists on explicitly naming Federico's role in the encounter. Furthermore, by using the third person "he" rather than "you" he eliminates Federico as the teller of his own story, and even as an interlocutor in this particular exchange. Manny does not say, "the next day *you* started it" as he would if he were including Federico in his revision. Instead, with his statement, "the next day he started it," Manny is addressing me alone, and excluding Federico from the narration of his own story. By using the third person singular, Manny eliminates the author from the present interaction and renarrates his role in the story. Manny's authoritative pronoun use appears to have been effective and the reframing of the initial story appears to be complete. After Manny's explicit statement, Federico adopts this version of the events, and rearticulates what happened when "we and the homeboys went down" in his story as "the next day I started a fight."

This unfolding re-telling of the story implicates Federico—and even leads Federico to implicate himself much more explicitly as a responsible party in the fight that led him to be expelled from school. The initial version of Federico's offense, "we— we and the homeboys went down" could have been revised in infinite ways, but due to the nature of my questions and Manny's willingness to fill in explicit agents for the actions involved, Federico ultimately pins responsibility for the final fight on himself. Manny debunks Federico's version of the story precisely by drawing on the linguistic resources Federico has used to convey his nonresponsibility—those that characterize the dropping out genre.

In a similar case, Rosa ends her story with a brief closing coda, "there," after which I start asking questions, initiating reframing of the "dropping out" story. In the following excerpt from "I Simply Asked Her to Watch It," the story author's peer supplies a revised version of events:

Excerpt from "I Simply Asked Her to Watch It"

response to problematic experience	ROSA: and I hit here an— an— we just got in a fight.
consequence	ROSA: And I got kicked out. But she didn't.
coda	ROSA: There.
Researcher initiated *REFRAMING*	BETSY: So why didn't she get kicked out?
	SYLVIA: I went to a lot of trouble for nothing, huh. 'Cause she— 'cause *she* started it.

After the coda and in response to my question, Rosa's friend Sylvia begins to reexplain the events of the story. Sylvia's initial statement begins to reveal Rosa's role in the fight. In her utterance, "I went to a lot of trouble for nothing," Sylvia reveals that she actually made up a story claiming that Rosa hadn't started the fight, the "trouble" being, in part, that she was lying. In this conversation, however, she is no longer protecting Rosa from school authorities and is more than willing to pin the blame on her friend. Like Manny, Sylvia won't let Rosa evade the narration of her own agency. She re-tells Rosa's story here using "she" and not "you." Like Manny's use of the third person singular, Rosa's use of the singular pronoun "she" here functions to eliminate the author from the present interaction and to renarrate her role in the story's action, explicitly naming her responsibility for starting the fight.

This story leads, in turn, to another, about the time when Rosa socked a teacher ("I Got Mad"). Again, while Rosa is hesitant to ascribe agency to her self, Sylvia is not. As this segment begins, Sylvia encourages Rosa to tell me why a teacher was looking for her. As Rosa continues to narrate her involvement as minimal (using the minimally agentive form of "get") and the teacher's actions as unavoidable and enduring (using progressive aspect), Sylvia explicitly intervenes assigning agency to Rosa, placing her as subject of transitive verbs:

Reframing of "I Got Mad"

Coauthor encourages ex- *plicit account*	SYLVIA: Oh yeah. 'Cause, why, tell her why now.
get	ROSA: 'Cause I *got in a fight*
progressive aspect	and *he was chasing* me.
DEBUNKING: Author as *explicit agent*	SYLVIA: He's— *She* socked him, liar.
get	ROSA: Oh [I *got in a fight*
DEBUNKING: Author as *explicit agent*	SYLVIA: [*She* socked him in the nose.
progressive aspect	ROSA: (Giggles)) And— and the teacher *was* *chasing* me.

Initially, Rosa characterizes her actions using resources of the dropping out story repertoire. The teacher was "chasing" her and she "got in a fight." Her agency is minimal, and in no way does she explicitly express her own responsibility for the consequences that followed. Sylvia, however, contests Rosa's portrayal of events precisely by rewording the way she describes them. In place of Rosa's usage of a "get" form, Sylvia uses a transitive verb ("to sock") with Rosa as agentive subject ("she socked him"). After Rosa counters by repeating "I got in a fight," Sylvia describes the events even more explicitly, adding exactly where Rosa socked the teacher ("in the nose").

By explicitly narrating the author's role in violent interactions, this sort of peer revision radically contests the identity primary authors convey in the initial kernel story. This occurs most explicitly when Sylvia explains the underlying nature of Rosa's troubles at school.

S: They kicked her out.
B: Why, do you think?
M: hhh
S: Oh because she was a troublemaker.

Sylvia's explanation for Rosa's expulsion, which centers not on ongoing rivalry or unbearable settings, but on Rosa, counters all the themes of the dropping out genre. She did not get kicked out because of injustice, ongoing unbearable conditions, or institutionalized inequity. As Sylvia puts it, Rosa herself "was a troublemaker." Using this past tense nominal, and resisting Rosa's attempts to portray her actions as emergent from enduring, unbearable conditions, Sylvia essentializes Rosa's identity, and debunks her efforts to contextualize her actions.

By redoing events of the "dropping out" story, renarrating each other's roles through these subsequent frames, narrators display an awareness of the identity construction underway. The examples above illustrate how students debunk each other's stories by revising their stories—eliminating those grammatical and indexical elements that exonerate students from their responsibility for violent actions. A more sophisticated kind of debunking occurs when students explicitly call attention to the genred nature of these narratives not by eliminating the typical genred elements of these narratives, but by calling attention to them and the ideology they construct. In this way, as will be illustrated in the next section, some peers resist the essentializing potential of these narratives.

Students Resist Their Own Essentialization

Although the "dropping out" stories led to much discussion, I do not want to create the impression that these stories unfolded effortlessly. There was often resistance even to my request for stories, and suspicion about my role as researcher. During the one taping session, a newcomer stopped me mid-sentence and asked, "What are you doing?" His painfully candid question led us into a discussion of how risky it is to tell one's stories, how "people" want to pretend this or that about gangsters and violent teenagers, glossing over the details of their lives, and their own human qualities. These explicit statements made clear what the students' strategic storytelling had begun to imply—that these students were going to be very careful about their presentation of self, and that they already suspected their commodification as "dropouts," "troublemakers," or "gangsters" and the tendency of outsiders to essentialize their identities.

These suspicions seem to be well founded, given the tendency of even well-meaning researchers like Michelle Fine (1991) to essentialize "older dropouts," for example, as "narrowed in vision, flattened in affect, and impoverished in their lives" (p. 124). As this young man, "Manny" would point out, his peers had obviously faced certain hardships and disappointments, but their ability to critique one another's vision, and to lead "rich" lives, did not seem stunted. As it turns out, Manny frequently took the role of debunker in these discussions. One way he debunked was by pinning responsibility on hesitant storytellers (as on Federico above), accentuating their own responsibility for their actions. He also had another, more sophisticated way of debunking. When it appeared that students were portraying an overly essentialized identity, or one that I might interpret as such, Manny would draw attention to the genred nature of their narrative by debunking the very way they explained their life. In this way, he would reframe their story more substantially than the previous debunking examples, providing a meta-explanation of what he thought I may have wrongly construed as "typical" dropout talk.

In one conversation, for example, a student, "Jerry," had been telling me the story of getting arrested in school ("Marijuana Story"). His glances between me and his peer, Manny, reveal the intricate identity negotiation going on in this complex participation framework. He begins by answering my questions, explaining how he got kicked out. Since I have asked the question, I am Jerry's primary addressee for the response. Jerry's gaze, directly at me, solidifies this expectation:

BETSY: What happened there. That— made you leave.
JERRY: Well. I got kicked out. ((sheepish glance to Betsy))

After explaining that he was kicked out, Jerry looks directly at me and smirks (see illustration in transcript above). At my further prompting, he continues his story, explaining that he was kicked out for "possession of marijuana" and that the police came into his third period class and put handcuffs on him. When I mentioned how embarrassing it must have been to be pulled out of a classroom by the police, Jerry replied that it wasn't embarrassing at all. He claimed he was "used to it" and at this point, it is clear that he is constructing his answer for Manny as well as for me, as he flashes a knowing glance and satisfied smile at Manny:

JER: . . . That was the first time I got busted.
BET: Wow that's embarrassing, in school like that.
JER: In school? Aww, I'm used to it. ((Jerry glances at Manny to his right))

Jerry's claim that he is used to being arrested could potentially accomplish any number of functions: He could be appealing to my sympathy, invoking the identity of "push-out" or victim of police injustice; he could be trying to impress his peers, and perhaps me as well, by his nonchalance in the face of authority (as his glance at Manny suggests); or, he could be trying to do both simultaneously.

Manny, however, finalizes Jerry's claim in a particular way, depicting his peer's story as a typical attempt to sound cool (though not necessarily *be* cool in actuality). After Jerry's statement, Manny enters the conversation. Though Jerry's glance perhaps invited him into the talk, Manny takes this opportunity not only to enter the conversation, but also to debunk Jerry's utterance that was directed at him. By drawing attention to canonical use of "get" forms, Manny constructs Jerry as using this grammatical/indexical resource as a way of "being cool." In this way Manny reveals his belief that Jerry believes that I want to see him as cool (and Manny's sense that I should be informed otherwise):

Reframing (Debunking) of "Marijuana Story"

Get

JERRY: . . . That was the first time *I got busted.*

BETSY: Wow that's embarrassing, in school like that.

JERRY: In school? Aww, I'm used to it.

DEBUNKING

MANNY: In a way, see, that's what I'm saying. The way that's what makes him think that "I looks cool," you know?

Exclusive 3rd person

JERRY: Well, *they— they didn't know* you know, why

MANNY: Why, but— [I mean

JERRY: The other pe [ople didn't know—

generic 3rd person + present tense

MANNY: [people— *some of them* think that it's cool you know when you look at them?

reveals use of "get" as an attempt to "look cool"

You know, "*get busted,*" and all that, "*getting cuffed*" all that stuff they think they look bad you know it just gives them a rep like aw you know "he went to jail *he got bo— he got booked.*"]

	JERRY:	((looks away from *Manny to table*))
	BETSY:	Uh huh
generic 3rd person + present tense	MANNY:	Sometime *they* think they give them more respect

By drawing attention to the use of "get" forms, Manny highlights the systematic nature of this way of portraying events, and reveals his own interpretation of the function of the dropping out genre. Through his own ventriloquation of this speech activity (the use of get forms, and specifically, the speaker's placement of himself as the passive recipient of a negative authority's actions), Manny indicates that this way of speaking (e.g., "he went to jail, he got booked") encapsulates an ideology—that talking about "getting cuffed," etc. is also an attempt to portray a particular kind of identity. Manny criticizes this form of talk by saying that Jerry is "trying to look cool" (and presumably not succeeding). In this way Manny reveals his own ideology about this way of speaking, and the flimsy kind of identity it upholds.

Manny also uses "they" and "some of them" when he takes over the narration, but he does not use them to describe the generic pursuing other, typical of the "dropping out" genre (e.g., "they got me" "they socked me," etc.). Instead, he uses them to describe *people like Jerry* and the delusions they have. Through this use of third person, Manny accomplishes (at least) two functions: (1) he invokes a generic kind of behavior, of people in general; and (2) he excludes Jerry as a direct addressee, indicating that this explanation is tailored for me, the researcher. Through his deployment of third person and generalization, his explanation comes off as instructions to me as to how I should interpret Jerry's talk. As in the previous examples, the debunker in this case uses the third person to exclude the narrator from continued narration of his story. At this point, as the transcript above indicates, Jerry disattends from the conversation, looking at neither me nor Manny, but down at the tabletop. Manny has effectively taken Jerry's place as primary narrator. He can now continue his reframing of Jerry's story, explaining to me what Jerry is trying to do with his "get" constructions, and then debunking that sort of identity.

In this excerpt, Manny uses the repertoire of the dropping out genre precisely to draw attention to the way it constructs an overly unified identity for Jerry. He draws attention to the typical, agency-resistant get phrasing to suggest that these phrases are used too easily and gloss over too much complication involved in the act of getting cuffed, busted, etc. This sort of debunking recognizes that any story is necessarily told from a particular perspective, and serves particular interests. Debunking then both recognizes the "dropping out" genre as a form of identity construction and resists its reification.

THE RAMIFICATIONS OF REFRAMING

On preliminary reflection, these young peoples' narrative renditions of public schools and the hardships they face there mirror Michelle Fine's (1991) description of dropouts as "pushouts," young people for whom school never provides, nor was ever meant to provide an education, students whom the administration and faculty are happy to see go. Elaborating on the distinction between "dropout" and "pushout," Dierdre Kelly (1993) writes, "dropout implies that the student makes an independent, final decision, whereas pushout implies that the institution acts inexorably to purge unwilling victims" (p. 29). Given this distinction, the term "pushout" does not seem as appropriate as a way to describe the protagonists of these stories. They do not situate themselves as victims of structural injustice, but in a set of conditions—some institutional, but most more generally social and interactional—that gradually expunge them. Kelly (1993) provides another, more adequate unifying metaphor for the trajectory of the underachieving student: A process of disengagement. Her description of leaving high school fits even more closely with that process evoked in these stories. As she describes it, "the concept of disengagement connotes a long-running, interactive process . . . it encourages us to connect events in students' lives over time and look for cumulative effects" (p. 29). This frustrating process of disengagement is portrayed in all the narratives about "dropping out" that I heard in the Friday morning sessions. These narrators usually preface their departure from school with a long accumulation of events—often including lists of former schools, cyclic gang retaliation, repeated victimization, a series of broken promises—not just *one* single encounter.

Furthermore, the descriptor, "pushout," is perhaps too solid an indictment of the structuring power of the institution, not because the role of the institution is small, but because this view lacks a recognition of individual and peer interactional roles in this process. As stories from the Friday afternoon discussion groups indicate, the stance of disengagement is not simply a structural outcome of an unjust bureaucratic system. This stance permeates the ways in which these students frame their own experiences and continue to construct their relationship to school (and other official and nonofficial sources of power) after they leave.

The purpose of this close analysis, then, is not to simply retell the story of dropouts or pushouts on a different level, but to suggest that the system reproduces itself on a micro-level in conversations among students and official others (including researchers like me) and that these reconstructions have ramifications. None of the students from the Friday discussion group stayed at City School. They became dropouts again, leaving an environment that tried to avoid all the "pushing out" activities of typical public schools.

As these small group discussions show, peer influence on the construction of self is very salient. But, as Kelly (1993) notes, "disengagement" is a potentially reversible process. The "debunker" role that emerged in this setting suggests one way this reversal could possibly occur at an interpersonal level. Debunkers both illuminate the identity norms certain to which students orient themselves, and illustrate how those norms are contestable in this situation—and alternative educational setting within which stories are open to reconstrual. Those systemic identities are recognized by some of these students and in some cases resisted. The "debunkers" here display a fluency with roles and with the repertoires in the genred presentation of self. They are not willing to pigeonhole themselves or the events of their lives as unitary and unchanging. The debunkers thus play a powerful meta-role in these talks.

Too often, though, schools have the capacity to reify overly unitary identities, those often structurally defined by the institution (e.g., Mehan, 1993). As Fine (1991) has noted, "low-income schools officially contain rather than explore social and economic contradictions, condone rather than critique prevailing social and economic inequities, and usher children and adolescents into ideologies and ways of interpreting social evidence that legitimate rather than challenge conditions of inequity" (p. 61). Schools, she claims, too willingly accept labels like "troublemaker" or "dropout" and apply them to their students. While some of the young men and women in these discussion groups were willing to see themselves as "troublemakers," most of them contested this role and were able to remake themselves in light of this self-awareness. Their societal critique, or course, varied in its degree of explicit articulation, but their recognition of the multiple versions that could be told of their lives introduced the potential for such critique. The subsequent narrative frames that have been explored in this chapter expose not just one identity (like "the troublemaker") but the multiple possible identities—and possible lives—students' stories can construct.

CHAPTER 5

Dropping In: Narratives of School Success

Think of it this way: Since you screwed up once . . . you might as well, you know, deal with it and do it better next time. Why come from where you messed up to here and then do the same thing?

—Nancy, 1994

This chapter analyzes stories told by a different set of City School students, a year after the original "dropping out" stories were recorded. While only one of the students from the original discussion group was still a student at City School, the students in this "dropping in" group, who had been at City School as long as but were not a part of my initial group, had either received their diplomas from City School or were nearing graduation. From this new set of students and graduates, a different sort of story emerged. In these narratives authors focus on their role as a returning student and distance themselves from their previous role as disengaging students. As one of the students, Nancy, put it, "Since you screwed up once . . . [you] deal with it and do it better the next time." The success stories analyzed here, though they recognize conditions described in the "dropping out" stories, are about "doing it better the next time."

The themes of these success stories become readily apparent when they are viewed with respect to the dropping out stories in Chapter 2. In the success stories in this chapter, speakers establish new moral frameworks: They narrate their pasts as "dropouts" in a radically different way than those who never found substantial success at City School. Like the students who told the dropping out stories, the authors of these success stories frame the events of their lives in a way that displays their own particular sense of the "right" choices to make. However, a different set of moral signposts frame these stories. These successful students emphasize how City School guided them away from unfortunate pasts and pointed them to bright futures. These storytellers denigrate pre-City School decisions and credit City School with giving them a fresh start. The textual structure and language of these stories clearly identify a turning point, after which the past self was no longer around and a new person could emerge.

This turning point, and the identification and abandonment of an old self are two features of "dropping in" stories that distinguish them from the dropping out genre. In the dropping out stories, narrators generally portrayed continuity between their current stance toward their actions and their stance as a character in the story. They narrated themselves as not directly responsible for their expulsion or departure from school, and in this way they mitigated their own current responsibility for possibly reprehensible actions. If the author ever identified his or her own role explicitly in blameworthy acts, usually it was because their peers had first drawn attention to it. The success stories are strikingly different in this respect. While tellers still distance themselves from their previous reprehensible actions, they do so by identifying a former self as the perpetrator of those actions. Rather than working to create a narrative context that justifies (or mitigates their responsibility for) previous actions, in these stories students locate their status as "dropout" in a previous self, who now no longer exists. By narrating a specific turning point in their stories, authors distance themselves from their previous actions.

The success stories also differ from the dropping out stories in how they invoke other people as motivators for their actions. In the dropping out narratives, protagonists often portray their actions as perpetrated on behalf of a gang or neighborhood, or to protect younger siblings. When violence was done, usually it is embedded in a narrative context that suggests it was unavoidable due to the need to protect others or remain loyal to them. In the dropping in stories, however, authors describe the abandonment of such loyalties, but they continue to portray their choice to return to school as a choice guided by their relationships with other people. Though their decision to create a new self has required considerable individual will, they describe the origin of that will as coming from their devotion to other people. As one student says, as a gang member one typically has to "show 'em [peers] you can prove it." As a returning student (and a young mother), however, this young woman has a different set of loyalties: "If I wanna be a good mom and a good example, I have to show it to my son." In dropping in stories, students typically invoke the voice of children or friends whom tellers say they can help not by being fellow gang members but by being responsible to their own future—and, most importantly, by getting an education.

These stories become testimonials to the abandonment of a rejected self, calling upon a particular set of linguistic and indexical resources to depict the turn to a new life. The investigation of these City School success stories read with knowledge of the stories of dropping out, reveals the losses and regrets—the abandonment of previous selves, and the discrediting of former commitments—inherent in choosing to return to school. In all these stories, maintaining a "dropping out" perspective and successfully completing school after "dropping in" are mutually incompatible.

THE INSTITUTIONAL EMERGENCE OF DROPPING IN STORIES

The contrast between the thematic concerns of "dropping out" stories and the "dropping in" stories can be partially explained through a closer look at the different institutional forces behind each set of narratives. As described in Chapter 2, the dropping out stories were gathered at the beginning of my research at City School. During this time, teachers encouraged the "worst" students to join my discussion group, and later they invited me to talk weekly with a class of young men who were considered the "leaders" (i.e., the major troublemakers, active gang members, graffiti taggers) at the school. During this portion of my research, I was encouraged to record officially the extent of the school's educational and social challenge to educate a group of young people who had been failed by all other formal educational institutions. This substantial failure of other institutions was clearly narrated in the dropping out stories.

The success stories, however, were recorded during the end of my research at City School. At this time, the school was threatened with closure and sought to bolster its public image by displaying not the "worst" students, but rather those students who would shine when subjected to more standardized criteria for success. One teacher even referred to these students as her "stars." At this time, I was encouraged to interview young men and women who had recently graduated from the school, or those who were almost finished. Considering the institutional context in which these stories were recorded, it is not surprising that these narratives portrayed such a different picture of the kind of choices City School students were making. But these transformed students, who seemed to have taken a positive turn in their lives, who had earned their diploma or landed paying jobs, were not those same students who had so strongly voiced the view of the dropout (see Chapter 2), criminal, or loyal gang member. This was an entirely new set of students, none of whom I had been encouraged to talk to during my initial visits to the school. Had I wanted to meet again with the "Dropping Out" story authors, I couldn't have—not at school at least. All but one of them had dropped out again.

I had been officially enlisted by Laura this time to document the results of her "intern" program, in which she placed students in volunteer positions in hospitals, schools, daycare centers, and offices for several hours per week. She had given me a list of students who had formerly held internships through City School and whom she felt had been successful. As she told me time and again, this portion of my research would be very important for City School's survival. She wanted me to record more student narratives and she wanted them to be stories of hope and success. "Use the best quality videotape you can" she would tell me, and promised that this footage was going to be seen by very influential people and help the school attain more grant money for summer programs.

By this time the school's existence was obviously precarious, and some of the teachers (including Laura) had spoken with me about their concerns, but Laura wanted to be sure I had some evidence of the "positive things" that happened there. It's not surprising, then, that she selected some of her "star" students to help me locate the former interns and set up group interviews. These students were also aware that our project might lead to more money for summer programs (and summer jobs for them), so they wanted to hear and record positive stories from their peers. As a presumably "neutral" social scientist, I felt slightly uncomfortable with Laura's mandate for upbeat stories, but I was eager for the opportunity to record more interaction at the school. While I had been recording classroom interaction and other student conversation at the school, I had begun to miss the Friday discussion groups and was interested in starting up something similar. I assumed this would give me an opportunity to record additional "dropping out" stories. Out of this combination of institutional and individual motivations, I began to record my last set of narratives. But I did not hear the "dropping out" stories I had come to regard as typical. Instead, students began to engage in a new discourse genre, the telling of "dropping in" stories.

THE CONVERSATIONAL EMERGENCE OF DROPPING IN STORIES

Like the dropping out stories, these narratives emerged from the institutional configuration that brought us all together as well as a particular interactional configuration. Though these students were selected on entirely different institutional criteria, I was determined to use Laura's request for upbeat narratives as a chance to get more dropping out narratives, and I decided to follow similar elicitation procedures. I organized group meetings and had only two general areas of inquiry: While I was planning to ask about internships, I also wanted to ask, as I had in the Friday morning groups, about students' previous school experiences. This way, I thought, I could accomplish Laura's task and simultaneously satisfy my own acquired curiosity about "dropping out" stories. At this time, I severely underestimated the power of both the institution and the participation framework to bring select views to the foreground. As I would soon discover, these variables led to a qualitatively different set of narratives.

As discussed above, these students were selected for entirely different reasons than those students in the Friday morning group, and the different selection led conversations to be organized very differently. One important difference was that some of Laura's students were now acting, along with me, as interviewers. Together we devised questions to ask, and I encouraged them to let the other students do most of the talking, but to ask follow-up questions for clarification, which, as I knew from the earlier discussion group, would lead to revealing addenda. As our first session began, narratives emerged generally in the same way that the dropping in narratives had, but students were sharing my role as conversation instigator, and in addition to asking questions about previous school experiences, we spent some time discussing former internships.

I had hoped that sharing my interviewing role with the students would make the discussion groups more relaxed from the start than the Friday morning groups had felt. Having students ask questions, however, had a different effect than I had intended. Rather than loosening their peers up, students' questions, because they had originally been my questions, often sounded more institutionally motivated and less personal than they would have had I asked them myself. Student interviewers were often very hesitant about asking follow-up questions when their peers were reticent. When students didn't feel like talking, their peers let them clam up, and eventually, these reticent students left after a very unsuccessful talk. When students did feel like talking, they elaborated on their narratives without much prompting, and delivered prototypical "success stories."

Student interviewers and interviewees were both very aware of the institutional auspices under which these discussions were taking place. "Is this for that summer grant?" one interviewee asked upon arrival. He proceeded to tell precisely the kind of upbeat story Laura had hoped for. Still, this particular story also revealed a great deal about the student and his relationship to the institution. While these stories can seem overly sanguine attempts to satisfy institutional desires, this does not negate their power for these students' identity construction. Many other students do not care to satisfy institutional needs (though they may do so unwittingly).

Although these students actively and positively oriented to the awareness that their narratives had an institutional audience, they did not explicitly draw attention to that audience. Despite the knowledge that these discussions were institutionally motivated, these young men and women did not tell stories that reconstructed the foundation on which these sessions were based. Rather, as Laura had hoped, they delivered shining testimonials to their success at school. Their narratives illustrate one such way that the identity of an achiever is constructed. Whether their interests were actually served by such an identity construction is a matter to be taken up in conclusion.

THE EXTERNAL FORM OF DROPPING IN STORIES

One way in which these success stories are prototypical is their distinctive use of external narrative structure. Though they follow generally the same narrative form as the dropping out stories, they all contain a crucial element that the other narratives do not: a turning point after which protagonists turn away from the "wrong path" and "start over," leave "all that behind," and concentrate on their future. In addition, the central problematic experience is not framed as a generalized "setting" as it was in the dropping in narratives, but usually is located in a former problematic self. Finally, the consequence of the protagonist's "response" is not departure from school (as it usually was in the dropping out stories), but a decision to return to school and abandon the old self. This consequence usually amounts to the emergence of a new self and a new way of behaving in the world. This new self is one put forward as a good example to a younger generation, or to peers who have not yet turned over a new leaf.

The general outline of the success story is as follows:

1. Abstract (not always present)
2. Central problematic experience (usually a Former Self)
3. Response (usually psychological) and Turning Point
4. Consequence (usually a return to school, an advice-giving New Self)
5. Coda (not always present)

This pattern, when seen in the form of a success story, reveals the difference between the two genres, dropping in stories and dropping out stories. In the narrative below, Gracie explains why she left high school and why she came back to City School. Her turning point is marked by regret over her previous life as a "gang member":

"I Was a Gang Member"

problematic experience
(Former Self)

GRACIE: I was a gang member.
BETSY: Uh huh.
GRACIE: A long time. Your friends, your surroundings. If you wanna belong to a group you have to show 'em you can prove it.
BETSY: Ye [ah
GRACIE: [Peer pressure.

response (psychological)
and Turning Point
consequence (New Self)

GRACIE: And *now* that I c— I regret it.
BETSY: Uh huh,
GRACIE: 'cause now I have to— I wanted to come back to school because of my son, so, .hhh if I want to be a good mom and a good example. I have to show it to my son.

Gracie narrates the problematic experience as an old self that had to be shed ("I was a gang member") and her turning point as the regret she "now" has over this past identity. Unlike the "dropping out" narrators who begin their stories with descriptions of externally inciting problematic events, Gracie begins her narrative by describing a problem about her self, or more accurately a *former* self, which led her to leave school: "I was a gang member." She then goes on to elaborate the problems that led her to leave school. Gracie describes her former actions, her gang membership, her concessions to ever-present peer pressure, but distances her self from that past by narrating "now" as a different time. She relegates these problems to the past when she mentions her response to them, and narrates this response as a turning point: "Now I regret it."

The reason for her regret is the recognition of the need to be a good example to her son. After this recognition, the turning point, she doesn't need to "show 'em" by being in a gang, but needs to "show" to her son that she can be successful in school. This story, like the dropping out stories, depicts the author as acting not only on behalf of herself, but on behalf of others. While students who tell dropping out stories explain their actions in terms of sisters or friends whom they must "protect" through gang membership, Gracie must protect her son in another way, by shedding her old identity as a gang member and taking on a new one as a successful student. She goes on to elaborate in the addendum, "gang's not going to give me an education . . . so I left all that behind."

Even in discussing their internships, students told narratives similar to Gracie's. Though they mention past problems, these narratives are equally distinct from the dropping out genre. In the excerpt below, for example, Abel discusses his internship at a probation office, responding to the question, "What made you want to work there?" In his response he constructs a narrative very similar to Gracie's description of leaving school:

"The Wrong Path"

abstract	ABEL: 'Cause I'm— I'm like interested in like helping out kids and stuff like that. Cause I understand cause I— I— my point of view li—
problematic experience (Former Self)	I used to be like on the wrong path,
response and Turning Point	but you know I'm *now*, when I came back like, like trying to set my life straight, you know I feel that I maybe the things that I— the changes that I've been
consequence (New advice-giving self)	through I could— give kids the same advice.

Like Gracie, Abel locates the problematic experience in his former self and narrates a distinct turning point. While he used to be "on the wrong path" he is "now . . . trying to set his life straight." He uses the switch from the past to "now" to indicate a new set of commitments, and to distance himself from the mistakes he can admit he made. Despite this story's status as a response to an internship question, even his reason for working at the probation office centers on his status as a former dropout, but one who now has "been through changes" and wants to pass on what he has learned, that is, "the same advice."

Like Gracie, who wants to be a good example for her son, Abel describes his job at the probation office as a chance to be an example to other kids and give them advice. These stories vividly contrast with the dropping out stories. While those stories generally offer extended and explicit description for the problematic experience and locate the problem in another "they," these dropping in stories present a very minimal problematic experience, and narrate this experience as one located in the author, not in a threatening, ominous setting, or in a pursuing "they." Just as Gracie positions herself in the statement, "I was a gang member," Abel places himself firmly in the subject position of the sentence and explicitly narrates his previous problem: "I was on the wrong path." His response to this problematic old self is still underway, "trying to get myself straight," but the consequence is that he has undergone changes, and ones which he would like to pass along to other young people (presumably those on probation).

In a similar way, Von moves from a story about his internship into a long description of his previous life and his decision to come back to school. The internship, he said, was his springboard, and he describes his desire, as he worked at an elementary school, to talk to the kids who remind him of himself at that age. When another student, Jesus, asks Von what he got out of his internship, Von describes how it gave him that recognition that he needed to return to school. His narrative is driven by his identification with younger students who might be making the same mistakes he did, and the importance of making a clean break from such a past. His description of his internship is constructed as an internal dialogue between possible past selves—musing invoked by the kids that Von watched playing at the elementary school where he worked. Rather than taking the role of potential advice-giver at the end of his story, Von intersperses his description of his internship with his own speculation on the value of advice between generations. The very recognition of himself as a *potential* advice-giver triggers his decision to dedicate himself to school.

"It Isn't Too Late for Me"

abstract	VON: Well, me, I got, the motivation to go back to school.
Setting-present self	Basically. I saw— little kids playin' and it's like—
Implied problematic condition of kids/former self	I wish I coulda went back to about that age. And then start all over again.
Present self	And then I look at 'em
Implied problematic condition of kids/former self	and it's like I wanna tell them so much but you know I don't like preaching to anybody about— one certain thing too much

Hypothetical problematic *past self*	'cause it's like I know if I was sitting there it's like "who is— who is he? What is he telling me this for?"
Present self	So I sit there and enjoy it. Sitting there and just looking at 'em and playin' with them.
psychological response and TURNING POINT	*Then* it's like well it ain't too— it isn't too late for me. That's what I said to myself.
consequence	That's when I started, you know, to come— going back to school . . .

Like Gracie, Von describes how his decision to come back to school is motivated by his regrets. While he sits and watches the elementary school kids play, he thinks about both how he wishes he could start over, and how he knows anything he could tell them would be futile "preaching." Like Gracie and Abel, he contemplates the kind of example he could be for those kids, and all the things he could tell them to make sure they don't make the same mistakes he did. He concludes simply with his decision to return to school, but this decision hinges both on a recognition of his past mistakes and the decision to turn away from them, that "it isn't too late for me." Although Von does not articulate his role as "good example" as explicitly as Gracie and Abel, he sees himself as older and wiser now, a potential "preacher," someone from whom younger generation could learn (if they would listen). Yet it was his decision to just "sit there and enjoy it" that made him realize his own potential. It's as though the young kids playing in the schoolyard, by prompting Von's introspection, gave some advice to Von.

Like the dropping in stories, these success stories are elaborated in addenda which, typically, elaborate not on the internship, but on the kinds of conditions and states of mind from which these successful students have come. Von, in particular, elaborates his stories extensively on his own, spinning off new narratives with little prompting. Often, the students' addenda elaborate on the life they have "left behind," the kind of person they "used to be," or the destructive activities they "used to do." These stories and addenda frequently discuss events and schools similar to those discussed in the "dropping out" stories. However, the success stories depict these scenes as part of their past, now over, and the illicit activities as wrongs committed by former selves, rather than necessary acts committed in lieu of any reasonable alternatives.

GRAMMATICAL RESOURCES OF THE DROPPING IN GENRE

As discussed above, one way these stories distinguish themselves as a genre is through their story structure. Another unique characteristic of this genre, and one that distinguishes it from the dropping out genre, is the kind of grammatical resources narrators use to create narrative themes, and construct a certain identity for themselves. Across these narratives and their addenda (seven narratives in all), the students draw on a systematic set of grammatical forms to describe old selves that have been abandoned, to narrate a turning point, and to lay out the bright future. Specifically, as the sections below will describe in particular, these authors deploy grammatical forms in systematic and characteristic ways to (1) portray a distinctly *former* identity; (2) identify illicit activities that the protagonist "used to" do; (3) mark a turning point; and (4) animate City School and Education, portraying them as companions which can help the person to a new life (e.g., "it's me and City School from here on up").

Portraying a Former Self

In their use of past tense predicates to describe themselves, these narrators take the role that debunkers like Manny and Sylvia took in the story addenda analyzed in Chapter 3. Like the debunkers who explicitly assigned agency and roles to narrators of dropping out stories ("*he* started it" or "*she* was a troublemaker"), these speakers explicitly assign such roles to themselves. The use of the past tense, however, explicitly locates these identities as former identities, and ways of behaving as former habits. When Gracie begins to describe how she came to City School, for example, she uses language that identifies her generic previous identities, "gang member" and "dropout."

GRACIE: *I was a dropout.* Until I came to this school,
BETSY: Uh huh
GRACIE: .Hhh an—
BETSY: What made you— drop out of high school?
GRACIE: Friends,
BETSY: Y [eah.
GRACIE: [*I was a gang member.*

Gracie begins her description of her former experience as *already* a dropout, suggesting that she had been one for an extended time—until she came to City School. While the dropping out narratives also identify problems as preexistent, those problems are always external to the speaker. Here, Gracie identifies an ongoing problem—her status as a dropout—as one located within herself. Though she mentions that "friends" made her drop out of high school, she also explains how friends could have been such an influence by identifying herself with another generic identity: "I was a gang member."

Abel, who at the time of this interview had recently graduated from City School, also used the past tense of "be" as a verb of reported speech to describe the kind of attitude he used to have:

ABEL: Well my mom always told me you know she said "graduate. You should graduate. Try to go to— just go to school you know." At first like, "yes," but back then I wouldn't see her point you know, cause *I was just*, "awww what you talking about you don't know anything."

Here, Abel uses quoted speech to indicate the generic sort of thing he used to say. By introducing this use of quoted speech with the copular "be" (specifically, the phrase, "I was just"), he also frames this kind of speech as a generic way of thinking, an attribute of himself at the time, the kind of thing he always used to say. That is, in the past, when his mother would tell him to go back to school, he *was* the kind of person who would say "awww what you talking about you don't know anything." Abel's use of "was just," above, functions to introduce what he felt at the time, and in turn, the he as a person was like (cf., Tannen, 1989).

Another graduate, Von, used the past tense to describe the state of affairs he faced before applying himself at City School:

VON: *it was* almost over with *for me*

Here Von uses the existential "it" in a way reminiscent of the dropping out narratives. But, unlike those narratives, which use existential "it" to evoke an entire atmosphere of threat, Von qualifies his use of the existential "it" with the prepositional phrase "for me." In this way he isolates this state of affairs as one unique to his story, not an ongoing, ominous threat for any student. Furthermore, his use of the past tense isolates this experience to a particular time in the past, a time that he has come beyond.

Past tense predicates imply that these are old states of affairs and ways of thinking. The shedding of these identities is made even more explicit when the past tense is used in conjunction with the past habitual periphrastic modal, "used to."

Identifying Former Illicit Activities

In the dropping out stories, students also identified generic conditions at former high schools that made their lives more difficult, but in those narratives, by using progressive aspect or present tense departures from narrative past, narrators conveyed the ongoing nature of these events, their continuity with the present (e.g., "guys get stabbed in the bathroom," "if they want you bad they'll be waiting for you"). In contrast, in the success stories, past habitual verbs identify generic activities that "used to" be a part of students' lives but now are not.

For example, Abel contrasts his former "path" with his current attempt to get his life straight:

ABEL: *I used to be like on the wrong path*, but you know I'm now, when I came back like, like trying to set my life straight.

Like Gracie, who "was a gang member," Abel describes how he "used to be . . . on the wrong path." By putting himself in the subject position of this sentence, Abel acknowledges his own responsibility for previous actions, but by using "used to," he denotes this as a *past* habit. He does not describe himself as continuing on this "wrong path."

Similarly, Gracie's uses the "used to" modal to describe her old habit of getting into fights:

GRACIE: *I used to fight*. But not in this school. I never got into a fight in this school.

In contrast to the dropping out narrators, who always use the nonagentive "get" (see Chapter 2) to describe their involvements in fights (e.g., "I got in a fight"), Gracie firmly places herself as agent of the verb "fight" here. However, by placing this habit in the past, she assures us that this identity is no longer salient. Indeed, as she goes on to explain, she has never been in fights at City School.

Fighting is just one of the habits the tellers of success stories eschew. Von also fesses up to other acts he "used to" do:

VON: You know, doing what I *used to* do going out on the streets rob and steal and doing all that other stuff.

These stories describe not only speakers' former activities (fighting, robbery, stealing, and "all that other stuff"), but also the kinds of things they used to say (or think):

FABIOLA: 'Cause my Dad told me "I know you're not gonna graduate. I— I mean— you can— I know you're— even gonna— you're not even gonna— you can— you will— hardly graduate from Junior High." All like— all like that, "okay whatever." I ju— *I used to say that.*

Fabiola describes here how her father would belittle her and her ability to excel academically. But when he told her she would never graduate, she didn't care. "Okay whatever" she *used to* say. She implies that this is not the kind of thing she says anymore. Having recently graduated from high school, she embodies the retort to her doubting father and an alternative to the "okay whatever" attitude she used to have.

Marking a Turning Point

Unlike dropping out stories, where unpleasant school settings and ongoing peer antagonisms provide an explanatory backdrop for the problematic experience in the narrative, the success stories describe old selves and old habits as problematic in and of themselves. The response to this problematic self, then, is narrated as a turning away from the old self and its detrimental habits. One grammatical resource that facilitates narration of a turning point is the use of adverbials (e.g., the words "until" and "now") which contrast past states with present changes. In success stories, these words routinely mark a turning point after which a new and better life (and portrayal of self) begins.

In the dropping out stories, narrators often depart from the past tense, using present tense to universalize those conditions described. Like the agoraphobic narrator described by Capps and Ochs (1995), these narrators also used present tense to create an immediacy to their previous hardships and a continuity between distant occurrences and the time of narration. In contrast, the success story narrators use temporal adverbials to create a cut-off from former identities and to portray their current selves as no longer associated with reprehensible activities of the past.

The temporal adverbial "until," for example, indicates "temporal termination" (Celce-Murcia & Larsen-Freeman, 1983, p. 260) and in these narratives denotes the termination of old behavioral habits and previous selves. In the following narrative, Michael uses it to show the end point of his problems and the onset of his new life at City School:

MICHAEL: It's gonna be better. But then it never— ended up that way. *Until I came to City School.* And I started doing a lot of stuff for myself, and, like I started focusing my life, knowing what I want to accomplish.

While Michael previously kept switching schools, always thinking it would be better, that never happened. That is, "until" he enrolled at City School, where he suddenly attained agency, focused his life, and became a success. By using the word "until" to make a clean break with his past, Michael succinctly narrates the emergence of a new self.

Gracie even more succinctly sheds her old self, using "until" to mark the transition:

GRACIE: I was a dropout. *Until* I came to this school,

While these narrators do not directly qualify their past misdeeds, they do indirectly qualify them by appending the *until* adverbial, indicating that those states of being no longer exist.

The temporal adverbial *now* further isolates the current self from an old identity. As Gracie laments, she "now" regrets her old life as a "gang member." But "now" she has new goals because of her son:

GRACIE: And *now* that I c— I regret it.
BETSY: Uh huh,
GRACIE: cause *now* I have to— I wanted to come back to school because of my son, so if I want to be a good mom and a good example. I have to show it to my son.

In Gracie's narrative, "now" distinctly separates the old identity she regrets from the "good mom" and "good example" she now is struggling to be. As she concludes her narrative, she reemphasizes that she has left her old life behind and uses "now" to point to her current goals:

GRACIE: So. I left all that behind, and *now* it's my future.

Similarly, Abel contrasts what his life used to be (the wrong path) with his current attempt to get his life straight:

ABEL: I used to be like on the wrong path, but you know *I'm now*, when I came back like, like *trying to set my life straight,*

The use of temporal adverbials "now" and "until" explicitly relegate previous mistakes to the past. A "wrong [crooked?] path" of the past is rendered distinct from the right, "straight" life of the present. All the bad habits of the past, the fights, the robbery, the callow fall to peer pressure occurred, but only "until" "now."

Portraying School as a Companion

But what does "now" hold? After the turning point, what do these young men and women turn to, and what are the consequences? In most of these stories, City School is instrumental in their turn from the dark side, and in some cases City School is even anthropomorphized as a hero or comrade. In the example below, Gracie thanks the school, an action typically performed on an animate object:

GRACIE: and then I go, "I'm gonna take it's my ch— my only chance and my only way out."
BETSY: uh huh.
GRACIE: To get my education. *So I thank City School.* I'm still here.

And Von metaphorically joins hands with City School in his rise to the top:

VON: So I knew, from that point on I was goin— it's me and City School from here on up.

As these and other grammatical resources suggest, this "dropping in story" genre contains a series of grammatical forms—in patterned textual context— that distinguish this genre from the dropping out stories. Driven by institutional agendas, their peers, and their understanding of this conversational context, these young men and women are actively structuring the events of their lives according to certain concerns. They have left the unpleasant and unproductive life of the "dropout" or "gang member," joined hands with City School, and started down the right path.

A DEBUNKER IN THE MIDST

As discussed in Chapter 4 ("Reframing Dropping Out Narratives"), one way genres are distinguished from one another is their openness to reconstrual. As the debunking episodes following the dropping out stories indicate, even the basic facts of these stories were open to revision after the story had formally closed. Rarely, however, do the success stories meet with such contesting up-take. In this setting, students generally take each other's stories at face value, nod in approval, and add their own similar story to the mix. Their conclusions are taken to be the final word. Student interviewers helped to create this interactional atmosphere. Rather than asking follow-up questions, student interviewers would often turn to the next student and directly elicit a response to the same question with, as exemplified below, a transition phrase like "what about you?":

MICHAEL: . . . Until I came to City School. And I started— doing a lot of stuff for myself, and, like I started focusing my life, knowing what I want to accomplish (and what I want to do).
NANCY: *I see. What about you.*
MONICA: um. When I was in high school I like. I don't know I guess. I just started like. Not really going to class or whatever.

As this interview closes, Nancy concludes Michael's story with a finalizing "I see" and turns to Monica for a similar story, which Monica then delivers. In other cases, student interviewers just turn from one storyteller to the next and, on this nonverbal cue, a given student starts in with his or her own success story.

Furthermore, unlike the students who told the dropping out stories, the students rarely need prompting to add addenda to their own stories. Like politicians on a news broadcast, they use their position in the limelight as long as possible and continue to speak uninterrupted. Unlike the students in the Friday morning discussion groups, these students' initial narratives are often quite extended, and they will add to them with little encouragement. Their stories are detailed and long and, upon completion, usually meet with short, approving nods, or stronger agreeing statements. After Von concludes a lengthy narrative about his transformation at City School, Nancy agrees handily:

VON: and if it wasn't I— I think if I didn't go to that internship I think I'd
    still be out in the streets somewhere. Or if I would still be living. Or I'd
    still be on the streets period. I'd probably be in jail I don't know. But
    that helped.
NANCY: *This school has made a difference in everybody,* I mean. In my life
    too.

As Nancy's participation unfolds, she seems to be converted by these narratives. Von is a powerful speaker and he holds the others' attention. As his narratives suggest (and his audience seems convinced), were it not for City School, he would have wound up "in jail or dead." As Nancy's contributions throughout his story suggest, she is thoroughly impressed with his new take on life. This school, she adds, has made a difference on *everybody*.

Another student interviewer, however, exposes a chink in his accumulation of public relations armor. Like Manny, who subverted the stance that "getting cuffed" etc. is cool, Jesus does not seem to take Nancy's rapture at face value. Von seems to have inveigled his listeners with his conversion, but after Nancy's hearty agreement, Jesus lets loose a scoff:

VON: I'd probably be in jail I don know. But that helped.
NANCY: This school has made a difference in everybody, I mean. In my life
    too=
JESUS: *psh*
NANCY: =wouldn't a been the same.

Jesus's debunking, in this increasingly officialized genre, is minimal. In fact, in Jefferson's (1978) terms, his scoffs are "sequentially deleted," as Nancy continues her thought (with "wouldn'a been the same"), unaffected by Jesus's contribution. His "psh" suggests, however, that he is not entirely convinced that Nancy has changed so much. Indeed, this minimal scoff suggests that Jesus has begun to assume the role of "debunker." As another exchange reveals, Nancy is not unaware of Jesus's role. In a discussion with another student intern, La-Quinta, Nancy had begun to contribute a great deal to the addendum, adding more and more about the need for people to leave their old lives behind once they come to City School. However, midmonologue, she turns aside, rebukes Jesus, who has said nothing, but who she senses is doubting her words. While he can't be seen on camera, Nancy's remark indicates she has been aware of his debunking potential:

NANCY: Why come from a— from where you messed up to here and then do the same thing. Not cause— cause I don't understand why people complain— about the work, about everything— cause I— I put my two cents into a lot of things— *JeSUS!* ((*aside to Jesus, off-camera*))
And um—
LAQUINTA: uh huh.
NANCY: You know i— i— it's just— it's bad.

As Jesus and Nancy have both admitted, their relationship is one of constant teasing—"like brother and sister," they say. This makes it understandable that when Nancy says that she puts her "two cents into a lot of things," Jesus might know exactly what she is talking about. While Nancy has just been reprimanding hypothetical others, her admission that she puts her "two cents" in herself suggests that she understands that others might interpret her as also being a complainer. With Jesus in the room, she is not able to maintain such a clearcut difference between herself and those reprehensible others. Putting on a shining public persona, as Nancy attempts repeatedly in these interviews, isn't always as easy when a sibling—or virtual sibling—is a witness. It is easy for such a character to crack the shiny surface, to needle exactly where it hurts. Jesus then, though he has said nothing, emerges in this setting as the closest thing to a debunker. And he also reveals the possibility that these narratives, like the dropping out stories—like all stories—are incomplete versions of the facts of dropping out and returning to school. As Jesus implies here, Nancy is not so sin-free as to be able to cast stones unself-consciously.

NARRATIVE AND REFORM

These two sets of narratives demonstrate the power of narrative not only to create a "self-portrait" (Capps & Ochs, 1995; Schiffrin, 1996), but also to conceal the complexities of life choices—complexities that can be buried by the institutional machinery that underpins narration. Institutions and institutional discourse play a powerful and subtle role in the concealment and simplification as well as the elaboration of identity (Cohn, 1987; Scholes, 1985; Willis, 1977). Through these two sets of narratives, we can see how an institution and its goals shape even the "personal" crafting of selves that went on in these discussion groups. Once this link—the link between institutional innovation and reform and student identity—is made, it becomes impossible to ignore the immense responsibilities of a reform movement. These stories vividly remind us that reforming a school, or in this case, creating a new charter school in order to reform an entire system, involves the lives of individual students. Sadly, this responsibility can be grossly abused, as students become pawns in reform movements, and learn to tell stories that reduce their lives.

These two sets of stories portray, then, not only the lives of the students, but these lives as told to serve the agenda of the reformers. In this way, the shaping power of school reform reaches beyond simply educating the child; it is the very shaping of the child. City School, like any school, provided an environment within which young men and women would become students, tell what it means to be a student, and embody that student. These stories are not simply momentary theater pieces. Each story told is living evidence of this process of becoming. Through telling stories, like these, lives are made. Neither the dropping out nor the dropping in stories are the "whole truth." There is no unitary truth, but there are the very real life events that these storytellers live through. The students who told these vastly different sorts of stories ended up having very different educational trajectories. None of the dropping out storytellers finished their education at City School. All of the dropping in storytellers had either graduated recently or were on their way. As this correlation suggests, the kinds of stories we tell are related to the kinds of lives we lead. But of critical importance here, and for the issue of reform, is that *institutions shape those stories that shape who we become.*

One of the best ways to deal with the necessary contradictions of life (and in this case, the paradoxical predicament of a dropout dropping back in to school) is to let stories become elaborate and complex, and to work through the contradictions through the telling. As the debunkers lurking in the background of these chapters well know, if a story perfectly serves one's agenda, it must be questioned. What is wrong? What is missing? While the stories in this chapter seem one-dimensional when viewed in light of the dropping out stories, so too do the dropping out stories seem one-sided when viewed from a nondropout perspective. After hearing those dropping in stories, and listening as students described an almost effortless departure from gang life and the constant fighting of their old schools, I had a different perspective on the dropping out stories recorded earlier, in which gangs and fights were made to seem so inescapable. How to reconcile these mutually contradictory, one-sided views?

One of the ideal outcomes of education, and of human development in general, is the elimination of the ignorance that leads to such one-sided views of life. The best of educational environments offer a "forum" for "negotiating and renegotiating meaning" (Bruner, 1996). The debunkers encourage this more multifaceted portrayal of the narrative events, but the impulse to create unitary narrative identities that "look good" is a strong one. At times, this "looking good"—shaped both by momentary peer group influences and larger institutional forces that create a certain forum for the telling—can happen at the sacrifice of more productive approaches to identity. As this chapter has illustrated, dropping out identities can be axed with machiavellian rhetorical strategies. Lives these young people lived and believed in for a number of years become, simply, "the wrong path." And frequently an abandonment of these old identities comes with increasing identification with the mainstream, and with new, genericized goals. Norma Mendoza-Denton (1996) has noticed similar patterns of changing loyalty in her study of gang girls in northern California, who, as they grew up and attended college, began to adopt once reviled, stereotypically Euro-American cultural behavior.

But dropping out and dropping in perspectives need not be so mutually exclusive. City School did not always stifle contradiction, and at times the environment there created a forum for creative change. The following chapters explore cases where discourse does not portray such unitary perspectives, cases that facilitate a closer analysis of the tension between the two perspectives, dropping out and dropping in, as well as the multiple, nuanced, and evolving perspectives inherent in human interaction and the creation of community.

CHAPTER 6

Names

This is Little Creeper from Diamond Street.
Westside Barrio Diamond Street.

—Federico, 1993

At one point, one could enter any classroom at City School and inevitably see one or more students scribbling furiously on pieces of paper, not finishing up schoolwork but writing their nicknames again and again. Why? And why was this permitted? This chapter focuses on these nicknames, their capacity to index an entire identity and set of social ties on the one hand, and their equally powerful capacity to signify "troublemaker" (or worse) to institutions and teachers, on the other hand.

The analysis of names in this chapter draws primarily from a series of discussions I had weekly for 3 months with a group of "leaders" at the school. These students were chosen by the teachers because of their status as active gang members, taggers, and those most able to influence their peers (either positively or negatively). Several of the participants overlap with those who attended the Friday morning discussion groups. During these meetings, graffiti and names came up quite often in conversation. Therefore, this chapter examines another linguistic resource at work in narrative and the presentation of self: the use of names (first names, last names, gang nicknames, and nongang names) in various mediums (writing, speaking, gesture) as well as the practices and contradictory ideologies surrounding their use.

The various perspectives surrounding the use of gang nicknames illuminate complexities that cannot be bounded within a single narrative viewpoint. An individual's multiple names and their varied uptake reveal the inevitable multiplicity of selves within an individual. The use of both gang names and given names provides a way of exploring this multiplicity within individuals at City School, where some students freely used both gang nicknames and their own given names without fear of censure. At City School, for several months at least, students were protected both from rival gang members who might take offense at particular names, and from the type of school administrators who might use names as a means to expel students. As a result, gang members talk openly about their names and identities attached to them.

City School's open acceptance of the symbols of gang affiliation (not only name use, but also clothing styles and ways of speaking) also facilitated my own exploration into the background of gang nicknames and their meanings in different situations. This chapter explores one student, Federico, and his use of the nickname "Little Creeper" within a narrative. But this chapter will also indicate how nicknames used by Federico and other gang members have very different meanings outside of their social group. Names in general, while having unitary referents (i.e., the named individual) attribute very different qualities to a person, depending on the context in which that name is used. Depending on their uptake, proper names, like narratives, become resources for multiple identities.

Students' stories and explanations frequently attest to the changing power of names in and outside of school. Students who have been expelled from schools say that information about gang names and members' nicknames is very useful for principals and police. According to students' reports, a principal's knowledge of a student's gang affiliation or nickname is often considered sufficient evidence of wrongdoing to have that person expelled. While principals and police attach one set of beliefs to a gang member's name, they disregard another set of accrued social meanings. For young men and women in their own neighborhood, gang names serve to reinforce a positive social identity; in another context, these names acquire new meanings and are, in some cases, criminalized.

In this chapter I outline naming and its various functions as described by and used in the narratives of one student. Then I discuss how the meaning of a name can transform in different social contexts. And last, I will examine the implications of local knowledge—like that involved in naming practices—for school reform.

GANG NAMES AND NICKNAMES AT CITY SCHOOL

The analysis in this chapter focuses on the names and stories of a young man whose dropping out narrative was featured in Chapter 2. In that chapter, Federico, an active member of the Diamond Street gang who goes by the nickname "Little Creeper," described "getting hit up" by a rival gang in his narrative, "Everybody Rushed Me." Like the various naming practices discussed above, the meaning of these names—"Little Creeper" and "Diamond Street"—is not isolable from their contextualized utterance, but bound up in the culture and history of associations associated with "Little Creeper" and "Diamond Street." In the following sections, I illustrate the layers of context that give meaning to these names.

The Here and Now

The most obvious source of meaning for a name is immediate context. Anytime we introduce ourselves to a complete stranger we explicitly label ourselves. In the same way, when Federico introduced himself to the tape recorder, he showed directly the connection between himself (as marked by the personal pronoun "my") and his two names.

FED: My name is Federico.
       That's my nickname Creeper.

The Surrounding Talk

While naming can be relatively straightforward, as in the example above, most naming is not done so formally or explicitly. In the next example, Little Creeper is telling a story in which he is describing another time he was "hit up" (that is, confronted by a rival gang member and asked where—which gang—he was from). In quoted dialogue, he describes himself being asked the canonical opener to a hitting up activity, "Where are you from?" Rather than giving the answer, "I am from Diamond Street," or even sillier, "I am from Guanajuato, Mexico" (which someone not familiar with getting hit up might say), he responds with the statement "This is Diamond Street":

FED: I go don't even get my sister into—
       to Eighteenth Street man
       "Why? Where you from?"
       "This is Diamond Street"

   The question "Where you from?" asks about group affiliation as well as individual identity. Federico's "This is Diamond Street" supplies an answer to both aspects of the question. By saying, "This is Diamond Street," Federico is not naming the street he is standing on. Rather, he is naming his group affiliation. To see how the use of the name "Little Creeper" is crucially connected to his membership in "Diamond Street," we can look to other examples where they co-occur, as below:

FED: The little— this is Little Creeper from Diamond Street.
       Westside Barrio Diamond Street. My name is Federico. That's my nick-
       name Creeper.

As the above example indicates, Diamond Street is associated with Creeper's proper name. Indeed, being part of this gang is a prerequisite for the effective use of the name "Little Creeper." Thus, being "Little Creeper" necessitates membership in the group "Westside Barrio Diamond Street" and familiarity with the institutionalized naming practices that accompany that affiliation.

The Causal Link to a Baptismal Event

Co-occurrence suggests a relationship between the name Little Creeper and membership in the group Diamond Street. Furthermore, only members of the gang Diamond Street are eligible to take part in the specific naming ritual—the baptismal event—that fixes the name "Little Creeper" to the individual, Federico. (For more detailed discussion on the relationship between baptismal events and the meaning of names, see Kripke [1977] and Putnam [1988]. For a detailed discussion of gang naming practices and their relationship to the anthropological and philosophical literature, see Rymes [1996]. See Rymes [1999] also for an overview on naming from an anthropological perspective.) Creeper's "baptismal event" comes in the form of a typical gang initiation, or "jumping in." Vigil (1993) describes such gang initiation as "a type of street ceremony or baptism" after which "the person can now state that he is 'wino' (or whatever nickname he has been given) and go on to graffiti his personal name along with the clique and barrio names" (p. 105). In the baptismal event described below, father figures (OG's, or Original Gangsters, the most esteemed and experienced gang members) initiate Federico into the Diamond Street gang through a typical gang rite; Federico receives his nickname and his right to use that nickname in conjunction with other gang members by getting "jumped in," or severely beaten by his future fellow gang members, or family-to-be:

FED: My daddy is black. Call him Creeper.
DUVAL: Your daddy black?
FED: Yeah,
DANNY: [Not his real dad—
DUVAL: [Who
FED: Not my real dad I call him dad, the guy that jumped me in? He gave me the name, Little Creeper? He's a black guy
DUVAL: Oh that's what y'all call your all big homies like oh dad— Y'all call (your all) dad,
FED: Well I call him my [dad
((others start laughing, talking at once))
DANNY: [not everybody
FED: Not everybody
DUVAL: He's O.G?
FED: Huh?
((overlapping stories))

FED: You know when they jump you like—Littleman's brother—Littleman's brother jumped me so I'm his son, so Big Creeper, I'm his son, uh, Vago I'm his son, and Cubby.

DUV: All those fools (up there)?

FED: Yeah

DUV: Oh Man, the OG's jumped you in, huh.

As the above initiation description suggests, for Federico, these names are not simply labels. Like all names, the fixing of the referent for the nickname "Little Creeper" is traceable to a particular baptismal event, in this case a gang initiation ceremony. Furthermore, the legitimacy of this baptismal event rests on the legitimacy of the group Diamond Street and the sociohistorical origins of this particular naming practice.

Names As Descriptions and Indexicals

The typical gang names (e.g., Fat Freddy, Triste, Creeper, Sniper, Littleman), give one the immediate impression of description. Indeed, within Los Angeles gangs, "personal approaches to members' behavior often are reflected in nicknames: Names like 'Loco,' 'Crazy,' or 'Psycho' often are given to the more volatile clique members, for example" (Vigil & Long, 1990). But as the above recollection of the baptismal event indicates, gang names are not merely descriptive of the individual. Rather, as in the case of Little Creeper, the name is indexical of his relationship with the OG or Veterano, "Creeper," who jumped him in. Indeed, many gang names are not immediately descriptive (e.g., Cubby, Buko, Casper, Mugsy), but as I have learned through my discussions with these young men, these names are frequently inherited from older or deceased gang members. This source of names also depends not so much upon the semantic value of the name, but the tradition with which it is associated.

Those names that may on the outside seem less obviously descriptive, like Cubby, are in fact indexical of an entire realm of cultural and personal associations. In turn, the descriptive aspect of more obviously descriptive gang names may be of negligible importance. In fact, when I asked Creeper what his name meant, instead of telling me what the verb "to creep" means, he told me the story of his baptismal event. Similarly, the gang name "Diamond Street" is not directly descriptive of the place where this gang congregates (or "kicks it"). If one went to the one block labeled "Diamond Street" in Los Angeles, one would find nothing resembling gang territory (see Figure 6.1). For members of "Diamond Street," their territory is not marked by typical city blocks or street signs, but rather by a more intuitive sense of where their friend can be found and by gang writing (see Figure 6.2). As Conquergood (1992) has noted, "Gangs possess and poeticize space, imbuing it with emotional intensity, aesthetic and

FIGURE 6.1: The Official Diamond Street in Downtown Los Angeles.

FIGURE 6.2: Diamond Street Gang Roll Call: Triste, Creeper, Frosty, Fat Freddy, Mugsy, Sniper, Chills, and Casper.

moral power" (p. 11). As described below, the name "Diamond Street" itself refers to a unique location and simultaneously indexes a brief history of the transformation of Little Creeper's original "'hood."

((Jack is asking Federico why he calls his gang "Diamond Street" when it
    seems like they don't hang out (or "kick it") on that street))
JACK: How come it be like— like your—
    like your hood is like, what's your street,
    you know Diamond Street right?
DANNY: Yeah.
JAC: An— An y'all kick it on— what it—
    [is (xxx)
DAN: [We kick it on Boyleston. Coit and Boyleston.
JAC: How come y'all don't kick—
DAN: We used to kick it right here.
FED: We kick— we used to kick it right here on Diamond Street but
    [they started—
JAC: [Yeah that's what I'm saying]
FED: They started making some buildings. So they kicked e—e—everything
    to the hill. But if you go right there you see the original street. Diamond
    S— Diamond Street. That's our street right there.

As this excerpt illustrates, a great deal of social knowledge is involved in understanding what the utterance "This is Diamond Street" means. Speakers have to know the background of Diamond Street to know that it is not just a street, but a social institution with long-standing conventions that legitimize naming practices. This knowledge is a prerequisite to (1) the baptismal event that fixes the reference of "Little Creeper"; (2) the use of the name "Little Creeper" by others; and (3) introducing oneself by giving one's gang name.

Context-bound Use

The social meaning of Diamond Street is also developed in opposition to an understanding of the rival gang Eighteenth Street and its similarly nondefinite location. Just as the name "Little Creeper" indexes a relationship, as much as an individual, the name "Diamond Street" indexes an opposition as much as it does a specific a place. In the contrast between Eighteenth Street and Diamond Street, the potential social effects of being from the Diamond Street gang are revealed. This potential meaning is not inherent in the name Diamond Street, but developed through parallelisms set up in talk about gangs and the naming of other gangs. As with Diamond Street, the location of Eighteenth Street (one of the most powerful and famous Los Angeles street gangs) is also amorphous.

Clearly the efficacy of being from Diamond Street, and claiming to be "Little Creeper from Diamond Street," is context dependent. Accordingly, Federico only uses his gang name in certain circumstances. At school and at home gang members will usually use their "given" names. In the discussions I had with these young men, I always had them sign in by writing their name in one column and their nickname in another. They would laugh at this practice, perhaps because they were not used to using both their names in the same context. The young gang members probably thought it was strange to see two of their social selves mingling on the same sign-in sheet.

While gang names seem slightly out of place on the school-based sign-in sheet, within the realm of gang talk and confrontation, gang names and nicknames take on great power. This is not only the power of presenting opposition (e.g., to Eighteenth Street), or of showing affiliation (e.g., to the *veteranos* or O.G.s from one's own gang), but also the power to protect one another and *deter* fighting. All of these functions of naming practice come into play in the stories these gang members tell of getting "hit up." As shown below, in stories of getting hit up, gang members use names to invoke their group affiliation and, consequently, their power as individuals to stand up for the gang and to prevent further fighting.

Naming in Stories: The Evolution of New Meanings for Names

While names are given at particular baptismal events, value accrues to those names. These names are "pegs" upon which to hang new meanings (Searle, 1958). But *how* do these meanings accrue? The following excerpt of narrative from Little Creeper begins to illustrate how his name accumulates particular value through the way Federico uses his nickname in a canonical story of gang confrontation. Through the way he tells his story below, Federico goes beyond the immediate context of the telling. He also goes beyond the sociohistorical information involved in the confrontation between rival gangs. In this narrative he uses his name to define himself uniquely as an important and powerful force as a gang member, as protector for his sister, and as a human being with a worthy mission. The story has been printed once in its entirety below (with names and gang affiliations in bold) and will be analyzed in smaller segments that follow.

Little Creeper in Narrative

FED: She's afraid of me though. 'Cause I kick her ass all the time.
LEO: Is she from *Diamond Street* too?
FED: Uh. She's from *Eighteenth Street. Morena.*
LEO: *Morena?*

FED: *Morena from Eighteenth Street.*

DUVAL: Oh is that right? ((Laughing a little))

FED: *Tiny Locas*

OTHERS: Heh heh heh

DUVAL: Oh your enemy huh.

FED: Well not actually though. The day I heard that she got jumped I went down there. That's the way I met that girl, *Smiley.* That's the way I met her you know 'cause I seen this bitch. The one that jumped my sister right. When they jumped her two of them— but it wasn't like— They couldn't accept it 'cause there was only two *jainas*— And—there was nobody to count. So supposedly my sister's from *Eighteenth Street* right now. They called her *Morena.* So I went back that day and I seen this girl and I go you're *Smiley* from *Eighteenth Street.* She goes yeah. And I go, "I'm looking for your *homegirl.*" She goes, "Who homegirl?" and I go, "Some homegirl I wanna talk to." So they took me with their homegirls *from Tiny Locas.* Got— I got there and I see like five bitches right there so I— I just socked one so bang I go don't even get my sister into— to *Eighteenth Street* man— "Why where you from?" *"This is Diamond Street" "Oh you're from Diamond Street"* and she goes, "but *they call you Little Creeper"* and she goes, "Oh you're the one who be talking to the punk" and then go, "You are?" and we started talking. So, my sister is afraid 'cause she thought I would not have the guts or the balls to go down there by *Eighteenth Street* and start talking shit to them you know.

Understanding the relevance of the naming in this passage requires knowledge of the opposition between Diamond Street and Eighteenth Street (and the Tiny Locas, a subset of Eighteenth Street) gangs. Generally, the claiming of Diamond Street followed by the claiming of Eighteenth Street should lead to confrontation, typically violent. Indeed, above, as soon as Federico mentions that his sister is from the rival Eighteenth Street gang, the others begin to chuckle at the problematic nature of having a sister as your rival. "Your enemy huh," says Duval. This background begins to set up a problematic setting for the rest of Federico's story.

Problematic Experience/ Setting	LEO: Is she from *Diamond Street* too?
	FED: Uh She's from *Eighteenth Street. Morena.*
↓	LEO: *Morena?*
	FED: *Morena from Eighteenth Street.*
	DUVAL: Oh is that right? *((Laughing a little))*
	FED: *Tiny Locas*

OTHERS: Heh heh heh
DUVAL: Oh your enemy huh.

As he continues, Federico explicates this problematic setting in more detail. First, he explains that no, she is "not actually" his enemy and explains how her "jumping in" baptismal event may not have even been legitimate:

Problematic Experience/ Setting (continued): Questionable Baptismal Event ↓	FED: Well not actually though. The day I heard that she got jumped I went down there. That's the way I met that girl, *Smiley*. That's the way I met her you know 'cause I seen this bitch. The one that jumped my sister right. When they jumped her two of them— but it wasn't like— They couldn't accept it 'cause there was only two *jainas*— And— there was nobody to count.

As this excerpt illustrates, Federico questions the preconditions necessary to legitimate his sister's baptismal event. He claims that there were only two "*jainas*," or gang girls present (implying there should be more), and nobody to count. For this reason there is doubt about the staying power of his sister's new designation as "Morena from Eighteenth Street." As he goes on to explain, however, the members of the Tiny Locas faction of Eighteenth Street are still convinced of her membership:

Problematic Experience/ Setting (continued): "Supposed" Name and Affiliation	FED: So supposedly my sister's from *Eighteenth Street* right now. They called her *Morena*.

While Federico admits that she very well may be "Morena from Eighteenth Street," he casts doubts on this contention by using the word "supposedly." Clearly, however, he was convinced that he could reverse this only semilegitimate naming process, and win back his sister. The next segment illustrates his response to the problematic status of his sister: He goes to personally confront the Tiny Locas:

Response to Problematic Name Part One: Socking	FED: So I went back that day and I seen this girl and I go you're *Smiley* from *Eighteenth Street*. She goes yeah. And I go, "I'm looking for your *homegirl*." She

goes, "Who homegirl?" and I go, "Some
homegirl I wanna talk to." So they took
me with their homegirls *from Tiny Locas.*
Got— I got there and I see like five
bitches right there so I— I just socked
one so bang I go don't even get my sister
into— to *Eighteenth Street* man—

In this first confrontation, Little Creeper, without even naming his own
gang, asks to be led to the pack of "bitches" from his rival gang and then
proceeds directly to a confrontation over his sister when he socks one of the
girls. Up to this point, however, the rules of "getting hit up" have not been
adhered to. It seems, in fact, that Federico has avoided naming his affiliation
with Diamond Street in order to be led into the lair of Tiny Locas. When Federico's hostility becomes apparent, however, Smiley asks where he is from, and at
this point, the importance of being "Little Creeper from Diamond Street" becomes the most salient. Federico communicates the importance of his own name
in this narrative by recounting the dialogue he had with Smiley:

Response to Problematic   FED: "Why where you from?" *"This is Dia-*
Name   *mond Street"* "*Oh you're from Diamond*
Part Two: Naming   *Street"* and she goes, "but *they call you*
                             Little Creeper" and she goes, "Oh you're
                             the one who be talking to the punk" and
                             then go, "You are?" and we started
                             talking.

This exchange begins with a canonical "hitting up" sequence, and seems
to quote the exchange directly, beginning with Smiley's question "where you
from" and directly followed by Federico's own response at the time, "This is
Diamond Street." Ordinarily, once one mentions a rival gang name in such a
speech activity, violent confrontation would follow. In this case, however, the
exchange ends when the two simply "started talking." Smiley's recognition of
"Little Creeper" seems to be enough to prevent further violence. In the subsequent coda to the story, Federico clarifies that this confrontation was successful.
His appearance as "Little Creeper" from Diamond Street is so clearly powerful
that even when outnumbered by rival gang members, it carries weight—weight
that he throws around to prevent the Tiny Locas from recruiting his sister:

Coda   FED: So, my sister is afraid 'cause she thought
                             I would not have the guts or the balls to

> go down there by *Eighteenth Street* and
> start talking shit to them you know.

By telling this story, Federico shows how his power, the power of being "Little Creeper" (and from Diamond Street), actually allows him to deter further violence between Eighteenth Street and his own gang, and further problems for his sister. In this way, a new meaning behind the name "Little Creeper" unfolds in the passage. This is a story of gang confrontation, where being Little Creeper from Diamond Street is very important as a show of power and affiliation with another gang, as well as a peace-keeping device, a deterrent, and a way to protect his little sister. The existence of rival gangs can cause confrontation, but the very power of being Little Creeper can curtail it.

When Smiley asks where he is from he says "Diamond Street," and (in Federico's narration) she immediately intuits that he is "Little Creeper." This is the brave gang member who confronted the punk (when he socked her and warned, "Don't even get my sister into Eighteenth Street"). He has just deceived the entire group of Eighteenth Street "bitches" and shown them that he will not allow his sister into their gang. Paradoxically, when Little Creeper finally identifies himself, this does *not* lead to confrontation. Rather, within Federico's quoted dialogue, his name now carries the power of deterrence and instead of fighting again, "they started talking." The conclusion to the story restates the reason Federico's sister is now afraid of him. It is not actually because he beats her up all the time; it is because he has managed to protect her and will continue to protect her by being Little Creeper, the one who had "the guts" and the "balls" to confront the Eighteenth Street girls.

In order to protect his sister from the rival gang, Federico has had to confront these girls, but at the end of the story, this violent confrontation has been subsumed into his name, such that his name has become so powerful that it is, in fact, a deterrent. For Little Creeper, using his own name is a matter of pride, not only because it indicates his membership in Diamond Street, but because it carries the entextualization of the confrontation where he acted on behalf of his sister and now continues to protect her. Thus, his name now has the power to transcend the dichotomous relationships of gang rivalry.

Federico restates the necessity for his role a few utterances later, when he explains how his name has a power that his mother cannot exert, even for her daughter's own good:

FED: I guess that's the only way I could get her off of trouble. You know my ma can't do nothing you know.

Just as Diamond Street maintains its sense of power and ubiquity, even while being pushed out of its territory by the real controller of material resources, the

FIGURE 6.3: The Hand Sign for Diamond Street.

downtown developers, Little Creeper maintains his own identity and sense of dignity in the face of hardship by contextualizing himself as transcendent of the gang rivalry to which his sister nearly succumbs. Naming therefore presupposes the entextualized value of an entire lifestyle, and allows Little Creeper and members of Diamond Street to create a sense of control and power for themselves.

Representing in Multiple Channels

This control is not only communicated through narrative. It is recreated in multiple mediums, most prominently grafitti and hand signs, but also through style and bearing. Members of Diamond Street and other gangs throw gang signs that signify the whole social context associated with gang membership and use graffiti to reinforce the relationship between their own nicknames and their gang affiliation (see Figure 6.3). Therefore, gang members will always write their name in connection with their gang (see Figure 6.4). Furthermore, gang members cultivate a unique style, a set of gestures, and a performance of attitude

FIGURE 6.4: Graffiti: Little Creeper from Diamond Street.

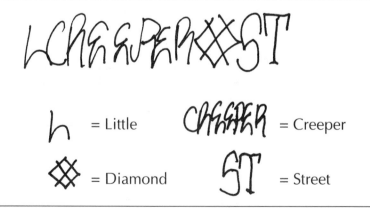

that signifies their membership in a unique group. Vigil (1993) describes these multichannel gang references as "role prescriptions" which include "standardized clothing styles, nicknaming practices (clique members often will not know the formal names of their fellows), tattoo and graffiti techniques, speech practices, and even distinctive patterns for face and hand gestures, body posture, and walking" (p. 64). All of these maneuvers tend to reinforce the notion that in order to express one's own individuality, one must simultaneously express affinity to the group.

ALTERNATIVE READINGS OF NAMES

Expressing one's affinity to the group, however, is interpretated differently in different contexts. While the previous discussion has linked "Little Creeper" and "Diamond Street" to identifiable, concrete events and referents in the environment, these links are not available to everyone who sees or uses gang names. Therefore, people develop different linguistic ideologies to account for the use of gang names and nicknames. Linguistic ideology "construes indexicality" or offers accounts about what names refer to (Silverstein, 1992, p. 315). As might be expected, names are linked to different events depending on the context of their use. Thus, if someone routinely encounters a gang name while watching an account of a drive-by shooting on the local news, this person will develop a different linguistic ideology about a gang name than one who routinely uses that name to refer to his group of friends or his surrogate family. As we saw in the success stories of Chapter 4, told by other students at City School, previous gang ties are sometimes eviscerated in the context of describing academic achievement.

Even currently active gangsters like Little Creeper recognize that their names mean different things in different contexts, and afford alternative readings. In the preceding discussion of gang names, I have focused on the meanings of gang names that develop in the context of gang relationships. Gang names have radically different possible meanings when they are embedded new and different cultural contexts. Societal institutions such as schools, the media, and the police interpret and act on gang naming practices quite differently than gang members themselves do. After reviewing possible meanings gang members' names hold within their community, I next provide some examples of how the meanings of gang names change when they are used in nongang communities.

Gang Members' Linguistic Ideologies

In his discussion of gang naming or "representing," Conquergood (1996) quotes a gang member who explicitly states what his representing means for him: "Our

struggle is to show love to each other . . . We all understand the love and meaning behind representing" (p. 40). This ideology about naming can be considered
an integral part of the culture of gangs (and emerges clearly in the dropping in
stories of Chapter 2). The system within which these signs are cultivated may
in fact be seen to parallel Bourdieu's (1985) notion of the field of restricted
cultural production, where artists or academics claim their realm as one distinct
from the standards and tastes of the mainstream. Products within this realm are
judged by a more exclusive set of standards—not usefulness, but meaningful-
ness of a kind negotiated between a small group of elite, a "mutual appreciation
society" that operates within an institution of "reproduction and consecration"
(p. 43). Within this realm, discourse takes place between "privileged interlocutors." The hand signs, graffiti, dress, and attitude of gang members can also be
viewed as exclusivity cultivated within a mutual appreciation society that claims
to be exempt from the demands or pressures of the field of large-scale production. Within this mutual appreciation society, self-sustaining linguistic ideologies, such as the one quoted above, develop.

In contrast to the field of restricted production, the field of large-scale
production is characterized by "the subordinate position of cultural producers in
relation to the controllers of production and diffusion media" and "principally
obeys the imperatives of competition for conquest of the market" (Bourdieu,
1985, p. 43). This is precisely the relationship to the power structure that artists
and academics seek to avoid through their independent enclaves and the development of group-specific styles and tastes. This also is what gang members
create for themselves through unique semiotic systems of gang references to
sociohistorical content as well as implicitly entextualized meanings. (Group-
specific naming practices are not limited to gang members, of course. Other
exclusive groups such as golf circles, the Shriners or the Masons, bowling
leagues, or the army may provide members with new names which, like gang
nicknames, might go through similar generations of community-specific meanings.) However, within "the market of symbolic goods," these isolated groups
are never exempt from the influence of the field of large-scale production. In
fact, gang members frequently fall victim to the language ideologies of powerful
others who interpret their names and naming practices in ways that damage
gang members.

Dominant Linguistic Ideologies

Within the field of large-scale production, new forms of meaning accrue to the
name "Little Creeper from Diamond Street." Powerful figures in the field of
large-scale production are quick to appropriate gang symbols and isolate them
from the more exclusive set of meanings and associations that have evolved
within the gangsters' culture, or more specifically, the moral frameworks emer-

gent in the telling of a narrative. Thus, outsiders use these signs to control gangs by reappropriating or claiming "extensional warrant" (Silverstein, 1987) to the products of the restricted cultural realm. In other words, players in the field of large-scale production attach new implicit meanings to gang names but maintain the explicit power of names to reference particular individuals. As a result, schools, the media, police, and politicians find gang names to be useful labels for anything bad that occurs in the city or its schools, and gangsters themselves as convenient scapegoats for such problems.

School-based Linguistic Ideologies

While my previous discussion has shown one set of associations linked to the name "Little Creeper from Diamond Street," it is precisely because these evolved entextualizations are implicitly (rather than explicitly) inscribed, that these meanings can be ignored by more powerful others. Principals of schools are not concerned with the baptismal event linking a name to a person or the social foundations legitimating that name in nonschool contexts. Principals are generally concerned with gang names because they associate them with problem students whom they want removed from their school. Principals and school staff are "more likely to pick out 'gang members' from among the students on the basis of the children's tendency to flash hand signals, pass encoded messages" (Monti, 1994, p. 46). Principals use information about gang hand signs and tags to incriminate students in the absence of any other information. Indeed, as we saw in Gracie's narrative in Chapter 2, some schools use yearbooks to track down "troublemakers," and as other students have explained, teachers often record the nicknames of various students above the students' pictures. This is one reason some students avoid having their yearbook picture taken.

Students have frequently told me of cases where whole groups of students are expelled from a particular school due to their suspected gang affiliation. Thus, for the principal of Federico's school, being "Little Creeper from Diamond Street" certainly does not involve the deterrent factor that Federico understands and conveys in the story presented in this chapter. The principal does not have access to the peace-keeping entextualized meaning involved in Federico's gang name. Rather, the principal appropriates the notion of gang rivalry, and the symbols that associate Federico with a particular gang as a means to transfer Federico out of his school:

FED: We had a little meeting with the principal down there. He started talking to him, "Nah, but your kid can't be here 'cause he's the only one from *that neighborhood* and we have all *these kind of neighborhoods* don't get along. *So we're gonna send him to Lincoln.*"

In the way Federico describes this event, the principal has appropriated Federico's gang affiliation as a tool for his own benefit: a means to get Federico removed from his school.

Media-based Linguistic Ideologies

But even this appropriation of the meanings of gang rivalry is relatively benign, in this case affecting only one individual. Larger scale influence is wielded by the media-spawned institutionalized misrepresentation of what it means to be a gang member. As newspaper reporters seek to cover stories of urban violence and, above all, to entertain in a timely manner, they rarely have time to talk to gang members individually. As might be expected, they tend to overemphasize the violent nature of gangs, building on stereotypes rather than seeking to understand. As Jankowski (1991) found in his study on media coverage of gangs, "the media emphasize the violence associated with gangs and the violent nature of gang members; but while violence does occur involving gang members, it is less central to gangs (or their members) than the media would lead one to believe" (p. 309). In general, the media uses gang activity as a commodity to sell newspapers, building on an increasingly prevalent linguistic ideology that associates gang names with disproportionate accounts of blameworthy violence. Like the school principal's approach to gang names, the media extracts the names from the communities in which one set of meanings has developed and thereby radically changes the meanings attached to those names.

Police Department Linguistic Ideologies

The police have an interest in sustaining the media-spawned impression of gangs. Their own public image is built on the negative press coverage of gangs. In fact, gangsters often function as a useful commodity for the LAPD. In the late 1980s, the police department's ability to portray gang members as hardcore, unrehabilitatable youth was crucial to the LAPD marketing plan. Large-scale crackdowns on "gangs" became a publicity stunt, creating a sense that these police were the only deterrent from the transformation of Los Angeles into a gang battleground (Davis, 1992). In their quest to impress the media statisticians and TV crews with as many arrests as possible, officers were permitted to "stop and interrogate anyone who they suspect[ed] [was] a gang member, basing their assumptions on their dress or their use of gang hand signals" (p. 272). For these officers, any sign of gang membership became grounds for arrest. Using their computers, police compiled gang rosters including nicknames and affiliations and used such lists to build their knowledge of gang territory. Instead of making legitimate arrests, officers would then use this information to drop solo gang members off in enemy territory, where they would be outnumbered by rival gang members.

In citing arrest records from Chicago gang members, Conquergood (1992) draws attention to a similar criminalization of gang-naming practices. One offense of disorderly conduct was written up as follows:

> The defendant was arrested for representing the Latin King street gang. The defendant was using hand signals and wearing street gang colors, thereby posing an imminent threat of violence. (p. 2)

Due to an accumulation of ideologies about gangs in the context of the dominant culture, throwing hand signs that indicate you are a member of the Latin Kings qualifies as "an imminent threat of violence." Within a gang and among fellow gangsters, however, a context exists that continually recalls the social origin of gang naming practices and which construes them as quite orderly.

Politicians' Linguistic Ideologies

In addition to school administrators, police, and the media, politicians have incorporated gang culture into their political rhetoric, and similarly extracted gang names and their meanings from their community of origin. In 1992, after the verdict of "not guilty" was read for all the four officers involved in the brutal beating of Rodney King, Los Angeles erupted in violence and looting. This civil disturbance was dubbed the Los Angeles "riots" by the media, but also known as an "uprising" or "rebellion" by those who saw the violence as not random, but a reaction to accumulated injustice. It provides a vivid example of the kind of renarration to which individual stories fall prey in the light of political elections. During the civil disturbance, politicians were quick to visit Los Angeles and offer explanations. News analyses immediately appeared, speculating as to who would benefit more from the "Los Angeles Riot" in the pending presidential election (e.g., Lauter, 1992). Furthermore, gang membership became crucial to description of the infamous L.A. Four, who attacked "innocent" truck driver Reginald Denny. "Eight-Trey-Gangster-Crips" became a household term, a commonly understood gang clique name in Los Angeles, and one that, for nonmembers, represented only the violence of the uprising.

CITY SCHOOL'S APPROACH TO NAMES AND GRAFFITI

In narrative, Creeper displays how this name, within the context of gang life, acts as a powerful deterrent to violence a means to protect his little sister. In the context of his story, being "Little Creeper from Diamond Street" in effect means taking a moral stance, though in other contexts, being Little Creeper may be considered, in itself, morally reprehensible, suggesting his responsibility for untold gang violence that has occurred in the past.

At City School, unlike traditional schools, both of these associations with naming practices were able to coexist. Indeed, by combining a recognition of naming practices (and graffiti writing) with the desire to end such practice, City School staff achieved two goals rarely met in these students' former schools: the elimination of nearly all graffiti vandalism and minimal confrontation between rival gangs. City School provided an environment in which the staff, abstractly respectful of the students' own knowledge, could actually recruit students, fluent in local perspectives and the cultural assumptions that undergird the writing of graffiti, to help battle the most damaging forms of this practice. These graffiti eradicators used their own knowledge of graffiti practices (and the referents of particular tags) in order to confront the perpetrators and ultimately rid the school of graffiti (cf., Sizer, 1984, and the successful use of student security guards). Nevertheless, many of these student "police" maintained their own ties to gangs or tagging crews and continued their naming practices, with the exception of those practices that would damage City School property or lead to fights in the school.

While the graffiti eradication program functioned smoothly at first, the role names played within the City School community changed over time and with the changing institutional demeanor of City School itself. During City School's final months of operation, graffiti began showing up sporadically on walls. Gradually it became clear that both student and teacher attitudes were changing: A teacher who had initially displayed great tolerance and pride in the graffiti eradication program (based on students' local knowledge) and the fact that rival gang members could openly name their affiliation without fear of reprisal, gradually displayed a greater degree of nervousness and frustration regarding gang names. One day during City School's final month in operation, I watched as this teacher irritably grabbed name-covered papers out from under the pencil of one of his students, who subsequently stormed from the room. After this minor melee, the teacher explained to me all the signs written on the confiscated paper, seemingly proud in his knowledge, but insisted that kids should not be broadcasting their gang loyalties like this at school. This was the same teacher who had, several months earlier, facilitated the group of student leaders that developed the graffiti eradication program by talking freely about gang loyalties (and antagonisms), casually writing their own gang signs on paper as they conversed. As City School's mission began to fail, this approach itself lost its integrity in the eyes of students, who were accordingly less eager to do the institution's bidding. At the same time, teachers began to display their own ambivalence toward the acceptance of local knowledge as a method of change.

NAMING, NARRATIVE, IDENTITY, AND REFORM

As the examples show above, police, media, teachers, and politicians have reasons to appropriate and reread gang names. Nevertheless, the fact that the name is explicitly tied to a referent continually returns these new meanings to the name-bearer. Because names hold both implicit meanings and explicit referents, the very fact of holding a particular name can become criminalized. Gangsters representing a gang name as a show of unity can be classed by police as "posing an imminent threat of violence," as the Chicago policeman wrote in his report.

The multiple resonances of names and the changing reactions of City School faculty to gang-naming practices illuminate how the acceptance of certain naming practices depict particular moral choices. The teacher who snatched a graffiti-ridden paper away from a student nervously displayed his sense of moral responsibility. The student who stormed from the room displayed his disgust for the teacher's insensitivity. As these contradictory reactions blatantly display, different people make moral assessments according to different standards. The multiple contradictory interpretations of even proper names also illustrate that different interlocutors bring very different assumptions to the table of moral judgment. Students and police certainly interpret gang names very differently, but so do the different students mentioned in Chapters 2 and 4. Contrasting interpretations even exist within the same teacher who, during City School's first months, accepted graffiti when written on paper, and during final months, snatched graffiti-laden paper away from a student in a display of frustrated indignation.

Naming practices at City School also illustrate the powerful role institutions have in shaping the moral framework from which students and teachers form judgments. During those first months, at the time when the leaders came up with their graffiti eradication program, City School accomplished real reform. By this I mean that it was clearly creating a context within which identities based on students' own local knowledge were validated—and were allowed to be powerful and effective in the school community. Again, language—in this case naming practices—is the medium through which individuals develop ways of being human. Communities create certain contexts where language can be used. And in this case, school reformers helped to create a community within which certain identities were not arbitrarily censored, others celebrated, but a community within which there was dialogue. For a time, City School transcended the distinctions Bourdieu (1985) has described and condemned. This transcendence was afforded by a respect for local knowledge.

The vivid case of gang names also illustrates, however, that accepting such local knowledge is not always morally simple. Understanding local meanings of gang nicknames, graffiti, hand signs, and associated practices can be much more difficult for a teacher than learning about *piñatas* or other comfortably different cultural practices. Because of the particular associations held by mainstream society about gang nicknames, schools are very apprehensive about trying to understand them or ask questions about their origins. To a school staffer, this can seem like negotiating with a terrorist. But some dangerous listening can lead to important growth for students and teachers. And, as naming practices at City School reveal, discussion and greater understanding of these names can possibly lead to some flexibility in their meaning and can act to deter their more damaging uses.

CHAPTER 7

When Friends Aren't Friends

Friends aren't friends, homes.

—Mario, 1995

This chapter analyzes what happens when Mario, a City School student closely aligned with the dropping in perspective, openly confronts two students who are currently active gang members. In this conversation, the dropping in and dropping out genres meet, and City School becomes, for a moment, a "contact zone" (Pratt, 1992) where different moral frames for organizing identity come face-to-face. The confrontation is not always productive, but it is captivating, and it exposes the complexity of the City School environment and the paradox of this educational project, where conflicts between gang involvement and abandonment and the purported value of gangs and education were confronted daily.

In this conversational contact zone, the word "friend" takes on very different meanings, depending on the kinds of allegiances one has. As we saw in Gracie's success story (Chapter 5), "friends" can be portrayed as bad influences, the embodiment of the peer pressure that involves one in gangs. In Federico's dropping out stories (Chapters 3 and 6), however, he conveys how friends and gang membership form the foundation of his identity, and he portrays this loyalty as honorable. In the conversation to be analyzed here, the meaning of friends and friendship is battled out between three primary conversationalists, two who are loyal gang members, and one who has abandoned gang life. As these three young men converse, their respective moral frames for friendship come into direct conflict.

One resource these parties call on to display their differing loyalties is the various apparently synonymous words for "friend" (e.g., homes, bro, homeboy, ése, and roll dog). These words are used by the former gang member Mario in his attempt to persuade the two current gang members, Jorge and Luis, to stop "gang banging." While giving advice to the two current gangsters, Mario uses these words systematically to index the fact that he is, though no longer a gangster, part of the same community as his addressees. At the same time, Jorge and Luis, whose friendship and gang loyalties are being attacked, contest Mario's use of these terms, and his presupposition of a shared perspective.

Like proper names, the meaning of reference terms can change depending on the situation and interlocutors' socially and historically shared associations (Kripke, 1977; Putnam, 1988; Searle, 1970; Strawson, 1955; Wittgenstein, 1953 [1945, 1946–1949]). For example, if I refer to someone as "Little Creeper from Diamond Street" rather than "Federico Valdez," I situate myself very differently with respect to the referent. Similarly, as this chapter will illustrate, the difference between calling a person a "friend," a "homeboy," a "roll dog," or a "chucho" can be significant among certain conversationalists and revealing of interlocutors' presuppositions about one another.

This analysis also shows how the meanings of these disparate reference terms are made and remade through talk as conversationalists use these words to put forward their contrasting points of view and maintain potentially self-contradictory social identities (cf., Donnellan, 1966; Hanks, 1990). Through creative use of reference terms and their systematic deployment in concert with other genred resources, Mario attempts to link dropping out and dropping in perspectives, but his attempt yields questionable success.

MARIO'S DROPPING IN PERSPECTIVE

"Friends aren't friends" is the lesson Mario has learned from the loss of his best friend due to gang violence. For Mario, a teenager who grew up in Los Angeles, there are many ways in which "friends aren't friends" anymore. Most immediately, his former best friend literally is not a friend anymore because he has passed away, a victim of gunfire. Following the loss of this friend, Mario left their shared world of the *barrio* and the friendships of gangland for a new kind of life. After he left the city and City School, Mario moved to the San Fernando Valley with his girlfriend, attended Valley Vocational School, and worked four nights a week at an ice cream shop in Westwood, an affluent shopping area abutting UCLA. He kept his distance from the Echo Park *barrio* where he lost his friend.

After City School closed down, I spoke with Mario many times at his job in the ice cream shop. During these conversations he elaborated on his former life as a "gangbanger" and his decision, after his friend's murder, to leave that life behind. Although these conversations were structured quite differently than the discussion sessions I conducted at City School, the way he described his turning point echoes those narratives of "dropping in" analyzed in Chapter 5. Like those storytellers, Mario refers to his previous activities as part of a former life, an old "dumb" (to use Mario's word) self that no longer exists. This old self wanted to protect "the neighborhood" through gang membership. As he puts it, these are the kinds of loyalties Mario "used to" have:

MARIO: *I used to say* the same thing: I'm gonna die for my neighborhood. So I didn't give a damn you know?
BETSY: [Yeah]
MARIO: [I say] a lot of stuff you know?

Mario's description of the kinds of habits he has abandoned draws on linguistic resources similar to those used in the dropping in stories told to me at City School. Like Mario, Abel and Gracie describe the kinds of things they "used to" say, and Von describes the kinds of habits he "used to" have before he came to City School (see excerpts in Chapter 5). All of these students are describing a way they "used to" be, a time when they didn't, in Mario's words, "give a damn."

While the former Mario didn't give a damn about certain things—school, the future—he did care a great deal about his "neighborhood" and his gang loyalties, and a particular best friend. As we saw in Chapter 5, in typical dropping in stories, narrators describe a turning point, after which former loyalties, now considered to be detrimental, are replaced with new loyalties—to a son, for example, or to people at City School. Similarly, Mario describes how he replaced his old gang loyalty ("a macho thing that everybody wants to carry around") with a new desire to start a family of his own:

MARIO: But I guess— it's just a macho thing that everybody wants to carry around. Mainly I think about it now is just I guess— when I was dumb when I say that because— I mean *now I'm thinking* about of— you know *I want to have a FAMily.*

Claiming to "die for your neighborhood," Mario now says, is just a "macho thing that everybody wants to carry around." "Now" however, he wants to have a family. And, he implies, this desire does not mix well with such macho pronouncements. Those are the kinds of things he "used to" say, when he was "dumb." Like the tellers of the other "dropping in" stories, Mario clearly separates that time, and that "dumb" person, from the identity he "now" has, of a future family man. As he goes on to say, his friend who passed away for those former loyalties will never be able to see a family of his own:

MARIO: You know he'd never got to have a family. He was still you know
BETSY: A ba[by
MARIO: [starting his life. YEAH you know.

For Mario, the death of his friend was the event that turned his life around. After that, he developed an entirely new set of commitments. Unlike the dropping in storytellers, however, he wants to discuss his former commitments at length, and he describes the loss of those commitments as substantial. His old friends call him now and then, ask him to come back to the neighborhood, and as Mario admits, their invitations are often hard to turn down. But in all our conversations, his commitment to his "new" life was firm. This commitment is probably made most vivid in the discussion of "friendship" I recorded at City School between Mario, Jorge, and Luis.

CONFLICTING COMMITMENTS IN DIALOGUE

This chapter focuses on an exchange between Mario and the two active gang-bangers, Jorge and Luis, which took place over a lull in a class, during City School's last month of existence. At this time, City School's class schedule and curriculum was at its most chaotic. Nearly half of the teachers had been let go as a money-saving strategy, but, as a money-obtaining strategy, more new students were being desperately recruited. City School received public funds from the school district based on student attendance. For this reason, maintaining a healthy enrollment became increasingly important as the school became financially strapped. Mario, Jorge, and Luis were three students recruited during this cash-strapped period. Their stated reasons for attending City School, however, varied: Mario came to City School in order to earn a high school diploma. As a former gang member who had spent months in juvenile hall, and who was now supporting himself through his minimum wage job, City School, he felt, provided the most practical educational alternative for him. For Jorge and Luis, the diploma and the need to schedule work hours were less important than satisfying their parole officers. City School's flexible schedule and vague academic requirements made this relatively easy. Furthermore, City School did not prohibit wearing gang clothing—baggy pants or special hats and jackets—so their identity as gang members was not challenged by dress codes or clothing restrictions, as it would have been in many other Los Angeles public schools. Probably the most difficult aspect of City School for Jorge and Luis was running into students like Mario, who wanted to persuade them to abandon their gang loyalties and who openly condemned the basis of their friendship.

In this conversation, Mario is trying to convince these two young men not to make the same "mistakes" that he did and to leave their life as gangsters before their lives were literally taken away from them. More specifically, Mario puts forth a very different view of friendship than that held by his addressees, Jorge and Luis. Jorge and Luis see sacrifice as a defining element of friendship. They show their willingness to sacrifice for their friends by being active gang members, "backing each other up" (fighting against rival gangs in the name of the home gang), and "getting locked up" for each other (going to jail for their friends' crimes). Mario, however, claims to have been through this kind of friendship and experienced its tragic finale: His friend was shot and killed by rival gang members. Jorge and Luis see their sacrifices as a valuable part of friendship, while Mario, as a consequence of the death of his friend, sees the sacrifices made toward a friend in a gang as an act of self-deception which inevitably ends in tragedy. Thus, in his discussion with Jorge and Luis, Mario tries to redefine what a true friend is—while Jorge and Luis insist on their own understanding of friendship. This series of redefinitions hinges on claims and denials about the referential value of the synonyms for friend.

These contradictory perspectives also resonate with the differences between the dropping out and dropping in story perspectives discussed so far. Like the tellers of dropping in stories, Mario is ready to disown a former self, and he sees Jorge and Luis as current embodiments of that former self. As he said to me once in conversation, speaking of Jorge and Luis, "I used to be *just* like them." Thus, his discussion with Jorge and Luis is not only an argument with these two peers, but also a conversational display that his former life is now over, that he has a different, more hopeful life ahead of him. Like the dropping in storytellers, Mario has reached a turning point in his life. This turning point came not when he decided to come to City School, but when a rival gang murdered his own best friend. The origin of Mario's turning point, as well as the presence of two currently committed gang members renders his need to discuss gang membership both more urgent and more complex than the discussions of gang involvement that emerged in the dropping in stories. Like those "successful" students, he rejects his former gang behavior, but unlike them, in this interactional context at least, he elaborates a great deal on those former ties, and their importance for him.

Mario, Jorge, and Luis's contradictory and deep-seated views on friendship can be traced in part by analyzing their use of a shared set of words that at first seem to be nearly synonymous. In addition to the word "friend," these three young men, and Mario in particular, use the words homes, ése, homeboy, family, familia, vato, roll dog, dog, and chucho at various times throughout their discussion.

NEGOTIATING CONFLICTING COMMITMENTS WITH REFERENCE TERMS FOR FRIEND

The meaning of these words—friend, homeboy, chucho, roll dog, family—is constructed and deconstructed in conversation as Mario confronts Jorge and Luis. As these three young men use these words to argue about the meaning of friendship and its relationship to gang activity, the meaning these words take on through conversation constructs two different versions of reality. As Mario struggles to use a shared language to promote change in others, and to communicate his own internal paradox, he relies both on the indexical associations (he believes) his words carry, and his own ability to use those words for new purposes.

Friends and Homies

Mario's internal contradiction—between valuing his former friend and distancing himself from the life and values he shared with that friend—is conveyed in the way he confronts Jorge and Luis. Toward the beginning of the conversation, Mario states the paradox that guides the discussion:

MARIO: Friends aren't friends, homes.

In this brief assertion, Mario makes a sad and universalizing point: The people you think are friends are not friends. The present indicative verb and the absence of articles with the pluralized nouns in this utterance are common characteristics of universalizing statements in English (e.g., "Germans are good musicians," Celce-Murcia & Larsen-Freeman, 1983, pp. 180–181). In the case of "friends aren't friends," no concrete referent is made explicit. However, as the conversation continues, it will become painfully clear that Mario is referring not only to "friends" of an abstract and universal sort, but also to the two friends sitting in front of him, as well as his own friend who has passed away. Mario complicates his statement, refracting the paradox, by adding the word "homes," which suggests that both his addressees are, indeed, *his* friends. While his first three words warn of the dangers of trusting "friends," his final address term "homes" indexes that his current addressees *are* his friends. In interviews I conducted later with Mario, I wanted to find out why he used the term "homes" so frequently in this conversation, and explained that "homes" for him means "friend":

MARIO: Homes is just like, the word like say friend.

But why use this address term with Jorge and Luis? And why not use a term like "friend" or "bro"? When I asked Mario if *homes* communicates additional respect, Mario answered no, although it might signal *dis*respect if used to address "a white person." For Mario, "homes" is a particular word that *Latinos* use for friends:

MARIO: Because saying like a white person comes in I tell him "hey homes, what's up?" I mean he like, he ain't gonna like that because, you know, he's not used to *that kinda slang=*
BETSY: Uh huh
MARIO: =*that Latinos, really use.*

For Mario, the use of the word "homes" identifies the speaker and the addressee as part of a particular group. He would never say "homes" to a white customer. They might take offense. But among fellow Latinos, "homes" is a standard address term that implies the person you are addressing is your friend. Furthermore, the term *homes*, like *ése* is also, for Mario, associated with gang membership:

MARIO: That's what— they use. Gangbangers use it more.
BETSY: Right.
MARIO: Yeah,
BETSY: More than homes,
MARIO: Bo— bo—
BETSY: Kinda the same.
MARIO: Both use 'em the same thing. "Homes," "ése" it's the same thing.

Given Mario's understanding of the word "homes"—that for him it connotes both gang membership and Latino ethnicity, and can connote friendship—it is telling that he uses the vocative "homes" *69 times* during the course of his conversation with Jorge and Luis. Though his statement "friends aren't friends" explicitly denies the possibility of friendship, his use of "homes" suggests he is attempting to establish a kind of common bond with his interlocutors. "Friends aren't friends, homes" then might, according to Mario, be heard as "Friends aren't friends, my Latino gangster friends." In this conversation, Mario wants to convey a lesson he learned the hard way: that friends can't be friends when they are associated with gangs. Still, his use of "homes" suggests that he considers himself to be a friend of Jorge and Luis, and similar enough to them to be able to give them this advice.

Thus, through a paradoxical association with universal truths about friends in general and the Latino gangster friends of the here and now, Mario opens the discussion to a debate about what true friends really are. The self-contradictory character of the sentence "Friends aren't friends, homes" is typical of paradoxes and parables in all languages. In this situation, Mario's use of paradox provokes an extended debate about the nature of friends, and, through such debate, continual reconfiguration of the referential terms themselves. In their discussion, Mario, Jorge, and Luis cycle through a series of words for friend: As soon as Mario explicates the dire consequences of having one kind of "friend," Jorge and Luis, sensing the application of Mario's moral to their own friendship, redefine the term, implying that Mario's definition is at fault, thereby preserving the value of their own friendship. Frequently their new definition involves a more specific word for friend. As shown below, as soon as Mario claims that friends aren't friends, Jorge counters that the reason Mario has this belief is because Mario has never been a true friend himself:

MARIO: Friends aren't friends, homes. I'll tell you that.
JORGE: Yeah. 'Cause you don't look at 'em as friends, that's why.
You probably backstab 'em and shit that's why they ain't your friends any-
    more.

In his response to Mario's utterance, Jorge transforms Mario's universalizing utterance about friends in general into one merely about Mario and the kinds of friends he has. Thus, through Jorge's collaborative completion of Mario's state-ment, the entire sentence becomes "Friends aren't friends (homes) because you [Mario] don't look at them as friends." Jorge then explains that Mario's state-ment simply refers to him and his friends. It is not universally true at all: For other people, friends very well may be friends, but Mario probably backstabs his friends, and "that's why they ain't *your* friends anymore."

As the content of Jorge's reply suggests, he does not believe that Mario has any true friends. As the conversation proceeds it becomes clear that neither Jorge nor Luis is buying Mario's affiliative use of the word "homes" either. In contrast to Mario's 69 uses of the address term in this conversation, Jorge uses it 3 times, as does Luis.

Family

Jorge claims that the reason Mario doesn't know what a true friend is because he never was truly loyal to *his* friends. However, Mario immediately counters with his own redefinition and a new term for "friend," namely "family," a word that may suggest an even greater loyalty than "friend."

MARIO: It ain't like that. I ain't considered them as my friends. I considering
    them as my family.

But in the next breath, Mario conveys that although he had friends that were so close as to be considered family, the reference term "family" is riddled with the same paradoxical qualities that "friend" is. Though both words suggest intimacy, relationships with so-called family and friends can lead to hurtful consequences. As Mario insists, Jorge and Luis's friendship is no different in this respect than his own former friendship:

MARIO: Where did your [family get you homes?
                    [((*points his hand at Jorge and looks at Luis*))
        Your [friends, ése?
            [((*points at Jorge again and looks at Luis*))
        He got you locked up, homes.
LUIS: That's 'cause I wanted to get locked up homes.

Here, gesture combines with words to "make maximal use of symbolic resources" (Streeck, 1993). Mario uses pointing and gaze and his knowledge of gang member language and morays to make his point about friends and simultaneously index his affinity to Jorge and Luis. As the videotape of this conversation shows (see Figure 7.1), the referential value of "family" and "friends" is clearly no longer in the realm of abstraction. In this exchange, Mario uses both referential terms and vocatives to make his point absolutely clear: While saying "family" and "friends," Mario points to Jorge (see arrow highlighting this gesture in Figure 7.1); by using the word "you," he picks out Luis as his addressee, and by using the address terms "homes" and "ése" he indexes a particular social relationship between himself and Luis. By appealing to a common vocabulary, Mario communicates his affinity with Jorge and Luis while at the same time using this impression of understanding to make his referent absolutely clear: The kinds of friends that "aren't friends" are seated right before him and these are friendships based on gang affiliation. In this brief exchange, referent and addressee are stacked with a specialized vocabulary shared by these three young men. By pointing at his referent, Mario shifts the grounds of the argument away from himself and specifically back to Jorge and Luis. While his pointing makes his argument more specific, by using the address terms "homes" and "ése" to appeal more generically to their common ground, Mario makes it hard for Jorge and Luis to claim he just doesn't understand their world. Paradoxically, however, Mario is simultaneously critiquing this world, the language of which he is mining.

FIGURE 7.1: "Where Did Your Family Get You Homes?"

Despite Jorge and Luis's gaze shift to the table, the concrete undeniability of his referent, the blame being heaped, and the sequential pull of Mario's questions (questions entail answers) draw Jorge and Luis back into the discussion. The efficacy of Mario's debunking, however, may depend on the addressees adopting some of the assumptions of the "dropping in" perspective (namely, that friends who "get" you locked up are no good). As Luis's next utterance indicates, he eschews these "dropping in" assumptions. For Luis, the fact that he went to jail for Jorge simply confirms their friendship:

MARIO: He got you locked up, homes.
LUIS: That's 'cause I wanted to get locked up, homes.

Luis's retort suggests that the differences between Mario and his two interlocutors Jorge and Luis are in many ways analogous to the differences between the dropping out and dropping in genres: While in the dropping in stories "friends" pose a threat to continuing one's education and achieving a successful future, in dropping out stories commitments to friends justify time spent in jail or expulsion from school. Thus, Mario succinctly articulates the successful student theme while debunking the assumptions of the contrary perspective. But his debunking has little impact: As Luis explains here, making sacrifices for another gangster (in this case, going to jail for him) is the *definition* of friendship.

A True Homeboy

Jorge and Luis counter Mario's criticism of their friendship with yet another redefinition of what it means to be a friend, and the reintroduction of the word "homeboy." Now, while they see that they have no words specific enough to elude Mario's understanding, they try to claim "extensional warrant" for the meaning of familiar, shared words (cf., Silverstein, 1987):

MARIO: You'd get locked up for a friend homes? That's something stupid.
LUIS: Fuck that, I don't get locked up for all my homeboys.
MARIO: Well do your time while their ass is out here=
LUIS: (shit)
MARIO: =you know getting smoked on and everything and what do you—
      what do you find out next time homes?
LUIS: I don't care.
JORGE: You ain't *a true homeboy* then. You ain't *a true homeboy*. You ain't *a true homeboy*.

When Mario argues that sitting in jail while your friend is out on the streets "getting his ass smoked on" (i.e., getting shot at) is not a worthwhile way to demonstrate friendship, Jorge claims, "You ain't a true homeboy then." For Jorge and Luis, a true homeboy is someone who goes to jail for you. For Mario, this is precisely what a true homeboy isn't. This is precisely why, as tellers of the dropping in stories would probably agree, "Friends aren't friends."

Indeed, Mario refuses to except Jorge's definition and continues to insist that "getting locked up" for someone is a misguided way to prove one's friendship. If this is the criteria, according to Mario, "family" and "homeboys" aren't real friends either:

MARIO: That ain't family, getting f— getting locked up for a *vato*.
LUIS: That's what we're trying to tell you though. The— that's my homeboy.
MARIO: Homeboy, family, whatever homes.
　　　　It ain't.
　　　　Well I'll tell you that much man.

In this segment, Mario further emphasizes his point that friends aren't friends by using the word *vato*. As he has discussed with me at the ice cream shop, for Mario, *vato* doesn't have the capacity to pick out friends. A *vato* is, in Mario's words "the same as a man" which is "just the definition of a person." This is not the kind of relationship deserving of great sacrifice. But while Luis's response shows he clearly understands how Mario is using the word *vato*, he insists Mario is wrong by again redefining his relationship with Jorge and insisting that Mario doesn't understand the definition of "homeboy." Luis didn't spend a year of his life in jail just for a *vato*. He did it for a homeboy. Mario, however, flatly rejects this claim. If you are getting locked up for this person, he is not a homeboy. Nor is he family.

Yet, all of Mario's criticisms of gang-based friendships imply the existence of an alternative, purer type of friendship. Like Gracie, who rejects the "friends" whom she used to try to "show" she was cool and replaces those friends with her son, whom the wants to "show" she can graduate, Mario has new commitments. Though old friends are abandoned, new connections exist. Abandonment of one set of commitments need not entail willful, self-motivated isolation. Similarly, when Mario takes the role of being someone in a community that says "homes," and "ése," friends aren't friends because one's gangster family of homeboys will never really be friends *outside* of this community, once one has changed and adopted a new self. They are only good for upholding this particular type of family and friendship, and it is this type of friends who, for Mario, "aren't friends" anymore. By implicitly maintaining this distinction, Mario salvages his own future and the potential for a better kind of friendship.

Mario's statements, which seem to degrade the value of friendship, in fact are the result of the pain he felt from his own very important friendship. How can one denounce gang-related friendship while at the same time maintaining that one speaks from the experience of having a very important, gang-related friend? Mario recognizes the value of commitments and best friends he used to have as a gang member. But he has also learned the fragility of these ties. As a consequence, he has spurned the loyalties and commitments of gang life.

Roll Dogs and Chuchos

While Jorge and Luis still speak from the perspective of active gang members and the associated definitions for "friend," Mario now speaks from a perspective that eschews such definitions. Nevertheless, Mario wants to convince Jorge and Luis that he, too, felt the importance of those former ties. Only by conveying the importance of his former ties can he convey that such ties must be abandoned. To accomplish this logically impossible task, Mario attaches his argument to a new reference term, first evoked by Jorge—"roll dog":

JORGE: We're *roll doggin'* it.
MARIO: Who you [think I wasn't a *roll dog* for my homeboy ése? Huh?
JORGE: [We've come through everything man.]
JORGE: Well we're still tight.
LUIS: Yeah.

In this exchange, Mario's own best friend, his "homeboy," is introduced as a referent—and a particular, special kind of homeboy, a "roll dog." Mario picks up on Jorge's use of this term (which Jorge uses to describe his friendship with Luis) and instantly associates it with his former friend, suggesting that his former friendship was based on loyalties just as strong as those felt by Jorge and Luis.

By mentioning his own roll dog, Mario's own adequacy as a friend is once again open for dispute, and Jorge jumps at the opportunity to put Mario's friendship to the test when he asks, "What happened to your homeboy?":

JORGE: What happened to your homeboy.
MARIO: He got shot homes.
GAB: ss.
MARIO: *My best roll dog*, homes, my *chucho* homes,
        he got shot, *ése*. Fourteen bullets homes.

Here, Mario is talking about the consequences of his *own* friendship, not the friendship of Jorge and Luis. As Mario explained to me on a different occasion, "chuchos," like "roll dogs," are the best possible kind of friend. Mario makes his point clearly and forcefully: Even friendships of the best kind—of which his own friendship with his roll dog is an example—can lead to tragic ends *when they are drawn into gang life* and the dropping out perspective. Even if your friend is a true roll dog, when "roll doggin' it" becomes a gangland activity, "Friends aren't friends." Not only do they "get you" involved in unsavory things, they "get" shot themselves.

Just a Homeboy

Neither Jorge nor Luis counter Mario's assertion by claiming that this bad end is also a part of being a friend. They appear mollified by the specter of death. While they do say that going to jail is a sacrifice they are willing to make, a sacrifice they consider to be an important part of showing friendship, they will not say that a friend *should* "get shot." Friends are too important, especially "roll dogs." Now Jorge and Luis begin to see into Mario's world: They are in agreement with Mario on the value of the "roll dog" relationship. They do not reject Mario's underlying assumption (that being shot is a negative consequence) as they did when the consequences were merely jail. After Mario reveals that his best friend was shot, Jorge and Luis do not say that he should be happy to have a friend die; but as the next utterance suggests, they are still not convinced that Mario was ever a true friend—a roll dog. To counter the serious claim Mario makes about the death of his friend (and his implication that the same fate could befall his addressees), Jorge and Luis suggest that Mario's friend was not really a roll dog at all, but rather that he was "just" a homeboy:

JORGE: So *that means that you just had a homeboy.*
MARIO: Where's he at now? *That was my roll dog ése.* I had a *familia.* My homeboys were my *familia,* but *that was my roll dog.* He got shot fourteen times homes. He was what, fifteen years old *ése. Where's he at now?*
GAB: Sh
MARIO: Underground, homes.
     You want your— *you want your best dog underground homes?*

Now the more gang-related word for friend is prefaced by a limiting "just" ("So *that means that you just had a homeboy*"). Here Jorge conveys his sense that a roll dog is something special, as Mario did above: a friend even apart from the dynamics of gang life. While Jorge may agree with Mario on the definition of "roll dog," he denies that Mario ever had one. Real roll dogs, he seems to be implying, don't get shot. Furthermore, by the code of gang retaliation, if they do, you retaliate—you don't forego the gang life. If, indeed, Mario's "best dog" was killed by gang-related bullets, and if Mario has done nothing toward retribution, the so-called roll dog was, actually, "just a homeboy." But the value of this cycle of violence, this way of defining friendship, is precisely what Mario is contesting. And for this reason, Jorge is still not willing to equate his own friend, Luis, with any friend that Mario had.

Your Best Dog

But Mario doesn't give up. He makes precisely that parallel—between Jorge's roll dog, Luis, and the roll dog that Mario lost. In the excerpt above, Mario asserts what has been implied in the former discourse and what he has told me in subsequent discussions: that he had a roll dog once and that to him, "roll dog" is the best possible term you could use for a friend. In this conversation, the terms "family" and "homeboy" had lost their agreed-upon status as terms that refer to valued relationships. Furthermore, they are words that *stereotypically index* gang affiliation, which in this conversation has come to index death. "Roll dog," however, has not been so emptied of positive associations. Both sides of this argument have used the term "roll dog" as a word for a very close friend. As Mario has told me, a roll dog is the person you are always there for, the person you are "tight" with, the person with whom you've "come through everything." By repeatedly asking Jorge "Where's [his roll dog] at now?", Mario tries to use the sequential force of a question to engage Jorge fully, or at least to make him acknowledge, verbally, that Mario did in fact lose a true friend, a roll dog. However, Jorge's response is minimal even in this sequential context. Nevertheless, Mario continues to question Jorge, and makes his next question explicitly applicable to his two addressees by making the parallel between his own lost roll dog and Jorge's best friend, Luis. He asks, "Do you want your best dog underground?"

Now Jorge and Luis have no choice but to consider the death of their friend(ship). There seem to be no new words, no new matters of definition or ambiguities of reference to come to their rescue.

Seemingly at a loss, Jorge stammers:

JORGE: Well don— don— don—
       come out with
       some stupid question like that man.

While it may be honorable to say you would die for your homey, it is not so honorable to say you don't mind if your homey dies. Jorge doesn't want his roll dog underground, but he doesn't have any other answer right now. Typically, the dropping out perspectives can evoke the honor of their gang ties by describing the deterrent force of gang membership, or the honorable sacrifices one must make for a gang. Jorge expresses loyalty for his roll dog, Luis, through their gang affiliation. For both Jorge and Luis, upholding this loyalty remains a powerful ethical imperative.

DECONSTRUCTING A GANG MEMBER'S MORAL FRAME

By tying such gang-related loyalty and sacrifice to the loss of his own friend, Mario attempts to deconstruct Jorge and Luis's moral frame. Without at least a minimal understanding of their world and the words to convey such understanding, Mario could never have confronted these two young men in this way. But Mario feels affinity with Jorge and Luis. As Mario remarked to me a few weeks later, he "used to be just like them—so stubborn." Even though Mario makes Jorge and Luis uncomfortable—forcing their gaze to the desk, or evoking stammering replies—Mario hasn't changed their minds. Nor has he found an easy solution to the paradoxical foundation of their own friendship, and his former one. There isn't a solution. However, by using a shared vocabulary to convey his own sense of experience of the gang life, and the life of a Latino, Mario attempts to convince Jorge and Luis that he understands them, and that all three of them are making choices in the face of admittedly difficult circumstances. Finally, he states this belief explicitly:

JORGE: I mean we grew up together since we were real small, that's what. You know?

MARIO: Yeah, and that's cool, homes, but what I'm trying to tell you homes is that— just expect it bro. Expect it homes. I'm telling you— my my look— here, homes, I don't know, it's just a lot of shit that, you know, that I've seen bro. But I— yo— I mean— *we all see the same shit man.* And still you guys don't see, man, that, it ain't worth it bro. None of this shit's worth it homes.

Again, Mario weaves immediate and community-specific terms of address throughout his more global claims about the world. However, the potentially gang-related "homes" and the more universally applicable "bro" are equally invoked. While Mario wants Jorge and Luis to leave the gang world and enter the world of "roll dogs" and "bros," and friendships defined by bonds other than those of the gang, he still reaches out to them with the familiar and gang-related term "homes." He understands that when we're all seeing the same hardship, it's no wonder that friendship as defined through gang loyalty becomes a last holdout against that "shit." But until Jorge and Luis see a brighter alternative, there really is nothing else more "worth it."

LANGUAGE, THE CONTACT ZONE, AND SCHOOL REFORM

The conversation among Mario, Jorge, and Luis reveals paradoxes that all students at City School had to deal with. How does one construct a worthwhile identity when "we all see the same shit"? Some students construct themselves as having loyalties that transcend that "shit." As Federico revealed in Chapter 6, the use of his gang nickname does not simply connote violence—the kind of violence Mario identifies as taking his best friend. It is also a powerful deterrent of violence. For Little Creeper, gang associations serve to protect his sister. Ignoring loyalties that uphold that deterrence is, for a committed gang member, heretical. For Gracie, however, such loyalties simply pull one into a life that takes one away from a worthwhile future, and from the possibility of being a "good example" to future generations. She deals with her former gang member-ship by relegating it to a past with which she no longer identifies. The conversation among Jorge, Mario, and Luis raises the conflict between "dropping out" of and "dropping in" to schools or gangs, a conflict that each one of these narrative genres ignores, but which these individuals must deal with daily.

As a place where such internal and interactional struggles take place with regularity, City School embodies a "contact zone," as defined by Mary Louise Pratt (1992). Pratt uses this term to describe colonial encounters and places that feature "complexity of interaction," where paradox flourishes. As she explains, certain narratives of the "anti-conquest" dissolve the boundaries between "who are the barbarians and who are the civilized" (p. 43). The kind of intertextuality I recorded at City School, and which is exemplified specifically in the conversation in this chapter, provides interactional evidence of a similar "contact zone" at City School, where different moral frames come into contact, and the virtues of either become unclear.

Genrefication of these different moral frames provides empirical access to these different moral orientations. Both "dropping out" and "dropping in" genres are highly self-sustaining and provide repertoires for their own narration. The nobility and necessity of gang-related friendship emerge in a "dropping out" narrative. The cycle of violence is portrayed in this genre as unavoidable, but through strategic adherence to ethical norms, one can maintain dignity, respect, loyalty to one's friends, and even deter neighborhood crime and violence. It is hard to argue with one who wants to protect his sister or defend a neighborhood in the clutches of gang violence. On the other hand, the hope for a better life and the eschewing of violent habits or bad influences of gang-related friends—the "dropping in" perspective—suggests the potential for a brighter future for these young men and women.

Choosing between either of these perspectives is a moral matter, necessar-ily expressed through genred particulars. As Jorge and Luis proclaim, Mario "ain't a true homeboy" because he has eschewed the loyalties and commitments that his former gang affiliation entail. He is the type who "backstabs" his friends, who wouldn't "get locked up" for them. But Mario sees Jorge and Luis as blinded by their shortsighted gang loyalty, the ethos of crime and violence, and their desire to "get locked up." They are the embodiment of his old self who lost a friend to that world. They are ultimately not loyal to friends at all, because their commitments will inevitably lead to the loss of those friends. Such "friends" potentially "get" shot. "Expect it," he warns. As Mario questions the value of Jorge and Luis's lives and loyalties, reference words proliferate, being remade and unmade as Jorge and Luis's world begins to tumble before them in conversation. Can words—or Mario—save them? Or new words like "chucho" and "roll dog"? Of course not. But in this conversation, these multifunctional, highly indexical words provide a medium for further talk, confrontation, and fighting out those issues that many other adolescents may never confront with such a life-and-death force.

There were certainly conflicting commitments all over City School, just as there are conflicting commitments within the Charter School movement. The three conversationalists discussed here embody some of that contradiction. Mario might embody the ideal charter school student, one for whom the school provides a perfect alternative format for him to reframe his life. Jorge and Luis together embody a more cynical approach to charter schooling. For them, City School is the easiest place to satisfy the requirements of their parole while maintaining their gang style and commitments. And, in their case, the welcoming arms of City School might be quite cynical as well. They were welcomed into the institution at this point, because City School was desperate for attending bodies. The school's financial picture was increasingly gloomy, and the more students they could count, the more money they would get from the state. The recruitment of these students then exemplifies the "sordid side" of charter schools—the fact that they have many financial incentives that can overshadow educational ones (Zollers & Ramanathan, 1998).

It requires little research to see both cynical and idealistic motivations behind any school community. But research that involves listening to conversations and observing the particular can reveal what sorts of identities are being created within reform-oriented environments, regardless of the multiple motivations that initially form these communities. Given that dropping out is, from one perspective, the endpoint of a long process of silencing students (Fine, 1991), it is important to hear student voices—like those of Jorge and Luis—long before there is any hope that they might stay at school. To this end, whatever else City School did, at least it provided an environment—a contact zone—within which students' voices were heard. When words are negotiated, and genres are in dialogue, change is possible.

Ultimately dialogue is valuable, but every school's responsibility goes far beyond simply enabling dialogue. City School was not founded to guide these students to jail—even though students might claim to see this as a noble end—but to guide them to use their experiences productively to become educated and employable citizens. City School's goal was to "reduce the high cost of school failure." To do this, they could start by understanding the forces that led many students to drop out of school. However, the teachers at City School had a much greater responsibility than simply listening to students' stories, overhearing their conversations, or even understanding their perspectives. They were charged to work with such students to keep them in school and to teach them. But what happens when a teacher enters such student conversations? Does a teacher's institutional position carry more moral authority? Or does a teacher's lack of experience in the adolescent world counteract such authority? Or worse, silence students? These questions will be explored in the next chapter, in which students and teachers negotiate "rights to advise" in City School's contact zone.

CHAPTER 8

Rights to Advise

I decided that that was not proper

—Tim, a teacher, 1995

When former dropouts return to high school, they often present teachers with a knot of paradox similar to that faced by Mario in the preceding chapter. Teachers at City School had to contend head-on with the paradoxical blending of dropping out and dropping in perspectives, recognizing and honoring the complexity of students' own local knowledge while at the same time trying to provide them with mainstream cultural capital that could help them succeed in school, and later, in the legal economy. These contradictory goals led to a great deal of interactional work, especially when teachers were explicitly trying to give advice about personal issues, or convince students to abandon former perspectives.

As we saw explicitly in the last chapter, one issue over which the dropping out and dropping in perspective diverge is the value behind "getting locked up." As one might imagine, teachers generally align with Mario on this topic. They find the idea of going to jail not only depressing and degrading, but antithetical to education. Teachers at City School struggled daily precisely to keep young men and women *out* of jail. But as Jorge and Luis argued in the last chapter, going to jail for someone can form the foundation of "true" friendship. To them, Mario's discrediting of this notion only revealed his incapacity to understand such friendship. This chapter looks again at how the subject of jail is broached and debated, this time when a teacher is present—one who, like Mario, believes jail is "not proper."

The current discussion of "rights to advise" examines students and teachers in a discussion about "jail" and illustrates how "rights to advise" are established by students and teachers at City School. While we typically think of advice—practical suggestions for future behavior or attitudes—as imparted by a single individual to others (cf., DeCapua & Huber, 1993, 1995), conversations at City School illustrate how the status of advice-giver is a distributed status, achieved *collaboratively* in conversation. This chapter begins to illustrate how rights to advise are conversationally negotiated.

131

CONVERSATIONAL BORDERLANDS:
STUDENTS AND TEACHERS AT CITY SCHOOL

While all the teachers I interviewed at City School believe they share a common background with the students, primarily because they are either of generally similar ethnic or socioeconomic backgrounds, in many ways teachers and students at this school are worlds apart. Both their experiences and their ideologies about those experiences differ greatly, and these differences are well developed and interactionally sustained through genred use of language (as has been illustrated in Chapters 3, 4, and 5) or through what Jerome Bruner (1996) has called "minor oeuvres," habitualized identities with institutional histories. As might be expected, when controversial topics were raised (such as jail or gang violence), teachers did not readily align themselves with student perspectives. Often, students relied on local knowledge that teachers generally did not share. Nevertheless, as this chapter will illustrate, there is flexibility within the socialization process.

Teachers at City School generally respected students' origins, and learned about current gang rivalries and tagging (graffiti) practices. At the same time, teachers also wanted to change these young men and women and discourage the continuation of such practices. Respecting students' backgrounds while working to change them, however, requires intricate conversational negotiation. These contradictory goals lead to two difficult questions faced by teachers and students in conversation at City School: (1) How does one give advice and communicate wisdom in the absence of shared experience, and (2) How does one communicate respect for behavior one wants to change? In these conversations, where advice is achieved (or is attempted), indexical forms emerge as a crucial resource for conversationalists as they negotiate their own credibility as advice-givers despite the absence of shared experience.

INDEXICAL LANGUAGE

What students and teachers say to one another, the exact words they use, carries layers of social significance tied to a particular social history (cf., Silverstein & Urban, 1996). While institutional settings like schools are typically considered to inscribe rigid roles on students and teachers through day-to-day discursive routines (cf., Mehan, 1985, 1993), City School provided a much looser pattern of classroom interaction and more opportunities for noninstructional dialogue. As a consequence, the kinds of language used there are more variable and roles are more flexible and tend to emerge through talk. And in conversation, as I will demonstrate, indexical forms are one resource that participants draw on to establish momentary alignments.

In the following analysis of two separate conversations at City School, I will be looking in particular at the pronouns I, me, you, and him, as well as the nonpronominal indexical forms "people" and "everybody." These words become crucial resources for interlocutors because they have two important properties. First, their indexical objects can be collaboratively constructed across a single conversation. For example, the meaning of a word like "people" in a sentence like "People are strange" is something that conversation partners work out together, usually implicitly, as they talk. A second crucial property of indexical words is their capacity to facilitate the voicing of different perspectives simultaneously. Because there is some ambiguity regarding the meaning of the word "people," for example, two conversationalists can use it simultaneously to mean two different sets or types of people.

Because the meaning of indexical words is achieved collaboratively in conversation, and because such words facilitate the voicing of multiple perspectives, they play an important role in establishing a common frame of reference and bridging the experiences of individuals to create common—and changing—understandings. The shared construal of indices can evolve within conversation, but common understanding does not necessarily always occur, for such implicit agreement also relies an a certain backlog of shared cultural experience, or a common social history to draw from (Hanks, 1992; Silverstein & Urban, 1996). Conversations between students and teachers, for example, may not always display a seamless mutual understanding of indexical words. While teachers at City School respect students' backgrounds, students' and teachers' experiences are often quite disparate. Furthermore, most teachers ultimately want to work to change students' perspectives, and will not so readily align with them. The following discussions of jail illustrate the collaborative process of indexical meaning-making and how this process can function (or fail) as a foundation for authentic advice-giving.

INDEXICAL FORMS AND CONVERSATIONS ABOUT JAIL

Jail is both a subject with which many students in this school have more experience than their teachers, as well as a subject about which the particular teacher in these examples feels he must provide some wisdom and advice. Not surprisingly, perspectives on jail and time spent there differed greatly between the teachers and the students at City School, but as I will try to convey here, different perspectives also existed *among* students and teachers and even within single individuals in a single conversation. I will begin, however, by describing some generic teacher and student attitudes I observed, and then proceed by problematizing, rather than reifying, these generic types.

Many of the students at City School display an understanding that time spent in jail contributes to one's identity as a person who is tough, brave, and a survivor. Such a person is capable of withstanding the trauma of jail. Jail time can thus be a status symbol, and is marked in various ways: some students have teardrop tattoos that signify time spent in jail, and others occasionally sport "L.A. County Jail" shirts. Having done time, for many students at City School, is worn, like a Purple Heart, as a badge of honor. Because one often goes to jail to protect the identities of one's gang brothers or sisters, jail time is a symbol of suffering for a greater cause—that of one's friends.

As we saw in the conversations in Chapter 6, jail may even be portrayed as something students want to do. Recall Luis's retort to Mario's accusation of Jorge:

MARIO: Where did your family get you homes?
Your friends, ése?
He got you locked up, homes.
LUIS: That's 'cause I wanted to get locked up homes.

The practice of "getting locked up for someone" depends on an institutionalized need for police to arrest a certain number of perpetrators. As students have discussed in interviews, when police happen upon a crime scene, they want something to show for their work, and may even be indiscriminate about who they bring back to the station, as long as they arrest a probable suspect. Mario told me that police feel any brown or black teenager dressed in baggy gang wear probably is guilty of something. Given this police tendency to regard any gang-type youth present at a crime scene as a perpetrator, students have little difficulty being arrested for other peoples' crimes, as discussed in the example above. In this way, they show loyalty to their friends and affiliation to a particular peer group by standing in for their friends who are the real perpetrators. As Luis's remark exemplifies, some students say they would return to jail should the need arise.

Not surprisingly, teachers at City School generally do not align with this perspective and describe jail as a place to be avoided. The teacher appearing in the following segments views jail as both a punishment for young people and a wake-up call for them to change their lives. To exemplify this view, he occasionally tells stories of those one or two students for whom jail was truly reformative—who, for example, spent one night in jail, after which they never touched a graffiti spray can again. But as teachers have explained to me in interviews, they also recognize that the way jail time is meted out in this society is not always just.

In the following segment, one of the students has mentioned that he has just been released from jail. In response, this teacher, Tim, tries to invoke his own (vastly different) experience of jail, recalling a time when, many years ago, he was locked up for 5 days. In this conversation, the teacher presumably invokes his own experience of jail in order to lend authenticity to his more general points about the fact that jail provides a wake-up call and to invoke a meta-perspective on society and jail. However, the students listening barely take notice of his weighty conclusions. As shown here, the language that this teacher uses and the way his indexical forms are taken up in subsequent talk serve to distance him from student perspectives, rather than forming a bridge between his experiences and those of the students.

JOE: What you were locked up for?
TIM: Failure to appear on a traffic ticket.
JOE: .hhhheh [heh
TIM: [*They* put me in jail for five days,
FELIPE: *For what?*
GRACE: ((coughs twice))
JOE: *Five days that ain't nothing* five days.
    (1.4)
GRACE: Oh yeah.
JOE: *I* was locked up for two [months.
FELIPE: [*Where at.*
TIM: [It was a long time for *me. I* decided that that
                                was not proper.
FELIPE: *Where at though.*
TIM: At county jail downtown where, um
        [on Temple and,
FELIPE: [By glass house?

First, it must be said that a teacher discussing his own experience in jail is not a common occurrence in a school classroom. But at a school like City School, where teachers have articulated a desire to raise students' meta-awareness of society in order to empower them within mainstream culture, discussing jail can be seen as an important educational step. Indeed, for African American males like this teacher, going to jail for a traffic violation *is* a common experience, regardless of socioeconomic status, age, or profession. Accordingly, in his framing of this experience, Tim invokes "they" to address the injustice involved in his own trip to jail, leaving open to construal who that "they" may be. This is a "they," it seems, against whom the students, especially Joe who was just released from jail himself, might readily align with Tim. In the first several lines of the segment, it could appear that Felipe is aligning with Tim in this respect:

JOE: What you were locked up for?
TIM: Failure to appear on a traffic ticket.

JOE: .hhhheh [heh
TIM: [*They* put me in jail for five days,
FELIPE: *For what.*

The falling intonation of Felipe's "For what" suggests that he is not aligning with Tim against an oppressive "they" by displaying shock that "they" put Tim in jail for 5 days for a mere traffic offense. Instead, Felipe seems to be ignoring the fact that Tim was in jail for 5 days and reacting only to his minimal offense. He seems to be scoffing at Tim for revealing the humdrum nature of his own jail experience. As this conversation unfolds, Joe's contribution helps to solidify this interpretation and the potential for a shared alignment against "they" vanishes:

JOE: *Five days that ain't nothing* five days.
GRACE: Oh yeah.
JOE: *I* was locked up for two months.

Joe's reactions to Tim's account of his jail experience show no acknowledgment of Tim's use of "they." Instead of noticing that "they" were responsible for Tim's sentence, as "they" may have been for his own, Joe focuses on the second half of Tim's utterance—"for five days"—which Joe immediately and explicitly describes as "nothing" compared to his own sentence of 2 months. By drawing attention to the different nature of their experiences, rather than the common foe ("they"), Joe puts Tim on the defensive:

JOE: *I* was locked up for two [months.
FELIPE: [*Where at.*
TIM: [It was a long time for *me.*

The contrast, which Joe has made explicit, between his own jail time (2 months) and Tim's (5 days) has the effect of particularizing Tim's experience and focusing the conversation on what happened to *him* in particular rather than the power "*they*" have over all of them. Tim's use of the pronoun "me" further isolates this experience as something different from the students' and his remarks seem to pertain only to himself, even when he tries to make larger conclusions:

TIM: *I* decided that that was not proper.

Without considering the particular way this discussion has developed, there are two possible interpretations for Tim's statement that his time spent in jail "was not proper:" The injustice implied by the initial use of "they" and the minimal nature of Tim's offense may suggest that his conclusion, "that was not proper," is a point about the general injustice of spending time in jail. But the claim "that was not proper" could also be understood as a more conservative teacherly condemnation of the time spent in jail. This is the meaning of the phrase that seems to be made relevant in this conversation, precisely because the students do not align with Tim against the "they" he has invoked. Just as Joe's belittling of Tim's short sentence has colored Felipe's less explicit question (for what?) with a tone of mockery, it has also created a context that renders any subsequent lessons Tim has learned from jail more difficult to identify with.

Over the course of the conversation, students orient not to the broader injustice of Tim's jail time, but rather the particulars of it, and its distance from their own experience. Tim's strong assessment (that jail was "not proper") makes relevant some sort of alignment or disagreement in the next turn (cf., Pomerantz, 1984), but Felipe's response displays no recognition of the assessment at all: He simply reasks his question about the location of the jail ("Where at though").

It may be the facts of his particular jail experience (only 5 days, and for an unheroic traffic violation) that lead the students to discount Tim's experience. But I would argue that it is also, and more importantly, the *way* that Tim imparts those facts and the *way* they are received collectively by Joe and Felipe that impede any collaborative reconstruction of his experience as one the others can share. Tim uses his own jail time as an illustration of the injustice of jail. Joe and Felipe, on the other hand, see Tim's experience and the spin he puts on it as illustrative of Tim's teacherly, outdated view of jail. While Tim begins to invoke a generic "they," open to collaborative reconstrual by the students (one of whom has recently also been a victim of such a "they"), the students progressively disalign with Tim, focusing ensuing talk on how his experience was different from their own. Indeed, the students continue to push Tim to describe the *exact* location of the building, emphasizing the unique and different quality of Tim's jail time, and constructing his experience and its details as alien. They display no recognition of the universality of his experience of jail and the injustices inflicted by "they," or any shared understanding of his point that "it was not proper."

Nevertheless, Tim displays that he does want to make more universal points. This is not a time to focus on the logistics of his particular experience, but on the lessons he gleaned from it which he would like to impart to these young men. After 63 lines of transcript within which the students continue to attempt to pin down the exact location of Tim's experience of jail, Tim tries, once again, to raise more substantial, generalizable issues (which the students, again, resist):

TIM: No I mean what wh— wh what do *people* hope to gain by putting *you* in jail.
    (1.0)
FELIPE: Teach *him* a lesson or something.

TIM: Okay. Teach *him* [a lesson.
FELIPE: [And there's—
TOM: Do [you think that works?
FELIPE: [(but tha—) there's,
FELIPE: No. For— *some people.*
    (1.0)
TIM: Okay, *who* do you think it works for.
    (0.4)
FELIPE: For *the guys* don't wanna be in there again.

Here, Tim uses a generic "people" and has made his statement even more generic by using the term "you" as the object of "people's" actions. The impersonal "you" within a hypothetical narrated event potentially makes universal points about the logic of jail ("What do *people* hope to gain by putting *you* in jail?"). Subsequent talk does not elaborate on the injustices or overarching plan of "people." Furthermore, the generic "you" is not taken up as a joint construction. Felipe, rather than working with Tim to construct a profile of this universal "you," substitutes the new indexical form, "him," shifting the referent to someone other than himself. Switching to this pronoun succinctly deflates the universality of Tim's questions, making any answer less universally applicable. When Tim asks Felipe if he thinks jail does "teach lessons" (presumably like the one Tim himself learned, and spoke of earlier), Felipe further detracts from the universalizing "you" by replying that it may work for "some people," implying that it does not work for *all* people, and further, that it probably does not work for him. Pressed even further by Tim ("Who do you think it works for?"), Felipe becomes more evasive when he identifies a particular category of people for whom jail works: that is, "the guys" who don't want to go back. This is a category with which the teacher had already identified when he said earlier that jail was not proper. Tim's questioning (almost interrogating) format has induced Felipe to continue talking on the subject of jail, but he has not succeeded in evoking any explicit statements from Felipe that he is applying Tim's reasoning to himself. Felipe never includes himself with the teacher in the category of "guys who don't want to go back." By specifically delineating the category of people for whom jail is reformative (and not including himself), Felipe may or may not be resisting Tim's attempt to make universal points about jail, but the conversation presents no evidence that Tim's statements will affect him, or his attitudes about jail, in any way.

In this conversation, interlocutors never establish collaborative construal of indexical forms (e.g., people, they, you), and as a result, it seems that Tim never reaches students with his message about jail and reform. While he may potentially be invoking an ideology about the generic injustice of a system of which both he and his students have been victims, this message also goes unheeded, as students insist that his descriptions of jail apply only to him or others like him. Furthermore, the students never convey their own perspective on jail; they only convey a vague resistance to Tim's individual view. Throughout the interaction, indexical cues serve only to emphasize the distance between speakers rather than to create a shared frame of reference regarding jail. In this interaction, Tim attempts to convey advice indirectly (or to invoke meta-attitudes about jail to be taken in the future) by voicing a personal reaction to his own experience of jail. However, this attempt falls flat, for his interlocutors never indicate that his experience is remotely applicable to their own.

In these two excerpts and elsewhere, the teacher does not display awareness of the kinds of ties that can draw students back to jail again and again. His own story has no room for the ideas many students share about jail or its capacity to symbolize friendship and dedication to the group. This teacher, like most others, wants students to leave jail behind in order to focus on a brighter future.

It can be argued that students would like to maintain this distance from the teacher, that students expect their teacher to have different views from them and that this is a comfortable and perhaps even productive arrangement. One might even argue that just because students do not articulate their acceptance of the teacher/adult view here does not mean that they do not understand and are not influenced by this view. However, it is impossible to analyze here such "understanding," since student views of jail remain unarticulated in the conversation. In those segments, we only have conversational evidence of resistance to the teacher/adult view.

There is evidence elsewhere at City School, however (see Chapters 3, 4, and 6, and below), that many students understand the point this teacher is making, and are willing to align with the teacher/adult view on jail. However, due to the way indexical forms are constructed across turns in these segments, Tim misses an opportunity to draw on students' ambivalence regarding this topic. As I witnessed in many other conversations among students, despite the usual contrast between students' and teachers' views of jail, many students at City School have returned to school precisely to attain an education—and they are ready to abandon gang members' typical attitudes toward jail. Students frequently contest each other's self-portrayals as loyal gang members, and stories of going to jail as something cool and worthy of respect. Recall, for example, Manny's debunking of Jerry's portrayal of being arrested as a typical and misguided attempt to sound cool (see Chapter 4). As Manny says, sometimes students "think that it's cool" to get busted, and they *think* they look bad. But Manny implies that while they *think* this, they are deluded—because it very well may not be cool at all.

As this excerpt and the conversation with Mario in the previous chapter suggest, there are vociferous students around City School who do not hold the "student view" in its purest form but try instead to counteract that view. There are also persuasive students who are living examples of the purest "teacher view" about jail: that, however unjust, it can be reformative. The young man who works daily at the reception desk, for example, used to be an active tagger (graffiti writer). After spending time in jail, however, he became one teacher's favorite example of a young man for whom jail is truly reformative. His every-day, well-dressed presence behind the reception desk was living proof of his changed outlook. So there are normative beliefs about jail and differing norms among teachers and students. Teachers and students always orient to these norms, but this orientation may be to contest or deny them.

Given the prevailing ambivalence at City School, it is possible that Tom in the first example above could have reached students, or even engaged them in a discussion about jail, had the conversation taken a different turn. Perhaps he might have refrained from introducing his own jail experience as a means of drawing students out. Instead of pronouncing what was "proper," he might have asked students their views. Instead, as it unfolded, Tim's sharing his own experience was constructed by the students as heavy-handed and one-sidedly teacher-ish. In reaction, Joe and Felipe presented a one-sided and oppositional stance. They seemed bent on debunking the teacher's experience as minimal and nothing like their own—with the implication that he had nothing to teach them.

In other conversations with teachers present, however, students do display flexibility regarding their attitudes about jail. Likewise, there are times when, within student-teacher conversation, teachers show a greater understanding of the students' perspectives. This is in large part because the teachers at this alternative school also have an agenda of social change: they are not sympathetic to our justice system, which disproportionately punishes ethnic minorities, immigrants, and the poor. Their agenda is evident in many practices that are alien to teachers in more traditional settings. For example, teachers readily provide these students with a chance to avoid jail should they have to go. They will speak with judges to get sentences commuted, because they feel students could learn more from being in school than from being in jail or juvenile hall. Their agenda of social change and their sense that the system is unjust justifies their own willingness to intervene on students' behalf.

Furthermore, some teachers also recognize that students, faced with limited options, are embedded in a set of very strong peer ties that make it hard for them to give up their lifestyle and the associated attitudes regarding jail. Teachers try to gain a greater awareness of their students' ties to gangs in order to change these kids and the habits they are forming. While the teachers do not condone graffiti or gang rivalry, they try to become aware of their students' local knowledge in order to combat some of their most destructive practices. At times they use this local knowledge successfully to prevent both vandalism at the school and gang violence, by calling on students who are leaders among their peers to confront graffiti writers and to discourage gang fighting at school (see Chapter 5).

So attitudes toward jail at City School are complex. Most teachers and students express, at different times, aspects of both the "teacher" (or "dropping in") and "student" (or "dropping out") views of jail. These two views can also be categorized as views that accept and resist the norms of the larger society. And this acceptance and resistance is in flux at City School.

Of crucial importance to the establishment of "rights to advise," however, is the capacity for such flexibility to emerge in conversation between students and teachers. While one can easily say "I am open-minded," the same individual may have more difficulty behaving that way in a conversation. As the two segments from the conversation with Tim illustrate, sometimes the contingencies of a particular conversation (and the way indexical value is collaboratively construed across turns) can make it nearly impossible to reach a shared perspective. By contrast, in the segment below, student perspectives come into the foreground, and suggest that in order to convince students that jail is a place to avoid, one must also deal with the alternative ideology in play at City School, namely, that for some, "doing time" is a way of showing loyalty to friends. In fact, when "you" go to jail, some of your friends may already be there.

In the conversation below, between the same teacher, Tim, and four young women, a student, rather than the teacher, initially voices the view that her experience of jail is one she never wants to repeat. The student in this example, however, makes a much more effective case for avoiding jail because, with the help of the other conversationalists, she bolsters her arguments about jail by incorporating a recognition of the alternative view: that going to jail is also something one's peers may do quite often.

((The group had been discussing how there are so many good looking young
     men in jail. After a lull, Keneisha continues))
KENEISHA: *I don't NEVer want to go back.*
          (0.8)
TIM: I hear ya.
     (2.0)
LATASHA: Liar you just said that's where everybody at, you should go out
     and do something else, huh.
KENEISHA: Who me?
LATASHA: Yeah trying to get through [there.
KENEISHA: [Oh no! I didn't care about anybody be-
                                    ing there [*I* wanted to go home.
LATASHA: [*Everybody* was like "*I*'m going to jail, all my homies in jail."
What *you* [wanna go to jail for.
VICKI: [*People* be like "*I'm*— *I'm* going to jail." As soon as *you* get there=
LATASHA: That's STUpid.

VICKI: = "*I* wanna go ho [me."
KENEISHA: [*You* be wanting to go ho— *I*'m telling *you* man.
LATASHA: See I couldn't be in jail 'cause all that.

As this conversation begins, one of the young women is contesting the
prevailing student view on jail, saying that she doesn't want to return:

KENEISHA: *I don't NEVer want to go back.*
          (0.8)
TIM: I hear ya.

There is a long pause, however, after Keneisha's statement. The other young
women are not quick to take up this alternative view. After all, they had just
been discussing the quantities of good-looking men in jail. The teacher, however, supports Keneisha's view, adding his empathic, "I hear ya." At this point,
Keneisha looks like another example of the prevailing teachers' view on jail:
living proof, like the young man behind the reception desk, that jail does have
reformative powers.

     After an even longer pause, however, another one of the young women
(LaTasha) responds, not to Tim's empathic remark, but to Keneisha's original
claim that she doesn't want to go back to jail. Rather than taking the teacher's
point of view, LaTasha denies that jail has reformed Keneisha at all, and even
suggests that she probably wants to do something to go back there.

LATASHA: Liar you just said that's where everybody at, you should go out
          and do something else, huh.

With this pronouncement, LaTasha is voicing the typical student point of view,
that jail is a place associated with friends, a place through which you regularly
pass in and out. The interactional question has become clear: Which of the
young women agree with the teacher that jail is undesirable? Despite the prior
conversation in which they all expressed the dominant student view, Keneisha
continues to express the opposite view here. Her experience of jail is still very
fresh in her mind, and she did not enjoy it or find that her friends there made it
worthwhile:

KENEISHA: Who me?
LATASHA: Yeah trying to get through [there.
KENEISHA: [Oh no!
          I didn't care about anybody being there
          I wanted to go home.

LaTasha claims that Keneisha really likes jail—to the point of committing another crime to go back. However, even after LaTasha's challenge, Keneisha reasserts her position. She didn't care how many potential friends were in there; she wanted to go home.

Despite the apparent disagreement between the two girls in the next several lines and in a matter of seconds, the authenticity of Keneisha's remark as well as LaTasha's alignment with it are reestablished. A reworked, shared viewpoint is achieved largely through the collaborative use of indexical pronouns. This shifting of indexical meaning occurs as more voices enter the conversation and LaTasha begins to express the views of "everybody" else who has gone to jail. Through the use of an indexical "everybody," LaTasha invokes the voices of students expressing the dominant view on jail. She introduces these voices through quoted dialogue:

LaTasha: *Everybody* was like "*I'm* going to jail, all my homies in jail."
  What *you* wanna go to jail for.

LaTasha has invoked the voices of normative students, here, who proudly say that they are going to jail and that all their friends are there. This is a view that all the young women, except for Keneisha, have endorsed moments earlier in conversation.

The question "what you wanna go to jail for?", however, suggests that LaTasha may not be solidly aligned against Keneisha. The view that LaTasha endorses now is still indeterminate. LaTasha's question could have at least two different meanings in this conversation. She could be asking a sarcastic, rhetorical question, likely to be posed by teachers or other more pro-jail members of the student community. In this case, she would be taking a stand against Keneisha and her claim that she doesn't want go back to jail. Or, she could be asking a question of "everybody," scoffing at them for actually wanting to go to jail. In this case, she would be aligning herself with Keneisha and her newly voiced anti-jail stance.

As the rest of the conversation illustrates, the meaning of LaTasha's question, and the momentary establishment of her own stance toward jail is achieved largely through the entrance of more voices into the conversation, voices that echo LaTasha's characterization of what "everybody" says:

Vicki: *People* be like "*I'm*— *I'm* going to jail." As soon as *you* get there=
Keneisha: That's STUpid.
Vicki: ="*I* want to go home."

"People," like "everybody," want to go to jail. And Keneisha is quick to point out that both people and everybody are "STUpid" to have this desire. As Vicki continues her utterance, she claims that while people initially want to go to jail, as soon as they get there they say exactly what Keneisha says after she went to jail, that she wanted to go home. At this point Vicki's utterance is as indeterminate as LaTasha's question. She could mean at least two things, depending on the indexical value of "you." First, the "you" could index Keneisha specifically. In this case Vicki could be making fun of Keneisha for first claiming she wants to go to jail and then, after actually experiencing jail, backing off. This could be a pro-jail view, denouncing the babyish change of heart displayed by Keneisha. Second, the "you" could be an impersonal "you," referring to "everybody" and "people" who talk about jail as a great place but who, upon experience, realize it is not. In this case, Vicki might be bolstering a particular anti-jail view possible for students, a view that incorporates experience of and subsequent disillusionment with the jail experience.

Much of meaning in this conversation hinges on the construal of the indexical value of "you," and this value is emergent as the talk continues. What the word "you" means depends on how it is said (including the intonation involved in quoted speech) and the way it combines with the quoted speech surrounding it. Keneisha has invoked a cast of characters that go to jail and say certain things about it, and from her quoted interactions with these characters, she can make generalizations about what "you" say and do. In the next line, by combining "you" with her original statement, Keneisha speaks as if Vicki means the second of the above possibilities. She repeats her original remark ("I wanted to go home"), but now it has been transformed from a statement of a singular "I" to a more universal statement about the impersonal "you":

KENEISHA: *You* be wanting to go ho— I'm telling you man.

The meaning of Keneisha's statement is still indeterminate here, but her use of "you," by tying her statement to Vicki's quoted speech in a way which suggests that "you" is equivalent to "people" and "everybody" potentially establishes that Vicki and LaTasha agree with Keneisha, that jail is an unpleasant experience, one not worth repeating. Though LaTasha initially seemed to contest Keneisha's view, her acceptance of this formulation unfolds in the subsequent discourse. In the next line, LaTasha provides temporary stability to the meaning of her own and Vicki's remarks by agreeing with Keneisha. She couldn't go to jail, either:

LATASHA: See I couldn't be in jail 'cause all that.

Against the view she had expressed earlier, LaTasha has now agreed that jail is not desirable.

We can understand the meaning of LaTasha's initial question ("What you want to go to jail for?") and Vicki's quoted speech ("I wanted to go home") only by examining subsequent context, and the interactional structure that emerges later in the interaction. In these subsequent lines of conversation, an interactional organization for participants emerges and the three young women ally themselves against the dominant student view of jail. In general, speakers depend on such emergent interactional structure to give meaning to utterances. Part of the structure that allows us to understand what LaTasha means is in the interaction itself—in the particular context set up by participants in this instance and in the interactional alignments among participants, both of which are established through the use of indexical forms (e.g., I, you, everybody, people).

In this conversation, it may be that conclusions unfold more favorably for Tim's point of view precisely because it is not Tim who voiced this view. Indeed, it appears that the girls here have a rapport with which Tim can not fully participate. This does not detract from the point that collaborative construal of indexicals can be an important component in establishing rights to advise. It does suggest, however, that such collaborative construal is more achievable among peers, who are capable of invoking a shared context for indexical reference. Indeed, the girls here may even be achieving advice despite Tim's presence rather than because of any particularly careful guidance. Tim and the school, however, do provide an institutional framework within which student talk and local knowledge is viable.

This conversation also provides Tim with an important cross-section of student local knowledge—something unable to be gleaned from his conversation with the boys. While the teacher's spoken role is minimal in this interaction, his nonspeaking role as listener and provider of a venue for talk is invaluable for the recognition of student views that may be an essential component to his future teaching.

GENREFICATION OF MORAL DISCOURSE AND EMERGENT MUTUAL UNDERSTANDINGS

So far we have seen how genres of speech—for example, the systematic deployment of certain forms and thematic concerns—can be used as a way to present a moral self; that is, to portray one's actions as understandable given a set of circumstances—to portray oneself as a good person. We have also seen how those same genred specifics can be used to debunk that moral self and how different versions of this "good" self emerge through different genred uses of language. But as we saw in Chapter 7, when conflicting genres come into contact, intricate linguistic negotiations must take place, and meaning—in particular, what it means to be a good person, to "do the right thing," to be someone's "roll dog"—does not emerge with such clarity. Instead, the contact between different genres creates a paradox and asks the question, "What is a 'good' person?" When contradictory, habituated discourse genres meet in conversation, interlocutors can be threatened with the deconstruction of each other's assumptions and moral frameworks for experience. The results of such encounters can range from intolerance to tolerant coexistence to meaningful social change.

As this chapter has illustrated, reaching any one of these results is a matter of both presuppositions brought to a conversation and the emergent meaning of indexical language within that interaction. Indexicality has been of crucial importance in the foregoing analysis because indexical language is dependent on conversational and sociohistorical context for construal and thus facilitates the collaborative construction of contingent, localized understanding. Such emergent understandings are the foundation of rights to advise.

I have been discussing primarily noninstructional discourse, but the interactional work involved in these informal conversations suggests that similar collaboration may be involved in other forms of classroom learning, and emphasizes the importance (and difficulty) of integrating students' own perspectives and experiences with more standardized educational goals. As Moll and Diaz (1987) have written, "[J]ust as academic failure is socially organized, so can academic success be socially arranged" (p. 302). The conversations I have discussed here only begin to suggest the complexities of such social arrangement. I hope that by focusing on the conversationally contingent emergence as well as the sociohistorical nature of indexical meaning, I have been able to illustrate some of the interactional and linguistic rudiments of the social organization of advice.

Through analysis of student-teacher conversations, the conversations in this chapter have demonstrated how people establish alignments as well as how people talk past one another. This analysis of indexical forms and their emergent function in conversation also illustrates one way of wedding discourse analysis with educational research, a marriage that potentially will result in a finer grained understanding of the complexities of both human interaction and individual and institutional capacities for development and change.

Lest these conclusions about the power of indexical language appear too sanguine, I must emphasize that indexicals also provide a means to shut out those who have different viewpoints, to render certain genres closed to contributions from others. Opening up one's own viewpoint to meta-analysis by others is (as we saw in Chapter 7) not always a comfortable experience. Indeed, such meta-examination, rather than leading to mutual understanding, may pose a threat to strongly embedded moral frameworks that structure an interlocutor's life as meaningful and worthwhile. The boys discussing their own jail terms early in this chapter, for example, may have moral reasons for eschewing Tim's suggestion that jail was "not proper" and for constructing his experience of jail as very different from their own. Aligning with a teacher who did what appears to the boys as meaningless jail time (for a traffic ticket) may threaten their presupposition that jail time provides evidence that one is a loyal friend, rendering their own experience of jail as meaningless, which is how they view Tim's jail time. In this case, these boys use linguistic means to distance their own experience from their teacher's, and ultimately, to render mutual understanding impossible. They remain like strangers in adjacent hotel rooms, the connecting doors locked from both sides.

Tim's conversation with the girls, however, suggests that understanding the nature of these differing perspectives can open the doors between contradictory viewpoints: One can move back and forth between the adjacent rooms and learn a great deal about the inhabitants of either. Whether such learning will lead to mutual understanding is debatable, but certainly more likely than were the doors to remain locked. The next chapter turns to the desire for mutual understanding and the role of social science research in unlocking contact zones like City School. Through an exploration of the genrefication of moral discourse, researchers can discover both their own relationship to the community they are studying as well as the conflict and solidarity within that community. In this way, social science researchers can work toward an understanding of the deep personal commitments behind conflicting and possibly unresolvably different viewpoints.

CHAPTER 9

School Closure

But, I mean, that's society. That's how it's built up. It's always been that way. You know, everybody has their problems, but nobody says, "Hey, let's help out these kids!"
— Jaime, a teacher, 1994

On December 2, 1994, only one student was heading toward City School when I pulled into the parking lot. At 9:45, Aldo Rodriguez was early for Tim's scheduled Life Skills class, which I was also planning to attend and videotape. Together we arrived at the front door to find City School practically closed down. Another student, Chris, was manning the security desk, and behind Chris, the school's halls extended, dark and silent. Aldo walked with me to Tim's classroom, but as we made our way through the deserted, echoey hall, it seemed obvious we wouldn't find him there. In the middle of the dark hall, Aldo turned to me, angry: "This is fucked up," he said. He was tired of trying to graduate here and this was the last straw. He was going to go to a night school on Olive Street to finish up. This school was just "too much bullshit."

WHAT HAPPENED?

It wasn't difficult to understand how a student who had recently started attending City School would start to doubt the credibility of the program. (What was perhaps more surprising was that he would actually pursue his degree elsewhere.) For the preceding 2 months, City School had been embroiled in well-publicized controversy, and the district was threatening closure. Teachers had begun to spend a portion of every class period diffusing student anxiety over the current turmoil, using varying degrees of euphemism to explain the administrative and financial breakdown of their school.

As I slowly learned through these teacher explanations, as well as through subsequent interviews with teachers, and with Carlton Hobbes, one of the founders of the school, the problems had been going on for nearly a year, ever since City School had changed locations and quadrupled its enrollment. After this move, the program was constantly in flux, and the president of the school, Calvin Romaine, had become further isolated from the teachers. He had expensively furnished administrative offices on the fourth floor of the building, retreated there with a small staff, and was rarely seen. From this vantage point, Romaine began to lavish the school's money on a minority of the students (some of the "success stories" in Chapter 5), and to deny teachers' requests for rudimentary supplies, claiming budgetary inadequacy. As the months proceeded, students who had graduated became involved in the City School Associates program, through which they received a monthly stipend, and in return continued to attend City School, honing their computer skills and working in various unpaid internships in order to assess their options and prepare for college and/or a career. These 14 students were primarily mentored by Romaine, but the remaining hundreds of students rarely caught a glimpse of the president of their school.

In instituting the associates program and other curricular changes while withholding money for school necessities and claiming the board was behind him, Calvin Romaine had in fact been acting unilaterally. In fact, Carlton Hobbes, the university administrator who started the program with Romaine, had been diagnosed with cancer and had been hospitalized. He knew very little of the turmoil at City School, and did not have the presence of health to involve himself in its day-to-day functioning. The other board members were invisible, aside from their prominent position on City School letterhead. Gradually, a faction of teachers became frustrated with their isolation from Romaine, the lack of funding to run the school, and the repeated sabotage of programs for the sake of Romaine's idiosyncratic pursuits. Frustrated teachers finally filed a formal complaint, after which the school was officially audited by the district.

It would be hard to overemphasize teachers' frustration during these last months. And the history of City School makes clear that these frustrations were well justified. The president's idiosyncratic pursuits were by no means limited to curricular innovation. By January 1994, his isolated suite of offices on the fourth floor of the City School building was distant in every way from the instructional spaces on the first and second floor of the same building. The first and second floor was a study in contrasts from the fourth floor, indicative of the shift in priorities that had come over the school. The fourth floor administrative offices were carpeted, well furnished and appointed. Yet the first and second floor classrooms were barren, undecorated, and, as the year wore on, increasingly subject to graffiti vandalism. On the first and second floors, there was no money for teaching materials and books (even pencils and paper were in short supply), not to mention decorating upgrades. The framed portraits of notable minorities that had lined the wall of classrooms at the old building were now hung in the lavishly appointed fourth-floor boardroom. On the first floor, the art teacher used her own money to buy materials. On the second floor, the reading teacher brought her own books for students. These were teachers who had already chosen to take large pay cuts to come to City School, who, in the words of Laura, my initial contact, still wanted to "believe in the dream that brought them to the school." Meanwhile, the president's financial indiscretions extended far beyond the fourth floor. His expenditures also included the lease of a $39,000 sports car (with charter school funds), provision of a bodyguard, and a housing subsidy (Little Hoover Commission, 1996, p. 38). The president's priorities seemed to have shifted far from the instructional goals of the first and second floors to the isolated luxuries of his fourth floor suite and the demands of his small cohort of followers there.

Over the course of the year, and in the absence of Carlton Hobbes's guidance, Calvin Romaine himself seemed to have transformed from a bright, energetic, and charismatic spokesperson for the underserved youth of Los Angeles to a megalomaniacal, dictatorial, and unreachable man. Romaine's consistent feature was his uncanny leadership capacity. Two years previous to his demise, he had captured teachers' idealism and energy to lure them away from secure and better-paying public school positions. Now, most of these teachers had finally decided to take action against their president, but many students at the school were still devoted to Calvin Romaine, some even calling him "the father they never had." Some of these students stayed with him in his home (thus the "housing subsidy"), rode with him to school (thus the expensive car lease), and stayed with him at school from seven in the morning until seven at night. But even during the final months, it was not only students who fell under the power of Romaine's leadership. Select teachers also became part of his inner circle, as did his bodyguard, Joe Munson. This former officer of the Los Angeles Police Department was hired after Romaine filed claims that he was being stalked and threatened by the husband of one City School teacher. Joe Munson was another addition to the cohort at Romaine's home. With him 24 hours, this man also became a devotee.

I never saw the lavish offices on the fourth floor until City School closed. When I spoke with Romaine (and his bodyguard) while the school was in operation, we met at a downtown restaurant, several miles from the school. Not until the school closed, Romaine long gone, was I escorted through these offices. During this tour, I saw the appointments described above. But I also saw signs of the haste and panic in which the members of Romaine's inner circle had departed. The huge boardroom table, the framed pictures, the large desks and expensive chairs were still there. But file drawers had been left pulled out, files removed. Chairs were overturned, and miscellaneous paper and trash were strewn on the floor. "They left in a hurry!" my tour guide observed. Romaine, it was rumored, had fled to northern California with one of the teachers (the same teacher whose husband had been threatening Romaine) and at least one of the student associates.

On the morning of December 2 of that same year, the ramifications of these administrative complications were painfully apparent, to put it mildly.

Aldo and I found the door of Tim's classroom closed and locked. No note, no explanation. Aldo left immediately, and angrily, but I was determined to stay and wait for Tim. After waiting in the lobby for 45 minutes, however, I became sure that he was not planning to show. As I waited, the young man sitting at the metal detector began to fill me in on the story. With a hearing at the Los Angeles Unified School District pending, the school had been temporarily shut down. Teachers, he said, had tried to contact students, but many of them had not been reached, and like Aldo, they continued to arrive, only to be told that the school was closed today, that they would be able to return on Monday. Oddly, Tim had not contacted me either about this school closure. A chilly whiff of shame now wafted through the halls. After waiting 45 minutes for Tim, I met Pierre, an accountant and City School board member (whom I had never seen before, but who was now taking over the financial management of the school). He asked me to leave.

Outside, Joe, apparently transformed from Romaine's 24-hour bodyguard into school security guard, was busy pulling garbage out of the planters on the front of the building when I stopped to talk. He said it was such a shame about the school possibly being closed down and that he was going to do all he could to make sure it stayed in operation. As he pulled old beer bottles and condoms out of the plants (he advised me against helping), Joe also told me about what he saw as another ramification of the turmoil surrounding City School: Yesterday, one of City School's best students, Pablo, had been murdered in his neighborhood. Pablo was one of the students in the associates program, but the associates were "furloughed" when it was discovered there was no money to support them.

Joe was not only a security guard, not only a 24-hour bodyguard. He was devoted to Calvin Romaine. Over the months, Joe became increasingly involved in school politics—and a fervent believer in the school's worthiness—as his concern over City School's fate and his explanation of Pablo's death reveal. His contextualization of this murder draws dramatically on the premises of the "dropping in" genre, and Joe's own belief that City School had made a success out of Pablo.

According to Joe's version of events, as soon as the associates program was dropped (due to financial constraints imposed by the district, but before the school was forced to close entirely) Pablo returned to his neighborhood, and to the kinds of activities that led to his murder. From Joe's point of view, City School not only educated Pablo, but also took him away from the murderous street culture that ultimately took his life. Joe's explanation of Pablo's death registered a moral stance on City School ("This school was saving Pablo") as well as an indirect accusation ("Look what the school district has done to one of our best students").

After City School closed down, Pablo's death often came up in conversations with other City School staff members. This death seemed to crystallize people's views on the closure of the school. Everyone had a different take on this murder, and used Pablo's story to justify different forms of moral disgust. In hindsight, this diversity of views illuminates the varying goals and expectations that mingled in the City School community. Despite the dramatic transformation of Romaine and the obvious corruption at the upper levels of the school's administration, everyone still cared about the goals City School was meant to serve. Depending on their role in the school's demise, teachers and staff narrated Pablo's death quite differently, but all were attempting to salvage the dreams City School, and Pablo, might have fulfilled.

TWO VERSIONS OF PABLO'S STORY

Pablo's death illuminates a dilemma on which City School was founded, and which flourished for a while. City School had become a school for dropouts, a place for conversion, and yet a place of recognition of the complexities of city living and the circumstances from which the students came to City School. As this book has illustrated through analysis of stories and conversations that occurred throughout City School's brief history, a great deal of the moral import of a story is determined by the way the events of a narrative are contextualized in interaction. After City School closed, I continued to interview teachers and staff. In all these interviews, without any direct prompting on my part, the death of Pablo was eventually mentioned. It was as though interviewees, knowing I was following up on City School's closure, thought this story could best express the sadness of the school's fate. But each of these stories portrayed Pablo's death in a different light, and taken together they illustrate the multiplicity of perspectives that coexisted at City School.

On speaking with another teacher, Paula, about City School's closure, I found she characterized the cause of Pablo's death not as something precipitated by the district-mandated closure of the associates program, but as a result of the internal politics and financial mismanagement that the district finally recognized. Unlike Joe, the security guard who blamed the district for Pablo's death, Paula contextualized Pablo's death as something explicitly caused by the school itself. Her story differs dramatically from Joe's: Rather than isolating the district bureaucracy as the cause of Pablo's death, Paula located the problem within the school which had itself become untrustworthy, enabling students to return to their old ways. Before starting her version of the story of Pablo, Paula had been discussing this transformation in the school, the corruption of the school's president, and the effect it had on students long before the district intervened:

PAULA: And then you know the kids started like— the students started like—
    going back into their gangs, heavily.
BETSY: Uh huh.

PAULA: You know the— the ones that had like stayed away, an— an— were not doing drugs, and—
BETSY: Ye[ah.
PAULA: [They started just doing everything they were doing before.
BETSY: Oh jeez.

After describing the beginning of the school's failure, Paula begins her story of Pablo by describing his return to gang life, symbolized by Pablo's brother's shaved head, which appeared "all of a sudden":

PAULA: Well, uh, what happened was that his brother that had been staying away from gangs all of a sudden comes in with a shaved head.

Paula saw this return to a characteristic gang haircut as a deliberate attempt on the part of the students to show the school that they were fed up with the chaos and deception being perpetrated by teachers and administrators. For Paula, this new behavior was proof that the school was becoming a dishonest environment. The students, upon hearing the rumors of corruption among the administration and certain teachers suddenly realized that this school, like all the other schools they had attended, didn't care about them after all. As Paula put it, students started saying to themselves, and sometimes out loud, "Forget you! We're gonna go back to what we used to do. 'Cause you guys are a bunch of liars. City School—you're just the same like everybody else." Unlike Joe, Paula does not portray Pablo's foe as the school district that took Pablo's safety net (City School) away. Instead, Paula portrays the school itself as the villain, for failing to be a genuine safety net in the first place. In Paula's version of the story, the corruption of the school, just like the inadequacies these students felt in their old schools, precipitates Pablo's return to the mistrustful and defensive mentality that led to his death.

Carlton Hobbes's version of the Pablo story, however, resembles the view put forward by Joe Munson. Instead of emphasizing Pablo's return to the "dropping out" perspective, Hobbes focuses on the "dropping in" features of Pablo's story. Carlton's version of events stresses the disappointment of City School's necessary closure, but emphasizes City School's success up to that point:

CARLTON: What's so uh, I guess disappointing about it, is that there was never an argument that we were not successful with the students.
BETSY: um hm.
CARLTON: You know— um, 68 kids got diplomas that first year,=
BETSY: Yeah.
CARLTON: =who otherwise would not.
BETSY: Right.
CARLTON: Many of the students have gone on to college.

BETSY: um hm.
CARLTON: The president of the class had a four-year scholarship.

It was in this context that Hobbes brought up Pablo's death. Pablo was that class president with the 4-year scholarship:

CARLTON: Uh. And unfortunately he was the one who was murdered.
BETSY: Oh, I remember that.
CARLTON: Yeah. He had a four-year full ride.
BETSY: Jeez.
CARLTON: So— so there were many success stories of this experience and there's a lot to be learned.

For Carlton, Pablo was a "success story." The school's success is not diminished by his death, and may even be valorized through it.

As these two versions of Pablo's story illuminate, the tension between "dropping out" and "dropping in" is a salient one at City School. This tension is relevant not only for students battling out life choices within themselves, but also for teachers and administrators trying to justify the genesis and the demise of a program designed to help such students. Neither one of these versions of Pablo's death is "more true" than the other. But, like the dropping in and dropping out stories analyzed in this book, they both illuminate something about the people telling them, and the institutional forces behind their telling. Both Carlton and Paula view City School as playing an intrinsic role in Pablo's fate. While Paula sees Pablo's death as an indictment of City School, proof of its ultimate failure, Carlton, like Joe, sees Pablo's story as emblematic of City School's success, though illustrative of the shame of its closure.

A THIRD VERSION OF PABLO'S STORY

One teacher to whom I spoke, however, didn't contextualize Pablo's death in terms of City School's success or failure. This teacher, Jaime, instead saw Pablo's death as yet another example of the hardships generally faced by all the students at City School. Jaime didn't mention Pablo until the end of our conversation, when he began to talk about the kinds of difficulties City School kids faced generally. When the topic of Pablo came up, Jaime had been discussing the death—which had taken place over a year earlier—of another City School student, Jesse, murdered during City School's first months in operation:

JAIME: And there's other kids that you know that you see grow up ande—
       you know and—they—they tell you all kinds of stuff. There's one kid
       Jesse. Jesse Navarro, who died.

Jesse's death, as Jaime goes on to explain, came at the end of a very hard life, and symbolizes the "kinds of stuff" that "other kids" at City School were facing all the time. As discussed in Chapter 2, Jesse appeared at my first discussion group, dead tired, having been released at 4:00 a.m. from juvenile hall. As Jaime goes on to explain, Jesse was essentially homeless:

JAIME: Yeah, I don't know if you remember Jesse.
BETSY: Yeah.
JAIME: That was kind of a sad story about that guy.
BETSY: Yeah.
JAIME: You know he used to sleep on the doorstep of City School.
BETSY: Oh man.
JAIME: Yeah so—finally what they ended up doing is—they let him sleep in the child care center. 'Cause it had a carpet you know.
BETSY: Uh huh.
JAIME: I think they gave him like a blanket and stuff and—they have like those padding where the kids sleep.
BETSY: Uh huh.
JAIME: So that's where he would sleep. So. Until they killed him of course.

Here, Jaime uses the phrase "they killed him" as a generic way of talking about the seemingly ubiquitous gang violence that took Jesse's life. Jesse's death was tragic, but his life, as described here by Jaime, was tragic as well. City School provided him with a place to sleep at night, but Jaime mentions him not as a way of glorifying City School's contributions, but as a way of showing the complex lives of the students he tried to teach there. It is in this context that the death of Pablo arose:

JAIME: That was—pretty hard. [Jesse's death.] Then there was Pablo after that, you heard about Pablo's death.

Although Jaime does contextualize Pablo's death in terms of the hardships involved in many of the students' lives at City School, like Joe the security guard, Jaime sees Pablo's death as also related to the withdrawl of funding for the associates program:

JAIME: And uh, Pablo you know, goes "Well, what am I gonna do now?" So Pablo goes back to his old neighborhood. I think it was three weeks later he got killed? Something like that.
BETSY: Yeah.
JAIME: It wasn't that much after the associates program closed down at— you know.

Although Jaime links Pablo's death to the closure of the associates program, mentioning that it occurred 3 weeks later, he also emphasizes that Pablo's
fate is very common for many young people—and for others who went to City
School before its funding was curtailed. For Jaime, Pablo's death exemplifies
not necessarily the value of the associates program, but more generally, the lack
of options for these young men and women. As he said, many of the students
will probably make similar choices and meet similar ends. Now that City School
had closed down, Jaime conjectured,

JAIME: Pretty soon they're going to start showing up either in jail or in trou-
    ble or some other stuff like that.

In discussing his sadness over Pablo's death, Jaime did not focus on specific
bureaucratic machinery that closed down the school. Jaime suggests that society
itself is not concerned with "these kids," and never will be:

JAIME: But— I mean that's society. That's how it's built up. It's always *been*
    that way. You know, everybody has their problems but— nobody says
    "hey, let's help out these kids!" Nah it doesn't work. There's never, no-
    body ever really cares about them. "As long as not in my backyard I
    don't care what happens over there. Put them in the projects, give them
    welfare. That'll keep them quiet." That's not right.

Jaime recognizes and remarks on larger structural forces that preserve a status
quo that exacerbates the pitfalls of poverty and its isolation in the projects, away
from a society that seeks mainly to "keep [these kids] quiet." But his frustration
at society in general and individuals' selfish nimbyism is matched by his frustration with the young people themselves. This frustration comes to a head when
he describes first why he suspected Pablo was murdered (drug dealing), and
then his realization that his death was part of a much farther-reaching and less
explicit ethos. When Jaime first heard of Pablo's death, he assumed Pablo had
been selling drugs again, since his income from the "associates program" had
dried up:

JAIME: Yeah, and Pablo says, "Hey, I don't know what to do for money and
    stuff," so he started copping dope again. So when I found out he got
    killed, "Was he selling drugs again?" You know that was the first thing I
    asked.
BETSY: Yeah.
JAIME: You know w— was that the reason. And apparently that wasn't the
    reason.

Instead, as Jaime learned from evidence at the funeral, Pablo's return to the "gang member mentality," and not necessarily to drug dealing directly, had led to Pablo's death. He was back in his neighborhood, defending territory, representing for his gang friends. While simply hanging out, representing the identity of a loyal gang member, he was gunned down. This appears to be the source of greatest frustration for Jaime—he laments that even a death cannot snap many young people out of their pursuit of social acceptance through gang membership. Evidence of affiliation with the "gang member mentality" was everywhere at Pablo's funeral, according to Jaime:

JAIME: And here's the gang member mentality. And— all the gang members are there. Okay. All of them are there. And so I'm kicking with my brother— I went with my brother Anthony, and— Anthony was a lot closer to him than I was. So we're— we're all kicking back looking at— uh— the wake and prayer and all this and that. And we— I— I— started looking around and I go look— look— Anthony look behind you look at all these bald heads. You know. Gang members. And look at all these little girls over here you know. They're all like— dressed up really pretty an— not really for a funeral, if you know what I mean. Not black, and you know they're kind of— exposed. It was a pretty cold night too, and they're kind of exposing themselves you know a little bit. So we checked this out and, to these guys, it's a social event. It's like going to a dance. You know?

On hearing this story, I was reminded of Mario's own frustration following his attempts to persuade Jorge and Luis to abandon their gang by appealing to the death of his friend (see Chapter 7). I now recognized this same frustration in Jaime. "Some people *do* get influenced by the death of a friend," I mentioned, thinking of Mario. Jaime's response again revealed the hopelessness he felt at the funeral:

JAIME: Yeah. But not these guys.
BETSY: Yeah.
JAIME: These guys are just— take it— one day at a time I guess.
BETSY: Yeah.
JAIME: That's pretty harsh.

Jaime's contextualization of Pablo's death, although it mentions the loss of the associates program funding, differs radically from the security guard's narrative. He describes the futility of working with, on the one hand, a society that doesn't care about poverty, and on the other, the embedded mentality of gang members, who need a great deal of help to abandon the role society has left for them.

"Dropping in" to City School, Pablo changed from his baggy gang wear to a suit and tie, and eventually to a position in the "associates program." His role as a drop-in was apparently not sustainable without the support system of City School, but Jaime doesn't contextualize Pablo's death by casting aspersions at the district bureaucracy that closed the school. Instead he reflects more generally on the complexities of the societal matrix in which Pablo and City School was embedded.

CITY SCHOOL'S DEMISE

From Innovation to Despair

City School's official motto was "Reducing the High Cost of School Failure," a noble and nearly impossible calling. As Jaime's story highlights, City School was doing battle with strong, embedded historical realities: "the gang member mentality," the selfish people who say "not in my backyard," and the inevitable inequities of "society" in general. These are the realities education, education reform, and even more specifically, charter school reform are meant to address. When Shankar (1988) hailed the advent of charter school reform as the true innovation needed to transform a school system, I believe a school like City School was what he had in mind. This was a school that initially sought out those who had been failed by every other school and constantly innovated to meet their needs. Only under the auspices of a charter school could a public school ever have attempted the kinds of dramatic innovations that took place at City School.

As Joe Munson and Carlton Hobbes discuss in their narratives, City School was promising an education and a future to those whom no one else could help. These narratives highlight the promise City School held out to such young people. There were students who truly did view Calvin Romaine as the father they never had. These students felt they had been saved, and perhaps they had been. At times, when I was interviewing members of the associates program, I felt their adrenaline rush in my own veins as they told their stories. I listened, energized, as one student described her triumph (through graduation!) over a father who never believed in her, and as another told of his own shock and gratitude at a party given for him after an internship—and a job well done—at a city office. These were students who had never experienced school success before and were now getting a substantial dose of it through City School. Other times, when I walked into a classroom and saw a teacher patiently reading aloud with a 17-year-old just learning how to read for the first time, I could tell that both that teacher and her student were experiencing tremendous accomplishment. I felt the pride in the voices of three girls as they described their trip to UCLA to perform a play that *they had written*. When I saw students who had never carried a book in their lives strolling the halls with beat-up, dog-eared copies of Luis Rodriguez's tale of Hispanic gang life in L.A., *Always Running*, I knew this school was reaching students who had not been helped by schools before. These were the beneficiaries of school innovation, of the type envisioned by charter school reformers.

However, as Paula's narrative highlights, and as the facts attest, Romaine had irredeemably taken advantage of the charter school funding legislation. Despite small success along the way, in the end, after only 16 months, this school became in the eyes of students, "just like everyone else." Innovation had initially encouraged the kinds of discussions I recorded during my first year. City School's innovations had broken the silences of those students used to skipping classes and being ignored when in attendance. But as the leadership went into hiding on the fourth floor, and as the school district suspicions began to grow, City School teachers and staff no longer felt free to innovate or to invite all viewpoints into discussion. With institutional changes came interactional changes, and City School did begin to feel more like typical public schools. Gradually, students began to clam up and to resist teachers they once had been happy to call by their first names, had confided in, and had called on for a place to sleep or to vouch for them in court. Student narratives became more contrived and artificial (see Chapter 5) and students' naming practices began to resume their illegitimate forms (see Chapter 6). Teachers found it increasingly difficult to reach students. There was no longer an institutional forum for innovation. Though comfortably residing on the fourth floor, the leader had gone underground. Innovation had been made to look very bad. Innovation had transformed into corruption. And City School, like many traditional and "alternative" public schools before it, had failed its students.

Innovation's Future

Although City School closed its doors and was marked by many as an educational disaster, its genesis must be remembered, for it represents a leap of faith in the power of a new sort of community to have a positive impact on the lives of young people. As Jerome Bruner (1996) has written, this belief in the power of social life, or "culture" to shape new ways of thinking is crucial to educational success. For Bruner, human development depends on "the continued growth of networks of mutual expectation" (p. 174), networks that are largely structured through language. The preceding chapters have shown that such networks of expectation—and presupposition—differ widely from group to group, even from situation to situation. This book has largely used language to trace the development and sustenance of such networks, and the potential for their interpenetration. As the stories of Pablo's death illustrate, upon the school's closure members of this community drew on narrative themes that had been developed through such "networks of communication" throughout the school's brief history. Analysis of narrative themes has served not simply as a descriptive analytic for community, but also as a way of seeing how such genres contribute to the positive development of a community—and the "continued growth of networks of communication."

Throughout the course of this book, I have also been careful to note that narratives are an important resource for *collaborative* identity construction. Schools are an inevitable context for this activity. All schools are potentially environments of constant intergenerational and interpeer group contact, but this contact is also subject to institutional and societal forces. Unfortunately, the institutionalized discourse norms of many school situations lead not to contact and interaction between groups, but to further isolation. For a short time, City School tried to counter this tendency, and became a liminal realm where teachers and students and their different forms of local knowledge and accompanying presuppositions were in dialogue. Through analysis of the discourse at City School, this book has shown emergent patterns in interaction and the ways that thematic concerns evolve and change within such a community. A close look at the discourse within City School has also been an attempt on my part, as a researcher, to respect the differing perspectives at play in such a community, while seeking to understand how an innovative school community, brought about by real reform, can foster real change.

The problems at City School and, more generally, the dilemmas involved in serving this population of students cannot be solved through a list of policy recommendations or the condemnation of certain irresponsible administrators, teachers, or students. Nor can they be resolved through ethnographic and discourse analysis. Closely examining the school's discourse and the potential within that discourse for change, however, can illuminate possibilities for future schools like City School and the ways in which contradictory viewpoints can constructively coexist. This ethnography of City School has analyzed discourse to understand how ways of seeing become encoded through language over the course of interaction, and over the history of an institution.

Since City School never survived, some might argue that the lesson it provided is simple. Don't do it that way. In the open market, failed companies rarely are emulated. Why would one try to emulate a failed school? Often charter school proponents argue this angle, suggesting charter schools' primary value is in the competitive incentive that they provide to other schools. But City School's contribution is much more than simply providing much heralded competition to the lackadaisical public school system. More significantly, it offered up an entirely alternative mind-set for understanding education and urban youth. City School was a failed attempt to educate this population. But it was an attempt. And the kind of dialogue it engendered, documented here, will, I hope, spark others to continue making these ventures.

In the next and final chapter, I build from the unfulfilled promise of City School, and the revelations of the interactions that occurred during its brief history, to salvage some hope for future reformers, and for current teachers who are working with students like those City School hoped to serve.

CHAPTER 10

On Teaching and Reform

Change where it counts most—in the daily interactions of teachers and students—is the hardest to achieve and the most important.

—David Tyack and Larry Cuban, 1995

An overarching theme of this book has been that adolescent identity and attitudes toward school are not only created by individuals, but are also facilitated, "coauthored," by society, policy makers, institution, peers, and teachers, through interaction. From this perspective, a layered understanding of the interactions in schools is essential for productive, positive, and humane change. Changes in institutions transform the kinds of interaction possible there. In turn, new interactional contexts can create opportunities for teachers and students to learn from each other. For me, as a researcher, the City School context provided a setting through which I could contemplate the human stories behind a radical reform effort. From listening to those voices, and hearing them together, I have come to some of my own conclusions—and recommendations for teaching and reform.

These recommendations do *not* come from a position that City School was a success to be emulated. It was not. Nor was it a complete failure. Like any life project over which energy, emotions, time, and concern are spent, City School was important, and the details of its existence should not be effaced from charter school history. The following recommendations come from the complex experience of having heard multiple voices within an idealistic, yet failed attempt at charter school reform and from my familiarity with the issues that were vital to the members of that community. Not one individual was ultimately happy with what happened at City School. But their voices provided insight into what students and teachers cared about and what might have made this charter school successful. Based on my research in this one innovative and ultimately unhappily dismantled school, this chapter provides two sets of recommendations—one for teachers of adolescents and the other for charter school reformers. In the sections below I suggest how teachers and charter school advocates can play a role in the coauthorship of students' stories in meaningful, important, and inspiring ways, and, in conclusion, how educational researchers can illuminate innovative reform efforts like charter schools by looking closely at the interaction within them.

INTERACTIONAL COAUTHORSHIP: RECOMMENDATIONS FOR TEACHERS WORKING WITH ADOLESCENTS

City School was a school for students who don't fit into school. This founding paradox was relevant in almost every interaction I had there. Students were always struggling with how to see themselves as students, when for so long they had seen themselves as not students, when so much of their identity was built upon being rejected from school settings. Likewise, teachers struggled to reconcile their role as traditional teachers and their desire to reach out to students who traditionally do not like teachers. How, as a teacher, does one work with students who don't fit in—who hate school? This was a question these teachers faced everyday. This is also a question that every teacher working with adolescents faces. After spending over a year listening to such students, I have some recommendations for teachers faced with similar challenges.

Listen to Narratives

Telling stories is the most universal means human beings have for conveying to others who we are, what we believe, how we feel, what we value, and how we see the world. I believe it is crucial to successful teaching to know this human side of our students. I know from my own teaching, however, that students often keep this human side hidden away. Therefore, it is important to create a space in classrooms in which narratives can be told. When I began this research I was amazed at how much more I was learning about the students as a researcher than I had learned about my own students as a teacher. I regretted not having had the insight as a teacher to ask students to tell me their stories and to spend the time necessary to listen and analyze them. Now, I recommend that everyone encourage storytelling, find those subjects that bring students' stories into interaction, and let those stories come and flourish.

Listen Dangerously

Few would argue that it is important to listen to the stories of our students. But why don't we? There are many practical reasons for a teacher not to listen. There is too much to cover, there are classroom management concerns, the bell suddenly rings, etc. But we also may be afraid of what we might hear, and the sorts of responsibilities that hearing would entail. As Susan Baur (1994) has written in *Confiding*, a book about her work as a clinical psychologist, "to adopt anyone's condition as my own is to agree to live among the vulnerabilities that shadow every life. It is to know that there is no way for anyone to sail home in safety" (p. 304). Hearing students tell about the kind of fear they live in, or the sorts of violence they have engaged in, and *empathizing* with them, really and dangerously entering their lives, makes it impossible to forget how stratified and unjust life is. In my case, I could no longer have an easy distance from gang violence or vandalism, writing it off as stupidity or foolishly irresponsible behavior. I became swallowed up in the human vulnerabilities that lead to gang membership or graffiti tagging, and I lived those vulnerabilities through narrative.

Listening can be dangerous, but it is necessary, for "dangerous listening is what it takes to change a mind" (Baur, 1994, p. 304). From my own listening it was not students' minds, but my mind that changed. Now, I would argue, to change one's own mind is the first responsibility of a listener—not to change the ethos developed through a story told, but to understand it, and to feel the vulnerabilities that give rise to a story.

Let Stories Build on Each Another

For some time, during storytelling discussions, you may need to sit back and listen, to let stories build on one another. As I found in my discussion group at City School, students told longer and better stories when they followed on the tail of a peer's story. During our first discussions I was discouraged that no extended narratives were told. It may take longer than one or two occasions to learn what students want to talk about. Eventually, though, students found the subjects that concerned them, through which they could most adeptly craft a narrative self.

During my last discussion group, with the successful students, I, to my own great disappointment at the time, learned exactly how *not* to encourage storytelling. As described in Chapter 5, I had appointed some students to act as interviewers in these groups. These efficient student interviewers were brilliant at closing down discussion, cutting stories short, and subverting collaborative storytelling. Like an efficient teacher soliciting student responses, these interviewers would turn from one storyteller to the next, abruptly ending stories and moving on. I witnessed the enactment of sound-bite mentality, as each student being interviewed strove to swiftly encapsulate an inspirational message.

Although I learned a lot about the institutional shaping of identity through these sessions, this was not dangerous listening. No minds were changed, and no empathy was displayed. Empathy was unnecessary because there were no vulnerabilities. And this is how classroom discourse often proceeds. These student interviewers were experienced in this form of safe, distance-maintaining classroom questioning and they reproduced it successfully. However, I am rec-ommending stepping away from this discourse pattern and letting student voices take over, letting stories tumble out one on top of another, so that, for a while, you can become a student of your own students' worlds.

Analyze Narratives

As recommended above, "dangerous listening" is a first responsibility for teach-ers listening to student stories and trying to learn about their worlds. This is the responsibility to be empathic, to identify, however uncomfortable or disconcert-ing that may be, with students' perspectives. Obviously, from my point of view, a teacher's responsibility is *not* fulfilled through censoring narratives or decid-ing what can and can't be told. Still, even as a researcher, after listening to a story about jail or some kind of violence, I felt I was shirking my responsibility as an adult role model if I let this sort of talk go on too long. I felt ethically unsure about my own role as I let talk perpetuate itself through laughing ac-counts of hitting a teacher or stabbing someone in the bathroom. I could feel a narrative-bound ethos developing before me, one that I felt I shouldn't condone.

While listening may be a first responsibility, it is certainly not the end of our commitment. After stories are told, and listened to, mulled over, contested, I found that looking back at and analyzing them was a more helpful way to understand—and take responsibility for—the ethos developing before me. By transcribing and looking back at stories, I was able to look *at*, not *through* language (Capps & Ochs, 1995) to understand exactly how language was con-structing the ethos that made me so uncomfortable. Language isn't just a means to convey information—though people often look "through" language to pull out the bare bones of a story. Language is also a way to craft a story in a way that says much more than "just the facts." Looking "at" language—the *way* a story is told—is a key to understanding the storyteller's world.

I also wanted to communicate this way of understanding to the students, helping them to analyze stories. I now urge teachers to have students partake in this analysis as well. Transcribe students' words and let them take a look. What do they see? Do they see the same patterns you do? I did often go over tran-scripts with students, but primarily in the preliminary stages of analysis. I would ask students about names, indecipherable words or phrases, and students would be entranced with their own words, so authoritatively transcribed on paper, and with their own voices coming through the headphones.

Were I to go back again, to have these students in my classroom as a teacher, I would encourage them to go through the next steps of analysis with me—to look for patterns, words, phrases that came up again and again, to use the computer to arrange text, to see their words as carefully crafted narratives. I don't have this opportunity, but I encourage teachers to try this with their students, to see how they can take responsibility for students' stories by encouraging students to look carefully at their own (inevitably fascinating) words.

Identify the Generic

By looking at language instead of through it, students, like researchers, literary critics, or critical media analysts (cf., Giroux, 1991, 1997) can begin to be aware of the generic in their own stories. And, after stories have been told freely and students have built stories on their peers' stories, making sense of them will be more fulfilling, because the material for analysis will be so rich. As students look across the kinds of stories they have told, they can see that they have common, shared expressions for talking about—for creating through talk—ways of experiencing the world. For example, they might discover the common use of "they" for the ambiguous, omnipotent other, or that they so glibly refer to the ritual of "getting hit up," or "getting jumped in," normalizing these practices.

Teachers can then ask students about the meaning of these patterns. What does it mean that everyone in the group talks about fights? What does it mean that "they" is always used to vaguely refer to their opposition? What does it mean that narrators always portray themselves as passive victims who "get" in fights, "get" kicked out, or "get" arrested? In contrast, what does it mean that so many students in one group mention a "turning point" in their stories, an "old self," a "then" and a much improved "now"? Why do they disparage the old friendships of the gang self, friendships that must have been very important to them at the time? How does an institution shape these narrative self-portraits?

By having students identify the generic themselves, teachers can encourage students to develop an awareness of how their identity is shaped not only by their own individual will and choices, but also by society, peers, and institutions, *through language*. Helping students to recognize how these forces all contribute to their narrative self-portrayals provides students with a stronger foundation for choosing their own future. Identifying the generic might be especially relevant for those students who feel they have had to cover up their ethnicity, accept labels like "ESL" or "troublemaker" or "good kid" (Harklau, 2000), or reinvent their linguistic or ethnic background to match society's expectations (Mendoza-Denton, 1996). Understanding the underpinnings of their own narratives—and how they adopt others' labels for themselves—can give students critical resources to understand context-imposed generic identities, and even to resist the impulse to adopt complacently and perpetuate the identities that institutional and societal forces discursively create for them.

Attain Local Knowledge

Though there has been voluminous research about going to students' houses and seeking "funds of knowledge" there (e.g., Gonzales et al., 1995) and even more talk among teachers about the value of such home visits, my research at City School shows that the students are themselves immense funds of knowledge. But again, getting at that knowledge requires care—dangerous listening, mulling over, and thoughtful analysis. It also involves asking questions and valuing students' perspectives enough to learn about what one doesn't understand. What does that writing signify? Why do you use that nickname? What does going to jail really mean for you? What do the phrases "getting hit up" or "getting jumped in" mean? Understanding local knowledge means recognizing it as that—knowledge. While local knowledge can be obvious and explicit (e.g., who the owner of a certain graffiti tag is), it is more often very subtle and takes careful and repeated listening and familiarity that can only come over time.

Attitudes about jail at City School are probably the best example of subtly distinct local knowledge and attitudes. As described in Chapter 8, the teacher Tim in one conversation tries to use his own experience of jail to teach the students a lesson about "what is proper." But tales of his jail experience do not resonate with the students. Instead, he ends up appearing even more distant and square than he would have had he not mentioned his jail time. In contrast, when the same teacher simply listens as a different group of students discuss jail, offering an empathic comment now and then, students' local attitudes about jail are revealed and the students, even without the teachers explicit prompting, end up revising their views. Comparing these interactions reminded me how important it is to seek students' knowledge before assuming ours will be meaningful to them. Since often we are ignorant of where and in what form that knowledge comes, sitting back, listening, and resisting the urge to provide our own views can sometimes be the best way of accessing that knowledge. In the best circumstances, when a teacher struggles to understand the words and worlds of the students, students and the teacher learn about themselves and each other.

Encourage Reframing

However, nothing a student says must be hallowed or left unexamined. These recommendations are concerned with listening, but also with participating in—coauthoring—student narratives, and encouraging students' peers to do the same. Reframing is probably the most explicit form of coauthorship. In discussion, listeners compare the way stories are told with their own views, and through reframing, more nuanced discussions of life evolve. In several instances at City School, reframing was the way generic attitudes were identified and critiqued by the students themselves. When Jerry talks about "getting cuffed, getting locked up," etc., he attempts to create a unified portrait of someone unfazed by the typical experiences of a gang member. His peer, Manny, however, resists Jerry's narrative self-portrayal. He reframes Jerry's statements as "what people say to look cool," with the implication that Jerry is *not* cool. Manny's recognition of the generic in Jerry's story, and his instant critique, forces everyone listening out of a complacent acceptance of the view Jerry initially offered.

This sort of reframing comes from a position of knowledge. Being able to create distance from a story and see how it is being crafted is a metalinguistic skill that requires insight into the power of language to mislead and deceive (Parmentier, 1994). Such meta-awareness is an important life skill. By encouraging students in this sort of reframing, a teacher can foster dialogue, encourage students to listen critically and to consider life's challenges from multiple perspectives. In this way, simple discussion, and simply encouraging student exchange, can lead to important development. Through reframing each other's narrative portrayals, they are learning to be aware of how the perceptions of others challenge or support their own views. They are learning how to learn.

Recognize Your Role as Coauthor of Students' Lives

Students are also learning how to *be*. As teachers, we need to recognize that talking is never simply just talk; it is a way of being and becoming participants in the world. There is a give-and-take between what we say and who we are. Encouraging the development of a narrative voice is also encouraging the development of an individual human being. This recognition is crucial, because it highlights the responsibility of coauthorship.

On the one hand, coauthorship can be a way of understanding how subtly, through language, "peer pressure" can work. As the stories in this book illustrate, the way in which stories are told is closely influenced by the way that other students respond to them. As stories unfold, tellers carefully attend to how their audience is receiving certain story details. As Federico, Ned, and Silvia told their stories of dropping out, for example, they all built on each other's similar portrayals of ever-threatening school contexts. Together they crafted a picture of school as a place where ominous rivals lurked around every corner. Together they told stories that made sense of their own disgust with and departure from regular school. This portrayal, worked out collaboratively through their stories, became a way of living, a way of seeing. Through their stories, students can create shared ways of viewing the world and understanding their actions within it. Telling these sorts of stories, comfortably, uncontested, may perpetuate certain identities. This is how language creates who we are, and how, subtly, through language, peers can coauthor who we become.

But these stories are not immutable. They are open to being examined, contested, and reframed. With this reframing, lives are reframed as well. Coauthorship can take the form of peer pressure, but it can also take the form of mentorship. And this is where the teacher's responsibility for narrative is so crucial. A teacher is always a coauthor of student voices. Standing mute over students will influence what they say as much as jumping in after each sentence to offer encouragement. In either case, the resulting story is shaped by the teacher's participation. The role, the responsibility of coauthorship is unavoidable, but the form of that participation is malleable. By carefully encouraging and even subtly shaping talk, dialogue, analysis, and the reframing of stories, teachers can facilitate students' intellectual development, students' capacity to make considered life choices, even change the course of a student's life stories, and, perhaps, a student's life.

As a teacher, your coauthorship will most likely occur in subtle ways. But at times, it can also be explicit and intentional. Whatever form it takes, playing a role of coauthor in these stories is an immense, ongoing, unavoidable responsibility.

INSTITUTIONAL COAUTHORSHIP: RECOMMENDATIONS FOR CHARTER SCHOOL REFORM

However seemingly independent a teacher is in his or her classroom, however unavoidable and immense that responsibility is, as I have argued in the preceding chapters, the kind of talk that happens there is always also shaped by the community norms at the school in general. Furthermore, the normative community that evolves is shaped in part by policy—like the charter school policy that enabled the genesis of City School. City School afforded a certain sort of discourse, and the school environment changed as the district began to become more influential, as administrative oversight and demands of media representation loomed. These differences made themselves apparent in discourse at City School. By looking *inside* City School at the kinds of stories told there and thinking about their relationship to charter school policy, this book makes a modest contribution to an understanding of charter school reform. It puts a face on, tells the stories of what might otherwise be abstract entities in policy argument.

Currently charter school policy has passionate, adamant defenders and concerned critics. Wells and her colleagues (1998a, 1998b) have conducted an extensive body of largely interview-based research on charter schools in California and, in their report *Beyond the Rhetoric of Charter School Reform: A Study of Ten California School Districts*, debunked many of the claims of charter school advocates. Charter schools are typically believed to be more autonomous, more efficient, needing less money to do more and achieve better outcomes. They are said to provide important choices for parents, to infuse the system with healthy competition, and to provide models of innovation for noncharter schools. Wells's data repeatedly suggest otherwise, and she has widely publicized her conclusions that charter schooling needs serious reassessment. Naturally, charter school advocates were incensed with Wells's report, and countered with evidence that disputed Wells's claims (Premack, 1998), reasserting the value of charter school innovation.

In the following recommendations to charter school reformers I do not mean to take a side in this debate. Instead, I intend to encourage reformers to reenvision their role, to see that while creating policy to affect learning, they are also creating environments where life stories are told, revised, contested, and retold. By putting a human face on policy, I also intend, more generally, to provide another angle to charter school debate, so that there is a place for untidy examples like City School to be influential beyond their status as sacrificial lambs (Little Hoover Commission, 1996). I encourage reformers to allow ordinary, particularizing, "human data" (Nussbaum, 1995), and "narrative truth" (Bruner, 1991) to take their role in shaping public thought, public life, and educational policy. And the way to do this, as outlined in the following recommendations, is to take control of the role of institutional coauthor by imagining as fully as possible the particularity of the human beings and the detailed community that reform policy affects.

Learn about the People in Charter Schools

Policy will always affect the lives of individuals, will always, inevitably, create contexts in which individual lives are authored. But unless reformers can imagine fully the lives of those individuals and see themselves as shaping the community through which those lives are narrated, the role of reformer as institutional coauthor will be arbitrary and only coincidentally effective. Reform policy has the potential to link the personal and the institutional, but without considering the individual lives that that policy affects, reformers will have little control over the job of coauthorship.

In *Poetic Justice*, Martha Nussbaum (1995) highlights the need for literary imagination and poetic vision in public life. Speaking specifically in terms of the law, she argues that judges need to familiarize themselves with the particularity, the nongeneralizability, of every case and every individual human being before them. Like a reader engrossed in a novel, deep involvement with the details of a case removes a judge from her own biases, immerses her in the world of those who will be judged. It is this involvement in lives—as opposed to a forced, impartial distance—that results in fair, unbiased judgment. Similarly, I am recommending that reformers immerse themselves in the inside stories of charter schools and recognize how the changes they initiate create communities in which certain kinds of stories, and certain kinds of listening, can occur.

I am suggesting reformers, in addition to asking the usual, typical questions like "How will the schools be held accountable?" also ask questions like, *"How, in this community, are stories told?"* At City School, students' stories were told openly and local knowledge was in free play as the project began. But as formerly idealistic teachers became frustrated, as the financial picture turned gloomy, and as pressure was increased for the school to display impossibly impressive tranformative power, the interactional environment became more rigid. Suddenly formerly valued student local knowledge was unimportant. Students and teachers alike were reduced to pawns in a policy game. As policy pressures changed, different kinds of stories—less illuminating kinds, I would argue—were told.

Attention to individuals and the unique environment of the reform community, its infinite variability, and the need for recognition of its unique complexity is a theme that crops up in the margins of many critical reform narratives these days. We need to stop thinking about students and teachers as "widgets" say the founders of a charterlike pilot school in Boston (Nathan & Myatt, 1998). "There is no such thing as 'school' reform," says a teacher-educator, "it's the people, the teachers and administrators who live and work in schools, who change or don't change" (p. 280). Similarly, policy specialists are calling for a new attention to the as yet unexamined particular. "The particular pathways to collaboration in new situations remain obscure," writes Fullan (2000, p. 582).

It is precisely the particular pathways of which reformers need to be mindful. Instead of remaining high above schools and speculating about how reform will make changes inside, reformers must open their imaginations to the multiple and diverse kinds of lives that are crossing paths in the corridors, classrooms, even the parking lots and storerooms at the schools they wish to change. As I found repeatedly in the conversations I overheard and recorded at City School, teachers can't affect students without understanding their motivations and the local knowledge that informs their stories. Likewise, a reform policy will be meaningless to a school if it doesn't take into detailed, human account the individuals within the community it seeks to affect.

Humans are generalizing and judging animals, quick to formulate points of view that gloss over the humanizing details. But this is not the way novelists think as they author the lives within a story. As a way of forcing themselves to make a link to concrete lives, I recommend that policy makers view themselves, like novelists, as coauthors in the construction of the narratives that will go on in the learning community they create. One way of entertaining this more detailed and concrete view of reform is to go inside schools. In *Possible Lives*, Mike Rose (1995) encourages policy makers to take themselves—literally—into the detail of lives in schools, for "the vantage point from which you consider schools—your location physically and experientially—will affect what you see and what you can imagine" (p. 430). Instead of portraying students in a school as "widgets," or potential earners of raised test scores, policy makers who see real contexts can afford a fuller vision and foster more detailed thinking about how students' potential might be realized to the fullest.

Be Familiar with Context-Specific Discourse Genres

Reformers can make the link between the particular stories of one school site and the policy that created it by learning about the discourse genres in reform communities. Communities are made up of individuals and their life stories, but these individual stories take genred forms that are similar among certain groups of friends or colleagues, and which change according to context. In the ideal charter school, a typical lunchroom story might be about the latest insight a teacher has had into how to motivate a certain student. In a stultifyingly dead educational community, a typical genre might be a lunchroom story about a "bad" student who is beyond rehabilitation. These genres don't emerge on their own. They are products of certain interactional environments. So in addition to asking themselves, "How are stories told?" reformers need to ask themselves, "What *kind* of story do I want to emerge in this school?"

In this book, I have described in detail some of the discourse genres that inhabited City School. Understanding those genres was my key to understanding how the institution shaped the community there. I would now argue that the more access one has to genred portrayals of events, the more complex a portrait one paints of the community. I also saw how changes in the viability of City School's charter status dramatically changed the genres of story told there. Based on this experience of discovery through narrative genre, I recommend that reformers also think about genre, that they consider carefully how they coauthor narratives and lives by creating policies and pressures that in turn shape viable narrative genres.

Encourage Access to Multiple Discourse Genres

To recap, reformers, in the process of policy proliferation, need to ask themselves, "How will stories be told in the context I am creating?" and "What *kind* of stories will be told there?" They also need to ask, "How will teachers and administrators be continually *aware* of the multiple kinds of stories told within the school community?" This is, generally speaking, an appeal to keep lines of communication and understanding open. At the beginning of City School's tenure, teachers, students, and administrators worked continually at keeping these lines of communication and understanding open. The evidence of this is their awareness of the multiple discourse genres there. The graffiti eradication program provides the most obvious evidence of opening up lines of communication by understanding differing student-, administrator-, and teacher-based discourse genres. Only in an environment that permitted telling stories of gang names and their meanings, and, in the same conversation, the airing of a teacher's concerns about vandalism, could enough information ever be shared to arrive at a policy to rid the school of graffiti.

Unfortunately, the lines of communication and understanding between teachers, students, and administration clearly broke down at the end of City School's tenure. As the interviews in Chapter 9 indicate, teachers and administrators each developed their own ways of talking about City School. Each drew on genred forms, but without awareness of other ways of presenting information.

Having access to these genres and encouraging dialogue between them is most important because it resists the normalization of certain conditions, genres, and ways of behaving. As soon as individuals see their way of describing things as a particular genre, that way of telling a story loses its solidity. For example, when they are viewed in combination with the "dropping in" stories, "dropping out" stories appear as only one of many particular possible viewpoints. Or, when LaTasha reveals her knowledge of the generic view of jail and explains how her experience conflicts with that generic view, she makes a good case for staying out of jail. This is a case she could only make, however, by voicing the opposing generic view. Though these examples are specific to City School, every school community has multiple, generic, narrative viewpoints. Keeping them in dialogue is the challenge. Therefore, reformers need to think about how to create communities where all players are aware of multiple viewpoints within the school. When genred views are in dialogue, continually reframed and rethought, in the process lives will be lived in a considered, constructive way, and learning will take place.

Recognize that Institutions Shape those Stories that Shape Who we Become

In summary, institutions shape the stories we tell, they shape the general kinds (or genres) of stories we tell, and they shape the awareness we have of other sorts of stories that are told around us. In all these ways institutional reform is a coauthor of the stories within a community, and policy makers have some measure of control over how each individual life will be narrated and how that narrative will be understood, reframed, or elaborated within an innovative school. What kind of stories will be told and who will know about them are factors that can be considered when assessing any reform initiative. As people implement "high-stakes testing," for example, it might help to ask and to investigate the kinds of questions I have posed here. What kinds of stories does high-stakes testing engender in schools? What voices will come to the fore? What voices will be silenced? Will narrative genres be in dialogue? Considering these sorts of questions and the role individuals play in their answers is a responsibility of policy makers. By creating pressures that lead to certain answers to these questions, reformers are coauthoring the lives of every individual within the reformed community.

PUTTING IT ALL TOGETHER: STUDENTS,
TEACHERS, REFORMERS, RESEARCHERS

What makes kids drop out of school? What can prevent it? These questions are perennially relevant to students, teachers, reformers, and researchers alike. This book has tried to emphasize that the fate of students like those at City School is a result of the complex interplay of human beings at all these levels of interaction and bureaucracy. As the narratives within this book illustrate, dropping out is usually the result of a long series of encounters and experiences, and the building up of attitudes, views—an identity—that is compatible with leaving school. The narrative creation of such an identity is coauthored by other students, by an institution, and, even, in this case, by me, the researcher.

I have done a lot of close analysis in the foregoing chapters, and a lot of zooming out and recommending in this chapter. The point to this zooming in and out is to suggest that the system reproduces itself on a micro-level in conversations among students and official others (including researchers like me) and that these reconstructions have ramifications. Most importantly, seeing the micro instantiation of larger social phenomena suggests their reversibility. If the disengaged dropout identity is conversationally created and recreated, then perhaps it can be undone conversationally as well. Disengagement is a potentially reversible process. But, it cannot be accomplished without attention to the particularity of individual lives, the way those lives are narrated, and the role that peers, teachers, and institutions take in the coauthorship of those lives. This is why, zooming back out, in making recommendations to teachers and reformers, I have continually emphasized the tremendous responsibility of coauthorship.

City School, because it was so novel, because its curriculum was so flexible, and perhaps, because it failed, provided an ideal setting to document this intertwining of institutional and interactional coauthorship. It illuminated how peer debunkers contested narratively conveyed identity norms, how teachers were effective when they gained access to local knowledge and used it to understand kids, and how institutional changes dramatically changed the legitimacy teachers granted to this local knowledge.

Ultimately, City School also provided an example of a failed charter school, the failure of which left students let down once again by the system supposedly created to provide them with opportunity. As the teacher Jaime pointed out, at the very least, City School provided an option for kids that have so few options. But after 15 months in operation, it did not even provide that. I hope this book has salvaged City School as a worthwhile though failed site of innovation, and at the very least, as a blip in time of energy, excitement, grand emotions, and disappointment, a tangle of the highs and lows that should infuse every educational effort. Whether intentionally or not, City School and the charter school policy that created it briefly accomplished what Tyack and Cuban

(1995) have called the most difficult and most important kind of change, a change in the interactions between teachers and students. I hope the memory of City School survives as, if not an inspiration, a spur in the side of teachers, reformers, and researchers, reminding them of the unavoidable human side of educational innovation.

References

Alexander, L. (1993, June). School choice in the year 2000. *Phi Delta Kappan,* 762–766.

Alvarez, A. (1993). *An ethnographic study of student resistance in a predominantly Chicano public school.* Unpublished dissertation, University of California, Los Angeles.

Amsler, A., & Mulholland, L. (1992). *Charter schools. Policy briefs number nineteen.* San Francisco: Far West Regional Laboratory.

Atwood, M. (1997, March 13). Interview with Michael Silverblatt on KCRW's radio show *Bookworm,* Los Angeles, CA.

Bakhtin, M. M. (1986). *Speech genres and other essays.* (V. McGee, Trans., M. Holquist, & C. Emerson, Eds.). Austin: University of Texas Press.

Basso, K. (1984). Stalking with stories: Names, places, and moral narratives among the Western Apache. In E. Bruner (Ed.), *Text, play, and story* (pp. 19–55). Washington, DC: American Ethnological Society.

Baur, S. (1994). *Confiding: A psychotherapist and her patients search for stories to live by.* New York: HarperCollins.

Bierlein, L. A., & Mulholland, L. A. (1994). The promise of charter schools. *Educational Leadership, 52*(1), 34–40.

Bourdieu, P. (1985). The market of symbolic goods. *Poetics 14*(1–2), 13–44.

Briggs, C. L. (1986). *Learning how to ask: A sociolinguistic appraisal of the role of the interview in social science research.* Cambridge, England: Cambridge University Press.

Bruner, J. (1986). *Actual minds, possible worlds.* Cambridge, MA: Harvard University Press.

Bruner, J. (1990). *Acts of meaning.* Cambridge, MA: Harvard University Press.

Bruner, J. (1991). The narrative construction of reality. *Critical Inquiry, 18,* 1–21.

Bruner, J. (1996). *The culture of education.* Cambridge, MA: Harvard University Press.

Capps, L., & Ochs, E. (1995). *Constructing panic: The discourse of agoraphopia.* Cambridge, MA: Harvard University Press.

Celce-Murcia, M., & Larsen-Freeman, D. (1983). *The grammar book.* Boston: Heinle & Heinle.

Chalker, S., & Weiner, E. (1994). *The Oxford dictionary of English grammar.* Oxford and New York: Oxford University Press.

Charter schools: Pain and Gain. (1994, December 12). *The Los Angeles Times,* p. A8.

Cohn, C. (1987). Sex and death in the rational world of defense intellectuals. *Signs, 12*(4), 687–718.

Conquergood, D. (1992). *On reppin' and rhetoric: Gang representations.* Paper presented at the Philosophy and Rhetoric of Inquiry Seminar, University of Iowa.

Conquergood, D. (1996). Homeboys and hoods: Gang communication in cultural space. In Lawrence Frey (Ed.), *Group communication in context* (pp. 23–55). Hillsdale, NJ: Erlbaum.

Cooper, M. (1994, July). Reality check. *Spin,* 52–56.

Davidson, A. L. (1996). *Making and molding identity in schools: Student narratives on race, gender, and academic engagement.* Albany: SUNY Press.

Davis, M. (1992). *City of quartz: Excavating the future in Los Angeles.* New York: Random House.

DeCapua, A., & Huber, L. (1993). Strategies in the discourse of advice. *Journal of Pragmatics, 20,* 103–125.

DeCapua, A., & Huber, L. (1995). "If I were you . . . ": Advice in American English. *Multilingua 14*(2), 117–132.

Devine, J. (1996). *Maximum security: The culture of violence in inner-city schools.* Chicago: University of Chicago Press.

Diamond, L. (1994). A progress report on California's charter schools. *Educational Leadership, 52*(1), 1–41.

Donnellan, K. (1966). Reference and definite descriptions. In A. P. Martinich (Ed.), *The philosophy of language* (pp. 235–247). New York: Oxford University Press.

Duranti, A. (1986). The audience as co-author: An introduction. *Text, 6*(3), 239–247.

Duranti, A. (1994). *From grammar to politics: Linguistic anthropology in a Western Samoan village.* Berkeley: University of California Press.

Duranti, A., & Goodwin, C. (Eds.). (1992). *Rethinking context.* Cambridge and New York: Cambridge University Press.

Eckert, P. (1989). *Jocks and burnouts: Social categories and identity in high school.* New York: Teachers College Press.

Fine, M. (1985). Dropping out of high school: An inside look. *Social Policy 16*(2), 43–50.

Fine, M. (1986). Why urban adolescents drop into and out of public high school. *Teachers College Record, 87*(3), 393–409.

Fine, M. (1991). *Framing Dropouts: Notes on the politics of an urban high school.* Albany: SUNY Press.

Fine, M. (1994). Chart[er]ing urban school reform. In R. Rossi (Ed.), *Schools and students at risk* (pp. 163–181). New York: Teachers College Press.

Fullan, M. (2000). The three stories of education reform. *Phi Delta Kappan, 81,* 581–584.

Gates, H. L., Jr. (1997, February 24 & March 3). Marketing Justice, *The New Yorker,* 11–12.

Gee, J. P. (1992). *The social mind.* New York: Bergin & Garvey.

Giroux, H. (1991). *Border crossings: Cultural workers and the politics of education.* London: Routledge.

Giroux, H. (Ed.). (1997). *Counternarratives: Cultural studies and critical pedagogies in postmodern space.* London: Routledge.

Goffman, E. (1959). *The presentation of self in everyday life.* New York: Doubleday.

Gonzalez, N., Moll, L., Tenery, M. F., Rivera, A., Rendon, P., Gonzales, R., & Amanti, C. (1995). Funds of knowledge for teaching in Latino households. *Urban Education, 29*(4), 443–470.

Good, T. L., & Braden, J. S. (2000a). Charter schools: Another reform failure or a worthwhile investment? *Phi Delta Kappan, 81*(10), 745–750.

Good, T. L., & Braden, J. S. (2000b). *The great school debate: Choice, vouchers, and charters*. Mahwah, NJ: Erlbaum.

Goodwin, C. (1979). The interactive construction of a sentence in natural conversation. In G. Psathas (Ed.), *Everyday language: Studies in ethnomethodology* (pp. 97–121). New York: Irvington Publishers.

Goodwin, M. H. (1982). Instigating: Storytelling as social process. *American Ethnologist, 9,* 799–819.

Goodwin, M. H. (1990). *He said she said*. Indianapolis: Indiana University Press.

Greenfield, P. (1980). Toward an operational and logical analysis of intentionality: The use of discourse in early child language. In D. R. Olsen (Ed.), *The social foundations of language and thought*. New York: Norton.

Gutierrez, K. (1995). Unpackaging academic discourse. *Discourse Processes, 19*(1), 21–37.

Gutierrez, K., Larson, J., & Rymes, B. (1995). Cultural tensions in the scripted classroom: The value of the subjugated perspective. *Urban Education, 29*(4), 410–442.

Gutierrez, K., Rymes, B., & Larson, J. (1995). Script, counterscript, and underlife in the classroom: James Brown vs. Brown v. Board of Education. *Harvard Educational Review, 65*(3), 445–471.

Hanks, W. (1987). Discourse genres in a theory of practice. *American Ethnologist, 14*(4), 668–692.

Hanks, W. (1990). *Referential practice: Language and lived space among the Maya*. Chicago: University of Chicago Press.

Hanks, W. (1992). The indexical ground of deictic reference. In S. Duranti & C. Goodwin (Eds.), *Rethinking context: Language as an interactive phenomenon* (pp. 43–76). Cambridge, England: Cambridge University Press.

Hanks, W. (1996). *Language and communicative practices*. Boulder, CO: Westview.

Harklau, L. (2000). From the "good kids" to the "worst": Representations of English language learners across educational settings. *TESOL Quarterly 34*(1), 35–67.

Harris, M. G. (1988). *Cholas: Latino girls and gangs*. New York: AMS Press.

Heath, S. B. (1982). What no bedtime story means: Narrative skills at home and in school. *Language in Society, 11*(2), 49–76.

Heath, S. B., & McLaughlin, M. W. (Eds.). (1993). *Identity and inner-city youth: Beyond ethnicity and gender*. New York: Teachers College Press.

Heritage, J., & Sefi, S. (1992). Dilemmas of advice: Aspects of the delivery and reception of advice in interactions between health visitors and first-time mothers. In P. Drew & J. Heritage (Eds.), *Talk at work: Interaction in institutional settings* (pp. 359–417). Cambridge and New York: Cambridge University Press.

Hill, P. (1994). Reinventing urban public education. *Phi Delta Kappan, 75*(5), 396–401.

Jankowski, M. S. (1991). *Islands in the street: Gangs and American urban society*. Berkeley: University of California Press.

Jefferson, G. (1974). Error correction as an interactional resource. *Language in Society, 2,* 181–199.

Jefferson, G. (1978). Sequential aspects of storytelling in conversation. In Schenkein, J.

(Ed.), *Studies in the organization of conversational interaction* (pp. 219–248). New York: Academic Press.

Kelly, D. M. (1993). *Last chance high: How girls and boys drop in and out of alternative schools*. New Haven: Yale University Press.

Klein, H. E. M. (1999). Narrative. *Journal of Linguistic Anthropology, 9*(1–2), 167–169.

Kohl, H. (1967). *36 children*. New York: Plume.

Kolderie, T. (1994). Charters: An invitation to change. *Educational Leadership, 52*(1), 36–40.

Kozol, J. (1991). *Savage inequalities: Children in America's schools*. New York: Harper-Collins.

Kripke, S. (1977). Speaker reference and semantic reference. In A. P. Martinich (Ed.), *The philosophy of language* (pp. 248–266). New York: Oxford University Press.

Kroskrity, P. V. (1999). Identity. *Journal of Linguistic Anthropology, 9*(1–2), 111–114.

Labov, B., & Waletzky, J. (1967). Narrative analysis: Oral versions of personal experience. In J. Helm (Ed.), *Essays on verbal and visual arts* (pp. 12–44). Seattle: University of Washington Press.

Labov, W. (1972). *Language in the inner city: Studies in the Black Vernacular*. Philadelphia: University of Pennsylvania Press.

Larson, J. (1995). Talk matters: The role of pivot in the distribution of literacy knowledge among novice writers. *Linguistics and Education, 7*(4), 277–302.

Lauter, D. (1992, May 1). Political leaders' analysis of crisis varies. *The Los Angeles Times*, p. A4.

Little Hoover Commission (1996). *The charter school movement: Education reform school by school*. Report available online at *http://www.lhc.ca.gov/lhcdir/138rp.html*

MacIntyre, A. (1984). *After virtue*. Notre Dame: University of Notre Dame Press.

Mandler, J. (1984). *Stories, scripts and scenes*. Hillsdale, NJ: Earlbaum.

Manno, B. V., Finn, C. E., & Vanourek, G. (2000). Beyond the schoolhouse door: How charter schools are transforming U.S. public education. *Phi Delta Kappan, 81*(10), 736–744.

Martinez, R. (1993). The other side: Notes from the new L.A., Mexico City, and beyond. New York: Vintage.

Mehan, H. (1985). The structure of classroom discourse. In T. A. van Dijk (Ed.), *Handbook of discourse analysis, Vol. 3* (pp. 119–131). New York: Academic Press.

Mehan, H. (1993). Beneath the skin and between the ears: A case study in the politics of representation. In S. Chaiklin & J. Lave (Eds.), *Understanding practice: Perspectives on activity and context*. Cambridge, England: Cambridge University Press.

Meier, D. (1995). *The power of their ideas*. Boston: Beacon.

Meier, D. (1999). Needed: Thoughtful research for thoughtful schools. In E. C. Lagemann & L. S. Shulman (Eds.), *Issues in education research*. San Francisco: Jossey-Bass.

Mendoza-Denton, N. (1996). "Muy macha": Gender and ideology in gang-girls' discourse about makeup. *Ethnos, 61*(1–2), 47–63.

Moll, L., & Diaz, S. (1987). Change as the goal of educational research. *Anthropology and Education Quarterly, 18*(4), 300–311.

Monti, D. J. (1994). *Wannabe: Gangs in suburbs and schools.* Cambridge, MA: Blackwell.

Nathan, L., & Myatt, L. (1998, December). A journey toward autonomy. *Phi Delta Kappan,* 278–287.

NCREL Report (1997). *New leaders for tomorrow's schools, Fall 1997: Charter schools and homogenous student populations.* Report available online at *http://www.ncrel. org/cscd/pubs/lead42/42homog.htm*

Nussbaum, M. (1995). *Poetic justice: The literary imagination and public life.* Boston: Beacon.

Oakes, J. (1985). *Keeping track: How schools structure inequality.* New Haven: Yale University Press.

Ochs, E. (1988). *Culture and language development: Language acquisition and language socialization in a Samoan village.* Cambridge and New York: Cambridge University Press.

Ochs, E. (1993). Stories that Step into the Future. In D. Biber & E. Finegan (Eds.), *Sociolinguistic perspectives on register.* Oxford, England: Oxford University Press.

Ochs, E. (1995). Narrative. In T. A. van Dijk (Ed.), *Discourse: A multidisciplinary introduction.* London: Sage.

Ochs, E. & Capps, L. (1996). Narrating the self. In W. Durham, E. V. Daniels, & B. Schieffelin (Eds.), *Annual review of anthropology* (pp. 19–43). Palo Alto: Annual Reviews, Inc.

Ochs, E., Smith, R., & Taylor, C. (1989). Detective stories at dinnertime: Problem-solving through co-narration. *Cultural Dynamics, 2*(2), 238–257.

O'Connor, P. E. (1994). "You could feel it through the skin": Agency and positioning in prisoners' stabbing stories. *Text, 14*(1), 45–75.

Parmentier, R. J. (1994). *Signs in society: Studies in semiotic anthropology.* Bloomington: Indiana University Press.

Peirce, C. S. (1931–1935). *Collected papers of Charles Sanders Peirce* (Vols.1–6, C. Hartshorne, & P. Weiss, Eds.). Cambridge, MA: Harvard University Press.

Phelan, P., Davidson, A. L., & Yu, H. C. (1998). *Adolescents' Worlds: Negotiating Families, Peers, and Schools.* New York: Teachers College Press.

Philips, S. (1983). *The invisible culture: Communication in classroom and community on the Warm Springs Indian Reservation.* New York: Longman.

Pomerantz, A. (1984). Agreeing and disagreeing with assessments: Some features of preferred/dispreferred turn shapes. In J. M. Atkinson & J. Heritage (Eds.), *Structures of social action: Studies in conversation analysis* (pp. 57–101). Cambridge and New York: Cambridge University Press.

Pratt, M. L. (1992). *Imperial eyes: Travel writing and transculturation.* London and New York: Routledge.

Premack, E. (1998). *UCLA's Charter School "Study."* Online publication of the Charter Schools Development Center at the Institute for Education Reform, California State University, Sacramento, CA. Available online at *http://www.csus.edu/ier/charter/ news12698.html*

Putnam, H. (1988). *Representation and reality.* Cambridge: MIT Press.

Pyle, A. (1995, October 1). Schools quietly severing ties to L.A. district. *The Los Angeles Times,* p. *B1.*

Rampton, B. (1995). *Crossing: Language and ethnicity among urban adolescents*. London and New York: Longman.

Rampton, B. (1996). Youth, race, and resistance: A sociolinguistic perspective. *Linguistics and Education, 8,* 159–173.

Resnick, L. B. (1990). Literacy in school and out. *Deadalus, 119*(2), 169–185.

Rogoff, B. (1990). *Apprenticeship in thinking: Children's guided participation in culture.* New York: Oxford University Press.

Rosaldo, R. (1989). *Culture and truth: The remaking of social analysis.* Boston: Beacon.

Rose, M. (1995). *Possible lives.* Boston and New York: Houghton Mifflin.

Rossi, R. J. (Ed.). (1994). *Schools and students at risk.* New York: Teachers College Press.

Rymes, B. (1996). Naming as social practice: The case of Little Creeper from Diamond Street. *Language in Society, 25,* 237–260.

Rymes, B. (1999). Names. *Journal of Linguistic Anthropology, 9*(1–2), 163–166.

Sacks, H. (1974). An analysis of the course of a joke's telling in conversation. In R. Bauman & J. Sherzer (Eds.), *Explorations in the ethnography of speaking* (pp. 337–353). Cambridge, England: Cambridge University Press.

Sacks, H. (1984). On doing "being ordinary." In J. M. Atkinson & J. Heritage (Eds.), *Structures of social action: Studies in conversation analysis* (pp. 413–429). Cambridge, England: Cambridge University Press.

Sacks, H., Schegloff, E. A., & Jefferson, G. (1974). A simplest systematics for the organization of turn-taking for conversation. *Language, 50,* 696–735.

Sautter, R. C. (1993). *Charter schools: A new breed of public schools. Policy briefs, report 2.* Oak Brook, IL: North Central Regional Educational Laboratory.

Schegloff, E. A. (1972). Notes on conversational practice: formulating place. In D. Sudnow (Ed.), *Studies in social interaction* (pp. 74–119). New York: Free Press.

Schieffelin, B. B. (1990). *The give and take of everyday life: Language socialization of Kaluli children.* Cambridge and New York: Cambridge University Press.

Schiffrin, D. (1987). *Discourse markers.* Cambridge, England: Cambridge University Press.

Schiffrin, D. (1996). Narrative as self-portrait: Sociolinguistic constructions of identity. *Language in Society, 25*(2), 167–203.

Scholes, R. (1985). *Textual power.* New Haven and London: Yale University Press.

Searle, J. R. (1958). Proper names. *Mind, 67,* 166–173.

Searle, J. R. (1970). *Speech acts: An essay in the philosophy of language.* Cambridge, England: Cambridge University Press.

Shankar, A. (1988). Restructuring our schools. *Peabody Journal of Education, 65*(3), 88–100.

Shuman, A. (1986). *Storytelling rights: The uses of oral and written texts by urban adolescents.* Cambridge and New York: Cambridge University Press.

Silverstein, M. (1987). Cognitive implications of the referential hierarchy. In M. Hickman (Ed.), *Social and functional approaches to language and thought* (pp. 125–164). New York: Academic Press.

Silverstein, M. (1992). The uses and utility of linguistic ideology. *Pragmatics, 2*(3), 311–324.

Silverstein, M. (1993). Metapragmatic discourse and metapragmatic function. In J. Lucy (Ed.), *Reported speech and metapragmatics*. Cambridge, England: Cambridge University Press.

Silverstein, M., & Urban, G. (1996). The natural history of discourse. In M. Silverstein & G. Urban (Eds.), *Natural histories of discourse* (pp. 1–17). Chicago and London: University of Chicago Press.

Sizer, T. (1984). *Horace's compromise*. Boston: Houghton Mifflin.

Smith, B. H. (1981). Narrative versions, narrative theories. In W. J. T. Mitchell (Ed.), *On narrative* (pp. 209–232). Chicago: University of Chicago Press.

Stein, N., & Glenn, C. G. (1979). An analysis of story comprehension in elementary school children. In R. O. Freedle (Ed.), *New directions in discourse processing*. Norwood, NJ: Ablex.

Stein, N., & Policastro, M. (1984). The Concept of a Story: A Comparison of Children's and Teachers' Viewpoints, in H. Mandler, N. Stein, & T. Trabasso (Eds.), *Learning and comprehension of text* (pp. 113–155). Hillsdale, NJ: Earlbaum.

Strawson, P. F. (1955). On referring. In A. P. Martinich (Ed.), *The philosophy of language* (pp. 219–234). New York: Oxford University Press.

Streeck, J. (1993). Gesture as communication I: Its coordination with gaze and speech. *Communication Monographs, 60*, 278–299.

Talty, S. (1995, March). The power of King love. *Spin*, 61–66, 108–109.

Tannen, D. (1989). *Talking voices: Repetition, dialogue, and imagery in conversational discourse*. Cambridge and New York: Cambridge University Press.

Taylor, C. (1989). *Sources of the self*. Cambridge: Harvard University Press.

Trueba, H. T., Spindler, G., & Spindler, L. (1989). *What do anthropologists have to say about dropouts?* New York: The Falmer Press.

Tyack, D., & Cuban, L. (1995). *Tinkering toward utopia*. Cambridge: Harvard University Press.

Vigil, J. D. (1988). *Barrio gangs: Street life and identity in Southern California*. Austin: University of Texas Press.

Vigil, J. D. (1993). The established gang. In S. Cummings & D. J. Monti (Eds.), *Gangs: The origin and impact of contemporary youth gangs in the United States* (pp. 95–112). Albany: SUNY Press.

Vigil, J. D., & Long, J. M. (1990). Emic and etic perspectives on gang culture: The Chicano case. In C. Ronald Huff (Ed.), *Gangs in America* (pp. 55–68). Newbury Park, CA: Sage.

Wells, A. S. et al. (1998a). *Beyond the rhetoric of charter school reform: A study of ten California school districts*. Available online at *http://www.gseis.ucla.edu/docs/charter.pdf*

Wells, A. S. et al. (1998b). Charter school reform in California: Does it meet expectations? *Phi Delta Kappan, 80*(3), 305–312.

White, H. (1981). The value of narrativity in the prepresentation of reality. In W. J. T. Mitchell (Ed.), *On narrative* (pp. 1–23). Chicago: University of Chicago Press.

Whorf, B. L. (1937). *Language, thought and reality: Selected writings of Benjamin Lee Whorf*. J. Carrol (Ed.), Cambridge: MIT Press.

Willis, P. (1977). *Learning to labor: How working class kids get working class jobs*. New York: Columbia University Press.

Wittgenstein, L. (1953 [1945, 1946–1949]). *Philosophical investigations* (G. E. M. Ans-
combe, Trans.). New York: Macmillan.

Wolfson, N. (1976). Speech events and natural speech: Some implications for sociolinguistic methodology. *Language in Society, 5,* 189–209.

Wortham, S. E. F. (1994). *Acting out participant examples in the classroom.* Amsterdam
and Philadelphia: John Benjamin.

Wright, R. (1937). *Black boy.* New York: Harper & Row.

Zollers, N. J., & Ramanathan, A. K. (1998, December). For-profit charter schools and
students with disabilities: The sordid side of the business of schooling. *Phi Delta
Kappan,* 297–304.

Index

Abel (student), 79–80, 81, 82–84, 86, 115

Adverbials, in narratives, 85–87

Agency, mitigating, 51–53

Aldo (student), 148–151

Alexander, Lamar, 6, 7–8

Alvarez, A., 6

Always Running (Rodriguez), 159

Amanti, C., 166–167

Amsler, A., 6, 7

Atwood, Margaret, 23

Bakhtin, M. M., 23, 40, 58

Baur, Susan, 163–164

Belmont Tunnel, 1–2, 5

Best dog, as reference term, 125, 126

Beyond the Rhetoric of Charter School Reform (Wells et al.), 169–170

Bierlein, L. A., 6

Bourdieu, P., 106, 111

Braden, J. S., 8–11

Briggs, Charles, 16

Bro, as reference term, 113, 118, 127

Bruner, Jerome, 24, 90, 132, 159, 170

California, charter schools in, 7. *See also* City School; Los Angeles Unified School District

Capps, L., 23, 29, 31, 33, 46, 85, 89, 165

Celce-Murcia, M., 47–49, 52, 85, 118

Central City West
  described, 1–2
  dropout rate in, 5
  new schools in, 4

Chalker, S., 43

Charter schools, 6–12, 158
  City School as, 7, 8–12, 158, 174–175
  institutional coauthorship of reform, 169–173
  nature of, 7–8
  number of grants, 11–12
  policy-level paradoxes of, 9–11
  as real innovation, 7–8
  role of ethnicity in, 26–27

Chris (student), 148

Chucho, as reference term, 124–125, 129

City School, 2–6
  Associates Program, 18, 149, 151, 152, 155–156, 158
  charter status of, 7, 8–12, 158, 174–175
  child care center, 5
  closure of, 12, 18–19, 114, 148–152, 158–161
  as contact zone, 128–130
  described, 2–3
  fieldwork process and, 12–19, 25–26
  as fiscal disaster, 9–10, 116
  formation of, 3–5, 9
  funding of, 4, 6–7
  impact on charter school reform, 11–12, 162–175
  innovative scheduling and, 20–21
  local categories of identity and, 12–13
  paradoxes of innovation and, 9–11
  as real innovation, 8–9
  redesign of curriculum, 18
  relocation of, 18, 148

City School (*Continued*)
  student population of, 3, 4, 5–6, 9, 10–
    11, 12–13, 17. *See also names of*
    specific students
  teachers at. *See* Teachers at City
    School
Clinton, Bill, 7–8
Coauthorship, 13–14, 63–67, 162–173
  institutional, 169–173
  interactional, 163–169
Cohn, C., 89
Confiding (Baur), 163–164
Conquergood, D., 96–97, 105–106,
  109
Contact zone
  conversations between students,
    113–127
  defined, 113
  school as, 128–130
Continuation schools, 20–21
Cooper, M., 6
Cuban, Larry, 162, 174–175

Danny (Sider; student), ix, 95, 98
Davidson, A. L., 6, 15
Davis, M., 2, 108
Deaths of students
  Jesse, ix, 21–22, 154–155
  Pablo, 151–152, 154–160
Debunking
  of dropping in themes, 82, 87–89
  of dropping out themes, 62, 63–70
DeCapua, A., 131
Dennis, Paul (psychologist), 4
Denny, Reginald, 109
Devine, John, 4, 8
Diamond, L., 6
Diamond Street gang, 1, 5, 93–110
Diaz, S., 146
Discourse analysis, 13–14
Discourse genres, 22–23. *See also* Drop-
  ping in perspective; Dropping out
  perspective
  access to multiple, 172–173
  context-specific, 172

genrefication of moral discourse,
  145–147
  official discourse, 58
Disengagement process, 71–72
Dominant linguistic ideology, 106–107
Donnellan, K., 114
Drew (student), 50
Dropout rate, 5
Dropping in perspective, 73–91. *See also*
  Success stories
  of Abel (student), 79–80, 81, 82–84,
    86, 115
  confrontation with dropping out per-
    spective, 113–130
  conversational emergence of, 76–77
  debunking, 82, 87–89
  dropping out stories versus, 74
  external form of, 77–81
  of Gracie (student), 78–82, 84, 85–86,
    113, 115, 128, 135–136
  grammatical resources of, 81–87
  institutional emergence of, 75–76
  "It Isn't Too Late for Me" (Von), 80–
    81, 83, 84, 87, 88
  "I Was a Gang Member" (Gracie), 78–
    82, 84, 85–86
  life choices in, 89–91
  of Mario (student), 113–130
  marking a turning point, 85–86
  nature of, viii
  parts of, 78–81
  portraying school as a companion,
    86–87
  of Von (student), 80–81, 83, 84, 87,
    88, 115
  "The Wrong Path" (Abel), 79–80, 81,
    82–84, 86
Dropping out perspective, 20–72
  confrontation with dropping in perspec-
    tive, 113–130, 157
  context for talk and, 20–22
  debunking, 62, 63–70
  disengagement process and, 71–72
  dropping in stories versus, 74
  emergence of, 27–28

ethnicity and, 26–27
"Everybody Rushed Me" (Federico),
    38, 52–53, 61–62, 63–65, 93
external form of, 28–36
of Federico (student), ix, 28, 31–32,
    36–38, 45–48, 49–50, 52–55, 61–
    65, 68, 92–112, 114
of Fran (student), 28, 35–36, 37, 43,
    44, 46–51, 55
grammatical resources of, 40–53
identity in, 23–25
"I Got Fed Up" (Fran), 35–36
"I Got Mad" (Rosa), 34–35, 66–67
"I Just Got Bored" (Ned), 33–34, 35
indexical forms of, 53–56
"I Simply Asked Her to Watch It"
    (Rosa), 65–67
of Jerry (student), 28, 44–45, 55, 68–
    70, 139, 167–168
of Jorge (student), 116–130, 157
"Knife Story" (Ned), 32–33, 59–61
"looking good" and, 25–26
of Luis (student), 116–130, 157
of Manny (student), 28, 55, 57, 63, 65,
    68–70, 139, 167–168
"Marijuana Story" (Jerry), 55, 68–70
nature of, viii, 22–23
of Ned (student), ix, 20, 28, 32–34, 35,
    37, 40, 44–49, 53, 54, 59–61
parts of, 28–29, 31–35
reframing of, viii, 57–72
reinforcing dropping out themes in,
    59–62
of Rosa (student), ix, 28, 34–35, 37,
    43–47, 47, 49, 52, 65–67
of Sylvia (student), 28, 65–67
themes brought up through, 36–38
of Wendy (student), 28
Duranti, A., 14
Duval (student), 95–96, 100–101

Eckert, P., 15
Eighteenth Street gang, 98–101, 103
Elizabeth (student), 21–22
Empathy, 163–164

Ése, as reference term, 113, 119, 120,
    121, 123
Essentialization, student resistance to,
    67–70
Ethnicity, narrative and, 26–27
"Everybody Rushed Me" (Federico), 38,
    52–53, 61–62, 63–65, 93

Fabiola (student), 84
Family, as reference term, 120–122, 126
Federico (Little Creeper; student)
    dropping out perspective of, ix, 28, 31–
        32, 36–38, 45–48, 49–50, 52–55,
        61–65, 68, 92–112, 114
    gang nickname and, 92–112, 114
Felipe (student), 135–138, 140
Fernandez, Danny. *See* Danny (Sider; stu-
    dent)
Fieldwork, 12–19
    discourse analysis in, 13–14
    entering the field, 14–17
    school control over subjects of, 17–19
    success stories in, 17–18
    transcription conventions, 29–31
Fine, Michele, 5, 11, 57–58, 68, 71, 72,
    129
Finn, C. E., 7, 8, 10
Framing Dropouts (Fine), 57–58
Fran (student), 28, 35–36, 37, 43, 44, 46–
    51, 55
Friend, as reference term, 113, 114,
    116–126
Fullan, M., 171

Gang banging, as reference term, 113,
    114
Gang nicknames, 92–112
    administration attitude toward, 93,
        107–108
    alternative readings of, 105–109
    causal link to baptismal event, 95–96
    City School approach to, 109–110
    context-bound use of, 98–99
    as descriptions, 96–98
    Diamond Street gang and, 93–110

Gang nicknames (*Continued*)
  Eighteenth Street gang and, 98–101,
    103
  Federico ("Little Creeper"), 92–112,
    114
  immediate context of, 94
  as indexical forms, 96–98, 105–109
  linguistic ideology and, 105–109
  in multiple mediums, 104–105, 107
  naming in stories, 99–104
  positive social identity and, 93
  significance of using, 114
  surrounding talk and, 94–95
Gates, H. L., Jr., 23
Genrefication, of moral discourse,
    145–147
"Getting," 54–56, 69–70
Giroux, H., 166
Goffman, Erving, 23
Gonzales, R., 166–167
Gonzalez, N., 166–167
Good, T. L., 8–11
Goodwin, C., 13
Goodwin, M. H., 25, 46
Gracie (student), 78–82, 84, 85–86, 107,
    113, 115, 128, 135, 136
Graffiti
  City School and, 109–110
  gang nicknames and, 109–110
Graffiti taggers, 1–2, 5
Grammatical resources
  adverbials, 85–87
  complexity in, 41
  of dropping in stories, 81–87
  of dropping out stories, 40–53
  "getting," 54–56, 69–70
  hypothetical constructions projecting
    the future, 45–46
  indefinite place referent, 50–51
  indefinite pronouns, 50, 52–53, 55, 83,
    133, 138, 143–145
  nonspecific noun phrases, 48–50
  past tense in, 82–83, 84
  present tense in, 46–50, 52, 53, 83–
    84

  progressive aspect, 43–45, 52, 83–
    84
Greenfield, P., 46
Gutierrez, K., 11, 15

Hand signals, 104, 107
Hanks, W., 23, 53, 58, 114, 133
Harklau, L., 166
Harris, M. G., 6
Hart, Gary, 7–8
Heath, S. B., 6, 15
Hill, P., 6
Hitting up, 38
Hobbes, Carlton (founder of City School),
    3–7, 9, 148–150, 153–154, 158
Homeboy, as reference term, 113, 122–
    124, 125–126
Homes, as reference term, 113, 118–123,
    127
Huber, L., 131

Identity. *See also* Gang nicknames
  as "dropout," 58
  emergence of, 23–25
  local categories of, at City School,
    12–13
  narrative and, 23–25
  role of ethnicity in narrative, 26–27
"I Got Fed Up" (Fran), 35–36
"I Got Mad" (Rosa), 34–35, 66–67
"I Just Got Bored" (Ned), 33–34, 35
Indefinite place referent, in narrative,
    50–51
Indefinite pronouns, in narrative, 50, 52–
    53, 55, 83, 133, 138, 143–145
Indexical forms, 53–56
  in conversations about jail time, 133–
    145, 167
  gang nicknames as, 96–98, 105–109
  "getting," 54–56, 69–70
  indefinite pronouns and words, 53–55,
    83, 133, 138, 143–145
  in student-teacher conversations,
    132–145

Innovation
  in charter schools, 7–9
  City School as, 8–9
  future of, 159–161
  paradoxes of, 9–11
  in research, 11
Institutional coauthorship, 169–173
Interactional coauthorship, 163–169
"I Simply Asked Her to Watch It"
  (Rosa), 65–67
"It Isn't Too Late for Me" (Von), 80–81,
  83, 84, 87, 88
"I Was a Gang Member" (Gracie), 78–
  82, 84, 85–86

Jack (student), 98
Jail time
  in student-student conversations, 116–
    117, 120, 125, 131, 134
  in student-teacher conversations, 133–
    145, 167
Jaime (teacher), 20, 148, 154–158
Jankowski, M. S., 6, 108
Jefferson, G., 88
Jerry (student), 28, 44–45, 55, 68–70,
  139, 167–168
Jesse (student), death of, ix, 21–22,
  154–155
Jesus (student), 88–89
Joe (student), 135–136, 140
Jorge (student), 113, 131
  conversation with other students, 116–
    130, 157
Juan (Largo; student), ix

Kelly, Dierdre M., 20–21, 71–72
Keneisha (student), 141–145
Kernel stories, 36
King, Rodney, 109
Klein, H. E. M., 28
"Knife Story" (Ned), 32–33, 59–61
Kohl, H., 5
Kolderie, T., 8
Kozol, J., 5, 14
Kripke, S., 95, 114

Kroskrity, P. V., 27

Labov, B., 28–29, 41, 46, 47, 59
Language in the Inner City (Labov), 41
LaQuinta (student intern), 88–89
Larsen-Freeman, D., 47–49, 52, 85, 118
Larson, J., 11, 15
LaTasha (student), 141–145
Laura (teacher/administrator), 14–16, 17,
  20–22, 26, 57, 75–77, 149–150
Lauter, D., 109
Leo (student), 99, 100
Linguistic analysis, 13–14
Linguistic ideology, 105–109
  dominant, 106–107
  of gang members, 105–106
  media-based, 108, 111
  police department, 108–109, 111
  politician, 109, 111
  school-based, 107–108, 111
Listening, by teachers, 163–164
Little Hoover Commission, 6, 12, 150,
  170
Long, J. M., 96
"Looking good," 25–26
Los Angeles Times, 8–9
Los Angeles Unified School District
  charter schools in, 7, 151
  Pacific Palisades, 8
Luis (student), 113, 131, 134
  conversation with other students, 116–
    130, 157

MacIntyre, A., 24
Maldonado, Ned. *See* Ned (Cubby; stu-
  dent)
Manno, B. V., 7, 8, 10
Manny (student), 28, 55, 57, 63, 65, 68–
  70, 139, 167–168
"Marijuana Story" (Jerry), 55, 68–70
Mario (student), 131, 134
  conversation with other students, 113–
    130, 157
Martinez, R., 2
Mavropoulos, William J., 1

McLaughlin, M. W., 6
Media-based linguistic ideology, 108, 111
Mehan, H., 15, 72, 132
Meier, D., 5
Mendoza-Denton, Norma, 6, 91, 166
Michael (student), 85, 87
Micro-level linguistic analysis, 14
Minnesota, charter schools in, 7
Moll, L., 146, 166–167
Monica (student), 87
Monti, D. J., 5, 6, 107
Morales, Rosa. *See* Rosa (Sunshine; student)
Mulholland, L. A., 6, 7
Munson, Joe (bodyguard), 150–153, 158
Myatt, L., 171

Nancy (student), 73, 87–89
Narrative. *See also* Discourse genres; Dropping in perspective; Dropping out perspective; Grammatical resources
    at City School, 25–26
    discourse genres and, 22–23
    identity and, 23–25
    recommendations for teachers working with adolescents, 163–169
    role of ethnicity in, 26–27
Nathan, L., 171
Navarro, Jesse. *See* Jesse (student)
NCREL Report, 27
Ned (Cubby; student), ix, 20, 28, 32–34, 35, 37, 40, 44–49, 53, 54, 59–61
Network of communication, 159–160
Nicknames. *See* Gang nicknames
Noun phrases, in narrative, 48–50
Nussbaum, Martha, 170

Oakes, J., 8
Ochs, E., 14, 23, 25, 29, 31, 33, 46, 62, 85, 89, 165
Official discourse, 58

Pablo (student), death of, 151–152, 154–160
Parmentier, R. J., 23, 168
Past tense, of narrative, 82–83, 84
Paula (teacher), 152–153, 154, 159
Peirce, C. S., 54
Phelan, P., 15
Philips, S., 15
Poetic Justice (Nussbaum), 170
Policastro, M., 28, 29
Police department linguistic ideology, 108–109, 111
Politician linguistic ideology, 109, 111
Pomerantz, A., 137
Possible Lives (Rose), 171
Pratt, Mary Louise, 113, 128
Premack, E., 169–170
Present tense, of narrative, 46–50, 52, 53, 83–84
Progressive aspect, of narrative, 43–45, 52, 83–84
Pushouts, 71–72
Putnam, H., 95, 114
Pyle, A., 8

Ramanathan, A. K., 129
Recipient design, 13–14
Reference terms, 113–130
    best dog, 125, 126
    bro, 113, 118, 127
    chucho, 124–125, 129
    ése, 113, 119–121, 123
    family, 120–122, 126
    friend, 113, 114, 116–126
    for friends, 113–130
    gang banging, 113, 114
    homeboy, 113, 122–124, 125–126
    homes, 113, 118–123, 127
    roll dog, 113, 124–125, 126, 127, 129
    in student conversations with other students, 113–130
Reframing, viii, 57–72
    in debunking dropping out themes, 62, 63–70
    ramifications of, 71–72

in reinforcing dropping out themes, 59–62

Rendon, P., 166–167

Rivera, A., 166–167

Rodriguez, Luis, 159

Roll dog, as reference term, 113, 124–125, 126, 127, 129

Romaine, Calvin (president of City School), 4–5, 7, 9, 148–151, 158–159

Rosaldo, Renato, 12–13

Rosa (Sunshine; student), ix, 28, 34–35, 37, 43–47, 49, 52, 65–67

Rose, M., 5, 171

Rymes, B., 11, 15, 95

Sacks, H., 25, 29

Sautter, R. C., 6, 7

Schegloff, E. A., 13

Schiffrin, D., 52, 89

Scholes, R., 89

School-based linguistic ideology, 107–108, 111

Searle, J. R., 99, 114

Shankar, Albert, 6, 7–8, 10, 158

Shuman, A., 15, 25

Silverstein, M., 105–107, 122, 132, 133

Sizer, Theodore, 15, 110

Smith, B. H., 25

Smith, R., 25, 62

Spindler, G., 6

Spindler, L., 6

Stein, N., 28, 29

Strawson, P. F., 114

Streeck, J., 121

Student conversations
about jail time, 116–117, 120, 125, 131, 134
with other students, 113–130
with teachers, 131–147

Students of City School. *See also names of specific students*
dropping in perspective of, 73–91
dropping out perspective of, 20–72

as parents, 5

Success stories, 17–18, 75. *See also* Dropping-in perspective
nature of, viii

Sylvia (student), 28, 65–67

Tagging crews, 1–2, 5

Talty, S., 6

Tannen, D., 83

Taylor, Charles, 23, 24–25, 25, 62

Teachers at City School
agenda of social change and, 140
common background with students, 132
conversations with students, 131–147
difficulties of, 5
experience with jail time, 134–139
interactional coauthorship and, 163–169
Jaime (teacher), 20, 148, 154–158
Laura (teacher/administrator), 14–16, 17, 20–22, 26, 57, 75–77, 149–150
Paula (teacher), 152–153, 154, 159
recommendations for working with adolescents, 163–169
reduction in number of, 116
rights to advise students, 131–147
student demands of, 10–11
Tim (teacher), 134–142, 145, 147, 149–151, 167

Tenery, M. F., 166–167

Tim (teacher), 134–142, 145, 147, 149–151, 167

Tom (student), 138

Trueba, H. T., 6

Tyack, David, 162, 174–175

Urban, G., 132, 133

Valdez, Federico. *See* Federico (Little Creeper; student)

Vanourek, G., 7, 8, 10

Vicki (student), 141, 143

Vigil, J. D., 33, 95, 96, 104–105

Von (student), 80–81, 83, 84, 87, 88, 115

Waletzky, J., 29
Weiner, E., 43
Wells, A. S., 8, 11, 169–170
Wendy (student), 28
Willis, P., 89
Willow (student), 48, 50, 55
Wittgenstein, L., 114
Wolfson, N., 16

Wright, Richard, ix–x
"The Wrong Path" (Abel), 79–80, 81,
   82–84, 86

Yu, H. C., 15

Zollers, N. J., 129

About the Author

Betsy Rymes is assistant professor in the Department of Language Education and the Program in Linguistics at the University of Georgia. She received her B.A. in English literature from Swarthmore College, and her M.A. in Teaching English as a Second Language (TESL) and Ph.D. in Applied Linguistics from the University of California, Los Angeles. In both her teaching and her research, she approaches content learning by examining its relationship to social, cultural, and linguistic context. Her current research examines the cultural and social foundations of second language learning in multiple contexts in northeast Georgia. She has published articles and essays in such journals as *Language and Society, Discourse and Society, Linguistics and Education,* and (with Kris Gutierrez and Joanne Larson) *Harvard Educational Review.*